To all persons who enabled me to reflect positively

MEMORIES—2001

At 86 and 87 in years,
Irene and I feel very much matured.
We view our futures in the light
of all we have endured.
In over 300 accounts we've written,
we've identified blessings of the past
In life's performances we have parts
in an ever changing cast.
Two trips through the Panama Canal,
both east and west.
European tours seeking old and new
in a deepening historical quest.
Touring Mexico's Copper Canyon,
Puerto Vallarta and friendly La Paz.
In South America, Canada,
the Caribbean enlightenment our cause.
Renewing family ties in many places
warm and deeply cherished.
In smiles and friendly greetings
our spirits kindly nourished.
But the energetic anticipations
of travel in earlier years is spent.
Memories encourage happy thoughts:
those we saw, where we went.
Now a tour of a few miles in our city,
not very far away.
A cruise, a short boat ride

in San Diego's sunlit bay.
Yes, we've lived to enjoy
many rewarding, fruitful years,
In our laughter, in our health,
enjoying professional careers.

Blessings to you!
Sincerely, Irene and Evans Anderson

CONTENTS

Special thanks are due to my wife, Irene, for her editing, to Hartha Jackson, for her typing expertise, and to my daughter, Anita, for her interest and optimism.

I
FAMILY AND FRIENDS

FAMILY AND FRIENDS
Table of Contents

FAMILY AND FRIENDS

Carl Martin Anderson—My Dad

My Dad was born in St. Paul, Minnesota of Norwegian and Swedish ancestry. Shortly after his birth the Anderson family moved to a farm in the Upsala community some 25 miles southwest of Little Falls, Minnesota. There were four children in the family, three boys and one girl. The Johnson family, a family of relatives who had no children, prevailed on my grandparents to send one of their sons to live with them and work on their farm in the Eyota, Minnesota area (near Rochester). Willy, the youngest son was sent on the basis of the Johnson request but Willy was not easily disciplined so later my Dad was sent to replace him. It wasn't until several years later that my Dad came back to Upsala when the Johnsons bought a farm in that area. (I was born on that farm in 1914). My Dad wanted to be a locomotive engineer so when he failed visual tests for that kind of work, he was compelled to resort to farming. When he married my mother in 1910 he got a job in timber work in Onamia, Minnesota, but under familial pressures, he and my mother returned to Upsala so they could operate the farm that the Johnsons had bought several years earlier. My Dad was an avid reader and storyteller. His formal education ended at the fourth grade but he had gained an interest in reading that lasted a lifetime. He could easily read a 250 page book during the course of a long winter evening. Following his perusal of a volume, he would, by kerosene lamp, jot down a few notes which would guide him as he subsequently told the story to relatives and friends gathered at our house a few weeks later. Dad got quite a reputation as a storyteller. One wintry night, he began with a story early in the evening, and when he completed the last of the story, the sun was just arising in the eastern sky. Our guests gave him a rousing cheer for the evening's entertainment. Nobody present in those days had television, few had radios. Dad performed effectively in the absence of all of those modern day conveniences. When there was a math problem in the neighborhood, particularly concerning measurement, my Dad would be called up to provide the answers for he was an expert. He was also a musician, playing the harmonica and accordion at local parties. In addition he would be a square dance caller if such an event was scheduled. My brother Laurel, sister Evodia and I regretted that our Dad did not have the opportunities for academic training that we had experienced. He loved fishing and baseball. Even though his vocational opportunities were limited, he led a rich life in giving much strength to his family.

Agda Otelia Ryberg—My Mom

My Mother, Agda Otelia Ryberg, was born in Sweden, reared in South Dakota and Minnesota. She had one sister, Hulda, and one brother, Albert, who were also born in Sweden. One sister, Ida, was born in South Dakota. Early life in the Midwest was pioneer-style; my mother told how leaves would sprout in the logs of their cabin in the winter from the warmth of the indoors. She attended a one room school in the Upsala, Minnesota area and with teacher training in Little Falls she became a teacher. Her professional assignments were involved in one room rural schools where the teacher was instructor, administrator and custodian all rolled into one job. My mother and dad were married in St. Paul in 1910. Early in their marriage they lived in Onamia, Minnesota, which in the early 1900s was regarded as part of the domain of Indians. During their time in this area, my mother ran a store; my dad worked in the timber business. Subsequent to their tenure in this part of Minnesota, they moved to Upsala, near Little Falls, where they farmed until their retirement in the 1950s. Work on the farm was strenuous with no telephone, no washing machine, supplying the wood-burning stoves with fuel; work in our garden during the summer months was demanding. My mother's main goal was expressed in her desire that my brother, sister and I all earn college degrees. Her ambitions were realized when all three of us became professors at three different universities in Missouri, Minnesota and California.

Brother Laurel

I have only one brother, Laurel, who is almost a year and a half younger than I. He was the star athlete in our family, especially in high school days. He was a star forward in the Upsala High School basketball team as a 9th grader and first string catcher on the baseball team in grade 8. My brother was an excellent scholar, earned a Ph.D. at the University of Minnesota with subsequent teaching assignments at Kansas State and later at the University of Missouri. Militarily, he was a member of an armored division that fought its way almost the length of the Italian "Boot" in WW II. His three children carry on

7

the family tradition of excellence with one son an honored computer expert with IBM. Another son is a chemist researching medical answers as a health expert. Both sons have Ph.D.s from the University of Wisconsin and a daughter, a graduate of the University of Iowa, works as a speech therapist. His wife, Dorothy, musically inclined, is a former teacher and expert gardener. Previous to earning a Ph.D., Laurel taught in one room rural schools in central Minnesota. In retirement he builds furniture in his home workshop. Laurel and I have always been good friends as illustrated by the fact that he, on a meager rural teaching salary, supported me at the University of Minnesota during 1938–39, enabling me to earn a master's degree in school administration. This saving gesture proved to be critical in my life during the days of the Great Depression.

My Sister—Evodia Anderson

I was 3½ years older than my sister Evodia. She was the last of the three surviving children in the Anderson family. Two boys died early in life; both had preceded me. She was the last to start school in Upsala, the last to leave home to further her education. While waiting for a call into nurse's training in Omaha, she attended Lutheran Bible School in Minneapolis. During her training in Omaha, I had occasion to meet some of the classmates and generally enjoy Omaha. Upon completion of nurse's training she opted for college enrollment and a B.S. degree. Evodia was accepted at Bethany College in Lindborg, Kansas, eventually accepting a similar position at Bemidji State in Minnesota. Subsequently, she became a student at the University of Minnesota and at Harvard University. One of her earlier jobs was as public health nurse in northern Minnesota where she was responsible for a variety of programs in health maintenance. As college nurse at Bemidji State College in Minnesota, she became engaged to and subsequently married Wilfred Reinikka. Evodia and Wilfred spend their years in retirement in the iron country of northern Minnesota. Early in her life my sister had difficulty with nearsightedness, a condition corrected by proper visual focusing. This did not prevent her from becoming an expert seamstress, nurse and university professor.

Grandpa Ryberg

He was the only grandfather I knew since Grandfather Anderson died early in my childhood. Grandpa Ryberg was the head of the Ryberg household of which my mother was a part—she was the second oldest daughter in the family. My grandfather's surname was originally Carlson, but when he enlisted in the Swedish army the military rosters contained the name Carlson to the extent that a request was made that he change his name to Ryberg. As a youth he worked as a herder of sheep, a job that he accepted with a deep sense of responsibility. One day a wolf threatened to claim a sheep, at which point my grandfather shouted so loudly for help that from that day on he spoke only in a high pitched voice. Early in his life people in his neighborhood would discuss the Civil War in America which was raging at the time. Several years following the war he made arrangements to immigrate to America, first to South Dakota, then to central Minnesota where he developed a farm which eventually encompassed two hundred acres. He was a man tall in stature and fast afoot. In his success as a farmer he supervised the building of a new house and several durable farm buildings. He was proud to be an American citizen, was a religious Lutheran and an avid reader. Through great visits in Swedish, my grandfather would tell me about Swedish history and his Lutheran faith.

Uncle Albert

My mother's brother was Albert, the only boy in a family of four children. Because of his interest in farming he was always "close to the soil" in Sweden where he was born or in South Dakota and finally in the Upsala, Minnesota area where he spent most of his life. The early days in Minnesota were trying for all members of the Ryberg family, eking out a living by clearing plots of hardwood forests and breaking the soil for a crop production. As Albert gained more stature physically and socially he developed an interest in purchasing and developing new land in Canada. He pictured himself as a farmer rearing a family in some new part of central Canada. As his interest grew in the direction of this development Grandpa Ryberg became concerned fearing that he might lose his son. Consequently, he offered Albert an 80 acre farm that he could develop, adding to the 120 acres the Rybergs already owned. Albert accepted the arrangement, stayed single and for the rest of his life helped Grandfather plow, seed and harvest at the Ryberg farm in central Minnesota. Albert was a dedicated son strongly motivated by his parents. His sisters owed him many "thank yous" for maintaining the home farm in the Upsala area. Albert was a faithful Lutheran adept at conversing in English and Swedish. He was a good pioneer, a good son.

Aunt Ida

Ida was my mother's younger sister, born in South Dakota, the survivor of a twin birth. Early in her life she moved to Upsala with her family. She was reared in a log cabin, later replaced by a four bedroom house. Ida went to a rural school in the Upsala community. Following 8th grade graduation she continued to live on the family farm until her enrollment in the nurses training program at Emanuel Hospital, Omaha, Nebraska. Ida's effectiveness as a student nurse and later as a full time employee at the hospital gained her the position of Supervisor of Nurses. (My cousin Eunice Peterson and my sister Evodia both received their nurses training at the same hospital but at a later dates). Due to the declining health of her mother, Ida was called home to work on the family farm as well as to attend to her mother's needs. Following this involvement she continued her education until she earned a high school diploma at what was then Minnesota College in Minneapolis. Subsequent to this development, my sister Evodia, as a public health nurse in northern Minnesota, obtained a position for Ida as head nurse in a hospital in the county where she was employed. Ida never married but in a sense she regarded the Peterson and Anderson nephews and nieces as her children. In her later years Ida traveled extensively and wrote newsworthy articles, some in the Swedish language.

Thanksgiving: Big Fork

My Aunt Ida invited Virginia, Evodia and me to share a Thanksgiving weekend with her at the hospital in Big Fork, in northern Minnesota near the Canadian border. As head nurse at this facility she had a small apartment where she could accommodate guests. Evodia, my sister, drove on this occasion; she met us in St. Cloud and we continued our drive to Big Fork on a chilly November day. As always, Ida welcomed us with a generous Thanksgiving dinner with goose as the main entree. The day following our feast in the hospital we had a wiener roast in what was a POW camp during WWII. At 3 below zero our winter picnic in the snow was invigorating. During our sojourn out in the woods we also chose our Christmas tree for the upcoming holidays. On another occasion Aunt Ida invited me to be the speaker at a Lutheran Church program at Big Fork. Virginia and I drove on ice and through snow during a trip that covered several hundred miles, but any trip to "Ida's Hospital" and community was always amply rewarded with good cheer and good food. My speech on this trip was well received with a good crowd on hand even though the weather was so bad on this November weekend that even several football games were canceled.

Caroline

Caroline is a cousin of unusual charm motivated by friendliness and bubbling enthusiasm. Her Dad, Henry Carlson, was one of my favorite relatives. Caroline's family lived in Northern Minnesota in an area partly ravaged by lumber barons. Nevertheless the family thrived on relatively poor land that was made to prosper through strenuous physical effort. She left the farm in early adulthood, seeking employment in International Falls, Minnesota. Misfortune befell Caroline as her husband disappeared, leaving her to support two young sons. While still living in Minnesota, she met Bob Vanlandingham who was also supporting his sons alone. Early in their marriage Bob was offered employment in the construction of an electrical facility in California. He accepted and there followed years of prosperity for the whole family. With Bob working at his trade and Caroline succeeding as a brilliant salesperson in real estate, the entire family has experienced great success in California. Caroline's enthusiasm and dedication to success in her employment have consistently revealed her friendly charm and bubbling enthusiasm.

Lillestrand Cousins

My Dad had two brothers and one sister, Alice. The brothers had no children but Alice had four, three girls and a boy. Decades ago the Lillestrand family moved into Upsala where they operated a grocery store for many years. Following the death of the children's father, Arthur, the family continued to operate the Lillestrand grocery in downtown Upsala. The eldest child was Ethel who eventually married Kenneth Nelson. She became a farmer's wife residing in one of the very scenic areas in the Upsala community. They lived near Pine Lake, famous for its beautiful pines. Ethel has two sisters, Florence and Fern, both of whom married and reared families in urban areas, particularly in Minnesota. Willard, the only son, assumed the management of the grocery store at the time of his mother's retirement. Lasting impressions concerning our contacts with the Lillestrand cousins were to the effect that we enjoyed their friendships and their hospitality. Since the Andersons and the Lillestrands were reared in rural environments, we sensed a close and enduring familial relationship.

The Peterson Cousins

My mother's oldest sister and the oldest daughter in the Ryberg family was Hulda. She was born in Sweden, moved with the family to South Dakota, then to Upsala in Central Minnesota. Her husband, Fred Peterson, was also reared in the Upsala community where he and Hulda were married. The wedding was held at the Ryberg farm in what was the home community for both Fred and Hulda. Uncle Fred was a telegraph operator working for the Great Northern Railroad. After a number of assignments earlier in the Midwest and West, Uncle Fred was at length stationed in Alexandria, Minnesota. There the Petersons reared five children, identified by the Anderson children as the Peterson cousins. Luther became an optometrist, Eunice a nurse, Lyall an adjuster for the UP RR, Everett a captain in the US Army and Doris a journalism major. As we grew up on the farm we admired our "city" cousins for conveniences they had which we didn't have. Nevertheless, we enjoyed entertaining the cousins in the Upsala area; they in turn entertained us in Alexandria, a moderately large town in one of the lake districts in Minnesota. One very favorable impression that comes to mind as I look back on our relationship, occurred in Alexandria on the occasion of a Peterson family reunion. The only persons outside the Peterson family circle present were Virginia, my first wife and me. We felt like honored guests in the club house setting where the Peterson family reunion was held on that memorable occasion.

Friends: Virginia—Later United in Marriage

I met Virginia in a one room rural school near Forest City, Iowa, while I was supervising student teachers in my job as Director of Teacher Training at Waldorf College.

14

I was mightily impressed by the teaching methods she employed and by the friendly climate that prevailed in her classroom. On our first date I met her in the city library, then drove to Lake Mills on a relatively short get-acquainted tour. She proved to be a very good conversationalist, and was politely frank concerning her ideas regarding effective education. We were engaged to be married not long before I entered the Army in the early 1940s. While I was stationed at San Antonio, Texas, and later at Camp McCoy, Wisconsin, then at Camp Funtston in Kansas, she would come to visit me at a sacrifice of her employment and difficulties in traveling. In appearance she was very attractive, very assuring regarding her demeanor. She was skillful as an organizer and especially adept in her ability to converse in any situation. In respect for her I never had a romantic interest beyond the days of our engagement and during the years of our marriage. Deep sadness was my lot at the time of her passing in 1983, and particularly so as Anita and I visit her monument at Fort Rosecrans cemetery.

March Wedding

For more than two days in early March, storms swept through the Upper Midwest; I was in uniform then. During a pass from my assignment in Madison, Wisconsin, I braved the storm by rail and by car to Forest City, Iowa where Virginia and I were married the evening of March 7th, 1944. A large group of relatives and friends filled our Lutheran Church to capacity inspite of the storm. The Waldorf College choir added musically to the warmth of the occasion, as I was honored as a former faculty member at the college. Following a memorable ceremony and a reception at the church, Virginia and I accompanied two family guests to the MSL station where we stayed our honeymoon night, waiting for the train for Minneapolis to arrive through the storm. Uncle Oscar and Aunt Clarabelle had arrived for the occasion from Evansville, Indiana. Since Virginia and I would be hotel guests in Madison and Virginia's uncle and aunt would train to Chicago and beyond, the four of us continued our visiting as we rode by car to Mason City, Iowa, and from there caught the east bound train. When I reported back to my unit in Madison I was told that our leave had been extended which gave us the opportunity to include a brief visit with my parents in Upsala. The raging storm and the bitter cold of our wedding night made Virginia and I feel that we were ready to face any subsequent storms that we might encounter during our marriage.

My Daughter—Anita

Anita, my daughter, was born on the 7th of April, 1959. She was the only child Virginia and I had and for our good fortune, she became a rare jewel in our family. Except for a temporary feeding problem she did not cause us a great deal of worry or anxiety. Anita received the usual protective immunizations early, one which caused a minimum of distress. On the day of Anita's birth I literally "commuted" between Sharp Hospital in San Diego and my office on the campus of San Diego State. She was born during the course of the evening of April 7th with a weight of slightly over six pounds. I still have a copy of the San Diego "news" printed that day. I retired the tie I wore on the occasion of her birth and still possess the cigar box which earlier contained smoker's treats distributed for the occasion. Anita's first trip out of town was to Gunnison, Colorado, where I was visiting professor during the summer of 1960. She has always been a good traveler, even on international visits. To assure us of potential and academic successes I enrolled her in our San Diego State Campus Lab School on the day following her birth. Anita proved to be a good student in elementary, secondary and college levels. She earned a degree at San Diego State University, graduating with honors with special emphasis in Spanish. For an extended period of years, she has been an officer in the INS stationed at the United States–Mexico border.

Marilyn

Virginia had one sister, Marilyn, who was about five years younger than she. Marilyn had a somewhat darker complexion, she was about fifteen pounds lighter, laughed readily when a positive atmosphere favoring her prevailed. Virginia and Marilyn's mother were the primary supporters for the family since the father, Verne, was disabled. During her years in Forest City High School, there were times when the friends Marilyn chose were somewhat on the wild side. Following high school graduation Marilyn entered nurse's training. Again her scholastic potentials revealed themselves as she was graduated with honors upon completing her training. As a result of a party about that time, she found herself pregnant. A friend of hers and Marilyn decided to migrate from Iowa to California where she found employment as a housekeeper in the home of a San Francisco policeman. Eventually she wrote to her mother and Virginia, explaining her situation. She did this only after months of deepening concern regarding Marilyn's health and whereabouts. The policeman, Jack Symons, who was divorced and rearing two children, eventually married Marilyn. She added a son to the family with the birth

17

following her pregnancy. At a relatively early age, Marilyn was the mother of three children in a home in San Francisco. Jack proved to be a subservient husband with Marilyn in charge of rearing his one daughter and two sons. Family life seemed to calm Marilyn's, at times, wild and restless spirit. Over the years her employment as a nurse helped support the family over rough and lean days.

Marilyn's Husband, Jack Symons

In the summer of 1949 Virginia and her mother journeyed to San Francisco for a visit with Marilyn. As a student at the University of Denver, I was unable to accompany them but on other occasions I had the opportunity to become well acquainted with Jack. He possessed a good sense of humor and an especially kind attitude when entertaining guests. Over the years he proudly announced the arrival of two more sons in the family. The five children in order of birth were Jack, Jr., Barbara, Steve, Scott, and Shane. Virginia, Anita and I enjoyed visiting this family of seven in San Francisco and eventually Santa Rosa. Jack continued working as a police officer while Marilyn was a nurse in the state prison at San Quentin. They enjoyed their ranch in the Santa Rosa area and their cabin in Monte Rio. We had pleasant visits in both locations. Her earlier life left some remarkable impressions on Marilyn as she seemingly struggled with feelings of jealousy concerning her sister Virginia. "Thank yous" for gifts and other correspondence were much delayed. Jack was a relatively good influence for Marilyn but never to the point that he could convince her to stop smoking. Both have died in recent years, leaving various imprints on their children. Steve, Marilyn's boy, proved to be most successful, following the earning of a degree in pharmacy at the University of Wyoming. Anita, my daughter, still keeps in touch with Scott, Shane, and Steve. Events which we all remember: the tour in a Model T Ford through their prune orchard in their first Santa Rosa home, a picnic in Monte Rio, my riding with Jack in his patrol car, swimming in their refreshing pool, visiting wineries and good dinners at the ranch.

Uncle Oscar

We became well acquainted with Oscar, Virginia's uncle, when he and his wife moved from Indiana to California. Oscar was married and lived in Des Moines as a successful businessman until his best friend claimed Oscar's wife and two children. Following this turn of events in his life, Oscar established himself in Evansville, Indiana. He was employed in a department store in downtown Evansville where he met Clarabelle, his second wife. They lived in an attractive home made more attractive by the gardening skills that Oscar employed. When we visited them in their pleasant home we always felt like welcomed guests, especially as they showed us their zoo and beautiful parks, including a trip across the Ohio River to Kentucky. In the mid 1960s both Oscar and Clarabelle gave serious thought to moving to California. In circa 1966 they arrived in San Diego County and lived with us for awhile as our guests. One Sunday afternoon as we were touring in Chula Vista I saw a sign for sale in what seemed to be a very friendly neighborhood and suggested we tour the facility. Oscar and Clarabelle lived in that home for approximately ten years until Oscar's death. During their residency of the house in Chula Vista,

Oscar developed beautiful gardens and Christmas displays that were prize winners. They were very happy as residents in California, thanks in part for the friendly support we provided for them.

Uncle Charles

Virginia's mother had two brothers, Oscar and Charles. Both were very friendly, inclined to be effectively optimistic. Charles' view of his future was dampened, however, when his relatively young wife and Charles were divorced. Kay, a son from the marriage, went to live with his mother, a hairdresser with a shop in Clear Lake, Iowa. Eventually the son became a dentist with an office in Oklahoma. On one occasion as we were traveling from California to Wisconsin, we chanced to meet him as he was out for a stroll. The only time Anita had her teeth checked in such a situation was by this relative. We met Charles in an amusement part during our travels. With him in a comfortable seat on the train in the park, we managed to film him as he rode along reminiscing as he recalled good times from his past. Eventually Charles made his home in Lafayette, Indiana, where he located for the convenience of his sales business. While we visited him at that location, he invited us to share lunch with him on the campus of Purdue University. While we lounged in comfort at the student center, Anita played a few special selections on their grand piano. Sometime following this visit we learned of his death, the passing of a friendly, effervescent relative.

Oscar and Clarabelle

On occasions we planned with Virginia's uncle Oscar and wife Clarabelle to make a trip to Santa Rosa in northern California to visit Virginia's sister, Marilyn, and her family. The day had arrived for making such a trip in our station wagon with Virginia, Anita, and me hosting Oscar and Clarabelle, plus a surprise guest, Clarabelle's white poodle. With no negative evaluations, only expressions of cheerful optimism, we started out on our journey. We stopped for lunch in Solvang, a Danish community north of Santa Barbara. While the three of us did some shopping, Oscar and Clarabelle found it necessary to air the dog. With a good lunch and a good bit of stretching, we continued on our journey through San Francisco, over the Golden Gate Bridge, into Petaluma and beyond. A warm welcome awaited us in Santa Rosa at the Symons, Jack's and Marilyn's home. Following a refreshing night and a leisurely morning a suggestion was made that we visit a nearby winery. Oscar said he would watch the roast while several of us enjoyed the hospitality of the winery. When we returned dinner was about ready. During the course of the meal Oscar opted to eat portions that were burned. He had watched the cooking process so he felt he had to deal with a sense of guilt. Later in the week we all returned home safely with shared memories, hopefully most of them pleasant.

Laurel at Morris, Minnesota

My brother Laurel was a member of the faculty at the Agricultural School in Morris, part of the University of Minnesota system previous to accepting an assignment at Kansas State University. On one occasion during his tenure in Morris, he invited me to speak to the students at one of their assembly programs. In St. Cloud I left a concert by the Minneapolis Symphony Orchestra early so I would be able to arrive in Morris on time. My old Ford did not cooperate very well. Besides, the miles from St.

Cloud to Morris in western Minnesota seemed to be especially long. I was well received on the campus at Morris, nevertheless, and I will admit that I did enjoy working with the students. On another occasion a small group of us had dinner in Laurel's apartment subsequent to his marriage to Dorothy. This occasion also proved to be very rewarding in a very friendly atmosphere. On another occasion while I was teaching in an off-campus assignment in Montevideo, Minnesota as a faculty member at St. Cloud State, Virginia and I drove to Morris one afternoon to visit Laurel. I believe that it was on this occasion that he opened one of his desk drawers and found a mother cat with a litter of new kittens, all of which were very comfortable. Western Minnesota, where Morris is located, offers attractions of distinctive types of prairie display in contrast to the lake regions elsewhere in the area.

Family Reunions

With respect to three grandfathers who were born and reared in Sweden and for the identification of relatives, we conducted family reunions in honor of family founders who contributed to the well being of all of us. Each was a pioneer, developing farm land and farm houses in wilderness areas of Central Minnesota. My grandfather (mother's side) was J. A. Ryberg; his two brothers, Otto and Swen, all chose to develop land in the vicinity of Upsala. My grandfather who was a Carlson, as were Otto and Swen, changed his name to Ryberg due to the fact that there was so many Carlsons serving in the Swedish army that name changing occasionally was required. The reunions that Irene and I attended were held in Grand Rapids and Upsala where excellent arrangements had been made for programs, coffee breaks and dinners. I was favored by being chosen as chairman of the gathering in each location. (I used both English and Swedish in directing activities in both settings.) Name tags, family tree pictures and accounts of tourism in Sweden were all part of each program. Group pictures for the sake of identification and memories were made. Both Irene and I felt that we had effectively honored our grandparents, to some great-grandparents, through the warmth expressed in our reunions. Irene, my second wife following Virginia's death, is Swedish. She was warmly accepted by all relatives in attendance.

Friends—Later Irene and I United

The first time I met Irene was in 1984 when she was traveling in Scandinavia with her sister, Vernia. My daughter Anita and I were tourists on the same trip—a trip planned and led by our Swedish course instructor, Eric Palmgren. The first stop in Scandinavia was in a unique but pleasant hotel in Copenhagen, Denmark. Our itinerary also brought us to Stockholm, Sweden and Oslo, Norway with stops at very interesting locations between these destinations. Irene was an excellent tourist, expressing a whole-hearted interest in each attraction we visited. For a few days Irene and her sister Vernia left the tour to visit with relatives in southern Sweden. As our travels continued, the conversations I had with Irene became more interesting, even fascinating. When we concluded a very scenic trip on a fjord in Norway she even allowed me to hold her purse which in my way of thinking was that she had confidence in me. When we returned to San Diego our romantic interests became more pronounced as I found myself expressing my affection for her. She was a widow and I was a widower—we were married January 5, 1985, in Ascension Lutheran Church in San Diego.

Pomona, 1954

Immediately following the Labor Day weekend I reported to the San Diego State campus for a new faculty check-in. Forms were surveyed and signed, orientation discussions were scheduled; we were even fingerprinted. Following orientation procedures we were told that classes would not begin for a few days so Virginia and I decided to visit the Miller family who was living in Pomona. Mr. Miller was one of Virginia's uncles who for a few years had been a widower following the death of his first wife, one of Virginia's aunts. He had recently been married to Enid and now had a new family of two daughters, one of theirs and one adopted. Enid had one son from an earlier marriage who had a private room at Millers with a television set. The little girls were not allowed to use his TV so they were not tainted by bad programming. Following an overnight visit the suggestion was made that we visit Knott's Berry Farm. On our way to "The Farm" the girls recited numerous Bible verses from memory. At Knotts we saw what then was usual, especially the transplanted ghost town. We did enjoy being Miller's guests, enriched somewhat by the Berry Farm visit. Early that evening we had hamburgers prepared on the grill with other food served in an appetizing manner. This was the first of several visits to Pomona which included trips to their big country fair. Tours like this helped Virginia and me to become well acquainted with many of the attractions that Southern California has to offer.

Mr. Sandahl

When my parents lived in Onamia, Minnesota shortly after their marriage in St. Paul, they became well acquainted with the Sandahl family. My first introduction to Mr. Sandahl happened in Holdingford in 1924. Since I was very much interested in the rail traffic coming and going, my attention was directed to a passenger train that stopped in the Holdingford depot. My Dad was with me so we had the opportunity to say 'hello' to Mr. Sandahl who as engineer of the train was seated in the cab of the engine. He even gave me the thrill of seeing how the engine operated. A sad note regarding the portion of the Soo Line system where Mr. Sandahl worked; there was a heavily wooded crossing near the Blanchard Rapids Dam where one of my cousin's lost his life. Mr. Sandahl didn't see my cousin's car but the fireman in the cab did. He was transported by train to Pierz where he died. The last time I saw Mr. Sandahl was in Onamia in the summer of 1938 where we had the opportunity to visit regarding any possible openings in the Onamia School system. He was a member of the school board but at the moment knew of no vacancies. The visit was enjoyable, nevertheless, and my respect for Mr. Sandahl's character has always commanded my attention.

Everette Nelson

Early one Friday evening I heard sleigh bells right outside our kitchen door. The sound of the bells seemed highly appropriate for such a beautiful winter evening. When the bells stopped ringing someone called my name. It was Everette Nelson, one of our neighbors, who has stopped by to invite me to attend a high school basketball game in Upsala that evening. I promptly accepted the invitation, grabbed my cap and coat and we were on our way through woods and fields until we arrived at Upsala High School. As we entered the gym, the ticket taker asked each of us to pay 25 cents for admission to the game. I fumbled around in my pockets but no quarter—in fact, no money was there. About that time, Mr. Bourne, our seventh grade teacher and coach, appeared and asked me why I was so disheveled. When I explained to him he said, "Let me pay—go for it!" Those words were sweet to my ears. The way home was in the nature of the return ride in the luxury of the "one horse open sleigh." When we got home I discovered I had dropped my purse in my bedroom. The following Monday when I wanted to return the quarter, Mr. Bourne refused to accept it. He thought that I had already learned enough concerning lost and found.

Axel Gunnar Axeen

When our class was confirmed at Gethesemane Lutheran Church in Upsala, Minnesota, Walter Mattson, another member of the class, was a good friend of mine. When we had our group and individualized pictures taken in Little Falls two days following our confirmation, Walter told me that pictures of his sister Anna, also in our class, and himself would be sent to Sweden. In the same year that we were confirmed, 1927, Walter told me that a cousin from Sweden would be living with his family on the family farm near Upsala. When I first saw this cousin, Axel Gunnar Axeen, I knew that family connection must be close since Walter's dad's name was Gunnar Mattson. I also thought of the pictorial connection regarding the confirmation pictures. Axel spoke some English but still preferred using his native Swedish. I became a close friend of Axel's as he told about soccer games and girls in Sweden. (Soccer was a distant topic then but the game sounded interesting). He also gave me opportunities to learn more Swedish as I helped him following his enrollment in Upsala High School. Axel became a member of the Upsala High School basketball team, another opportunity for him to use certain soccer skills. After what seemed to be a brief time, Axel departed for southern Minnesota where he became a successful farmer. Axel gave me excellent opportunities to learn more about Sweden and especially regarding the area where my mother was born. To me, Axel was "Mr. Sweden" with his humor, friendliness and with his determination to succeed as Mr. American.

Mrs. Nicholas Johnson

Mrs. Johnson became a widow following the death of her husband when they lived on a farm in the Upsala area, subsequent to a move from Eyota, near Rochester, Minnesota. At the time that Mrs. Johnson was operating the farm near Upsala, my parents were living in Onamia, Minnesota. Both were employed and apparently foresaw a reasonably bright future in the area. Mrs. Johnson, however, felt that my Dad and Mother owed her somewhat of a debt in terms of social obligations. Eventually my parents moved from Onamia back to the Upsala area, at least partially to accommodate Mrs. Johnson. Both had lived in Upsala earlier so my parents were well acquainted in the area. To make more pleasant for all involved, Mrs. Johnson had her own facility that had been added to the house that originally was constructed on the farm. Mrs.

Johnson would occasionally have a guest, a Mrs. Sundquist, who would stop by to pass the time of day. My brother Laurel and I would listen to their conversations, which seemed to be mainly about physical ailments. Laurel and I did enjoy these visits. I seemed to be a kind of favorite of Mrs. Johnson because near the time of her death she offered me her wedding ring. There were times when Mrs. Johnson's personality was such that she would not compromise. Eventually she left the farm to live with relatives in Upsala. Wherever she went she seemed to project the feeling that life was unbearable and that the people she was living with caused her to have this feeling.

The Ed Nelsons

The Nelson farm was part of our neighborhood located southeast of Upsala. We enjoyed many occasions with the Nelsons, exchanging visits in our homes and on occasion, traveling together. Everette was the oldest son who invited me to join him in his "one horse open sleigh" for an Upsala High School basketball game. Raymond, next in order, was one of the kids who sought to bury me on my first day of school. Later he and I became very good friends. Jenner, the youngest, was enrolled in the fifth grade in the Upsala Elementary School when I taught fifth grade in '36–'37. Florence, the only daughter, was a good friend of my sister Evodia. While I was a student in graduate school at the University of Minnesota, Ed came to visit me in Minneapolis when he was a delegate to the Land 'O Lakes dairy convention. One evening he asked me to accompany him on a visit to Florence who lived in south Minneapolis. We both enjoyed the occasion even though we experienced a blizzard that evening. While we waited for streetcar service the main streets in the downtown area resembled snow blown canyons. Nevertheless, Ed and I had a wonderful evening.

The Charley Olsons

For anyone who would have wished to envision how the Upsala area looked previous to the time when pioneer settlements occupied the area, two of several places that could have been surveyed were my Dad's woodlot and the heavily wooded area on Charley Olson's farm. Mr. and Mrs. Olson led a secluded life with their farm buildings situated up against a heavily wooded background. They were dairy farmers but on a limited basis. The main crop grown on their tillable land was rye. In early June when the rye plants "blossomed" the fragrance from the field of waving grain was pleasantly intense. I helped thresh their rye crop one summer so I got a close-up view of their farm buildings. On another occasion I chose to stroll through their wooded area, which was stimulating to the eye and ear. A mother partridge fluttered before me as she warned her chicks to go into hiding, which they did with remarkable efficiency. Apparently the new owners of the Olson farm following its sale, saw fit to decimate the beautiful wooded area that was once a scenic attraction. When my parents sold their farm the new owners chose to sell some of the best timber to the Little Falls boatworks, the kind of action that continued to devastate a wonderfully wooded area and transformed it into an open prairie.

Our Farm Neighbors

We knew all of our neighbors whose properties adjoined our 100 acres; it was a blessing to be able to identify each family as part of our circle of friends. In identifying these families I will begin with the Thompsons to the east of us, then go around in a clockwise circle. Mr. Thompson, over the years, lost his vision but not his ability to play the violin. Their only daughter, Marian, was in my confirmation class and high school graduating class. Next to the south and southeast was the Lawrence family whose daughters were quite acceptable but the sons were a bit on the wild side. When the daughters were married the family went all out in accepting their spouses. South our farm adjoined the Slagel farm. Mr. Slagel was an expert at finding bee trees each fall. He also closely supervised his daughter Rosella, who according to my recollection never married. West was the Nordstrom farm. They were noted for parties, some of which would last for days. My brother Laurel and I would carry home pails of skim milk from their farm to feed our hogs. We always enjoyed the excitement of people and pets at the Nordstroms. Farther west our neighbors were the Krupas. On occasions I would be his hired man for planting and haying. North were the Petersons with their musical daughters and two sons, one of whom became a mortician, the other a merchant in Upsala. To the northeast was the Nelson farm where two of the sons owned threshing machines, much to my excitement. One of the daughters was a secretary of a bank president in Minneapolis. During the summers we prospered together in the absence of drought conditions. In the winter we were snowbound together, almost like a sizable family.

Westbergs

While my Aunt Ida was a student in Minneapolis she roomed with a Westberg family whose home was located near the school. The Westbergs were friendly people of

Swedish descent, parents with two sons. As an employee of the University of Minnesota, Mr. Westberg longed for the days when he could own a farm away from the noise and pollution of the city. Eventually he did purchase a farm near Milaca, Minnesota, where hopefully his earlier dreams would come true. His land was part of a cut over section of Northern Minnesota where careless lumbering practices had decimated the forest, leaving behind large areas where the soil would support pine and spruce but only sparingly corn and wheat. Over a period of time due to Ida's almost incorporating the Westberg family into ours, Vernon, the older son, became my uncle's hired man. There were family visits to Upsala and Milaca which brought our families even closer together. Vernon eventually was employed by the Northern Pacific Railroad, the younger son Robert became a mail carrier. Both had large families. Sometimes our relationships with the Westbergs were based on sympathetic understandings, sometimes on the warmth of family relationships. There were occasions when we'd meet with the children and grandchildren of the family, all of whom seemingly had a deep love and respect for Aunt Ida. These feelings were transferred to the Anderson family due in part to the respect we had for Aunt Ida.

John Hedstrand

Following my freshman year at Gustavus Adolphus College, I transferred to St. Cloud State Teachers College (now St. Cloud State University) for my sophomore year. The transfer was made primarily for financial reasons. At Gustavus I roomed in the same dormitory as did John Hedstrand, a student from St. Cloud. To the best of my knowledge, John sought employment so returned to his home in St. Cloud for a full-time job. One evening (since we were both living in St. Cloud) John called me and asked if I would arrange a double date. I asked one of the girls who was a classmate if she and her roommate would care for a date during a particular evening, even quite soon. I had dates as requested. The girl I dated was Eileen, attractive, friendly and a good conversationalist. In fact she was the first date I ever had. In high school and later in college I hadn't dated anyone, partly because I felt I couldn't afford that kind of socializing. I had at least two dates with Eileen but showed her no affection even though I liked her and she liked me. I had a lot to learn at this time in my life.

Ronnie Seedorf

Ronnie was a student at St. Cloud State during the time I was a member of the faculty on that campus. I don't recall all of the details involved in our meeting Ronnie for the first time, but it is possible that it was over a potential car deal. Virginia and I thought he might be interested following a test ride so he could visit with his girl friend who taught in the Sauk Rapids High School. He did not buy our car. Eventually he earned a teaching credential and married the teacher who was earlier employed in Sauk Rapids. Virginia and I moved to San Diego and for awhile we were not in touch with the Seedorfs. Then one day while I was perusing the contents of the Upsala New Tribune I was surprised to learn that the Seedorfs were living in Upsala where both were teaching in the local high school. One Christmas Eve while we were visiting my Aunt Ida in Upsala, she invited the Seedorfs to a holiday party at her house. We enjoyed the party and our visit with the Seedorfs and their daughters. Ronnie contributed to the conversation by evaluating the Upsala school system in detail. Apparently his work as a teacher did not completely satisfy him so he enrolled in a Lutheran seminary and became a minister. The last time we saw the whole family was at a dinner in Chisholm, Minnesota, at the Lutheran parsonage. Earlier during the course of the afternoon Ronnie had taken several of us for plane rides at the Hibbing Airport. According to holiday greetings we obtained subsequently, Ronnie and his family had moved to North Dakota where he was involved in construction work—what next?

Friends' Sorrow

The Barkers have been family friends since in early 1946–47 when Hugh joined the faculty at St. Cloud State University. He became a member of the biology department; I was a counselor on the campus at that time. When the Barkers arrived in St. Cloud their only child was Ellen, who eventually became an outstanding student at St. Cloud Tech High School. Subsequently two more children arrived in the Barker household, two boys, the older of whom, Judson, is my godchild. Over the years we visited in their new home whereas, especially Dorothy and the children, would visit in our various apartments. Beyond high school both Ellen and Judson revealed their academic skills to the extent that Ellen got a Ph.D. in psychology and Judson became a statistician employed by a well-known insurance company. Ellen had married and as a result of family violence lost her life. Hugh Barker, her dad, sought a place of refuge near the family northwoods cabin where he could inter her ashes. Dorothy, the mother, over the years earned a Ph.D. in science with an invitation to join the faculty at St. Cloud State. Several years earlier she was troubled by a cancerous growth at the base of her spine. The medical care involved in treating the cancer brought distress to her job, brought on social limitations and eventually claimed her life. Hugh with Judson and Eldon, his sons, continue to bear a burden of grief at the death of wife, sister and mother.

The Ervin Ortmans in Hibbing, Minnesota

I had known Erv since we were both students at St. Cloud State Teachers College in the 1930s. In more recent times we've continued our friendship as Virginia, Anita and I had a standing invitation to visit them in Hibbing, which we did on numerous occasions. During early visits with the family, Erv, Molly and their two boys and a girl, we spent many enjoyable hours relaxing in their accommodations in a large brick home which had earlier belonged to a city official. During later visits we shared a home which had been built by a local contractor. The house was exceedingly well built with many conveniences included. We were entertained royally with excellent conversation, good food and tours of the community. Hibbing, for example, was at one time one of the wealthiest villages in the world as its school system still shows. The largest open pit iron mine is still functioning within the area. At one time there was such a wealth of high grade ore located under old Hibbing to access that they tore down the old town and built a new Hibbing. Huge piles of iron ore tailings stand in parts of the community, reminding reviewers of the glory days of mining in Northern Minnesota. Erv on one occasion took me fishing, which really proved to be mainly an opportunity for a good visit. Paul, the younger son, played his guitar for all us to hear, but his performance was primarily for Anita's entertainment. Upon Erv's death, Molly retained the family home in Hibbing, along with gracious memories which we all share with her.

Marvin Bacon

Marvin and I were faculty members assigned to the Upsala Consolidated School, Marvin with longer tenure, I with two years of experience before returning to college. In the winter of 1936 we roomed together at Mrs. Andwood's, breaking the ice in a water pitcher in our room each morning as WDAY Fargo broadcast *"Nobody's Darling but Mine."* We froze our ears on our way to breakfast at the Johnson pool hall where Mrs. Johnson served us those good meals each day, Monday through Friday. '36 was the winter of deep snowdrifts due to minimal thawing during the bitter cold weather. One month the temperature never rose above 0 degrees. During the summer of '36, which was unduly hot due to drought conditions in much of the Midwest, Marvin, my brother Laurel and I stayed in the same rooming house as students at the St. Cloud Teachers College summer session. Marvin married Frieda after the summer session previous to the beginning of a new school year. During the winter of '37 I roomed at their house near the school. At lunch time Frieda served hot chocolate with delicious sandwiches. The other meals we had were just as good. During evenings we visited and listened to the radio at a time when the top song of the first few decades of the century was *"Smile Awhile"*—. On one occasion when Marvin was visiting us in St. Cloud while I was a faculty member at St. Cloud State University, he told us of the wealth he would gain selling insurance in Massachusetts. He and Frieda, plus their two boys, lived there for many years, apparently well supported.

Friends: Florence, U of M

She was a member of our class in Public School Administration at the University of Minnesota. Very few women enrolled in this class so she stood out in all of her femininity, with a beautiful smile and courteous demeanor. On one occasion after class I had the courage to visit with her briefly concerning some point that was made in that day's lecture. Our conversation continued as we walked on the campus in the direction of her apartment. As we approached the building she did not invite me in which I thought was acceptable behavior on her part. Sometime later she did invite me into visit with her family: one boy and one girl. This kind of introduction did not eclipse our friendship but I must admit my romantic interests in her were much modified. We did go to the news reel programs in Northrup Auditorium on Wednesdays and occasionally I helped her carry her groceries. From time to time she would come to the seminar room in the campus library for a chat. She was attractive, effective at visiting, but her smoking always disturbed me. When summer school began I introduced her to my friend Al Madden. Some years later I learned that she had married the agricultural teacher at Brainerd High School. Her goal of leaving widowhood was accomplished.

Ralph Floyd

When I was a student in graduate school at the University of Minnesota, I roomed in the same house as Ralph, about a mile from the campus. He had a radio, I didn't. He was employed full-time, I was a full-time student. Ralph would initiate rather brief conversations when I would meet him in our upstairs hallway. Eventually, the conversations became more involved, more friendly. He would remind me that I could use his radio whenever he wasn't in his room. One evening quite early he invited me to go for a ride which ended in treats by him. He was not asking anything of me, rather that I might be his friend (no sexual suggestions of any kind were ever made.) As time went on he would take me to carnivals, interesting restaurants, tours to interesting sights in the Minneapolis–St. Paul area and finally to his home south of the Twin Cities. There he taught me how to sail, which I regarded as thrilling. Ralph Floyd was a true, friendly person with an infectious smile and with a philosophy of life that extended kindliness to persons like me, and I am confident to others. His was a friendship of warmth and generous giving.

John Menozzi

John and I were both students at the University of Minnesota, Minneapolis, in the late 1930s. That is where I met John for the first time. He impressed me as being even tempered, friendly and well informed. As a student he was always abreast of current developments on campus, in the Twin Cities and beyond. While we visited on various occasions, John would ask me, *"Have you heard . . . ?"* in reinforcing my knowledge of current events. His reminders kept me well-informed without a hint of gossiping. John's personality placed him well above any attempt at spreading inadequate information or false rumors. He and I were "buddies" at the Psych. Research Unit in San Antonio, Texas. Later as a veteran

John was principal of a high school in northern Minnesota where Virginia and I became better acquainted with his family. Later we had excellent opportunities to visit as summer school students at the University of Denver. During the years of our friendship, John's optimism, his even temper and friendliness taught me the value of these qualities in all of my professional involvements.

Henry Schlag

Henry Schlag was the professor in charge of art instruction at Waldorf College where at the same time, I was Director of Teacher Training. He was a sophisticated gentleman in regards to his professional demeanor, someone you would like to meet. Nevertheless, if some person or event did not meet his expectations he was capable of expressing negative feelings, as was the case when he received a statue which he had ordered for his class work. He felt that the work of art, since it revealed a complete human form no covering was necessary. This caused a problem to others, causing Henry to very sparingly display his artistic choice. On occasions in our dining room where faculty were seated in a reserved location, he would emphasize that German literature was just as significant as English, an opinion which stimulated vigorous discussions. Henry had been married previously, but while he was at Waldorf he remarried another artist from "back East," Rhea. As a couple, Henry and his new bride were very friendly toward Virginia and me. We traveled together on a number of occasions; one of our outstanding tours was in the nature of a sojourn in Minneapolis and St. Paul. Henry resigned from his professorship at Waldorf in 1942, previous to his and Rhea's decision to live in California. On the afternoon of their departure, they drove by way of the southern route out of Forest City. As we waved significant 'good-byes' we felt that a segment of our lives had gone with them.

Walt and Irma

Walt Person and Irma Tauber were my office mates at Waldorf College, Forest City, Iowa. Walt was the director of business education, including placement services. I was the director of teacher training, including placement services. Irma and I were the Department of Education at Waldorf, a two year college supported in part by the Lutheran Church. The three of us enjoyed interesting chats, conversations and evaluations. Irma had taught in a mission school in New Guinea where she was afflicted by some tropical ailment, but fortunately had recovered. Following WWII, the Persons lived in Albany, Minnesota for a while until he eventually became a professor at Augustana College in Sioux Falls, South Dakota. Irma authored Christian materials for Sunday School pupils as well as for adults. In whatever she did she revealed great academic skills. They had two sons with whom I was not well acquainted. Walt and the boys would go pheasant hunting out on the South Dakota prairies each fall. Eventually he died of a heart condition; I was never informed as to the cause of her death. I remember both as devoted Christians and excellent teachers.

Tillie—A Waldorf Tradition

One of the great advantages of living in a dormitory at Waldorf College in Forest City, Iowa, was that you could enjoy your meals in the campus dining room. I had a room in the men's facility so I was a recipient of this privilege. Single faculty who lived off campus enjoyed the same privilege. Each day three meals were served in this facility: breakfast, lunch and dinner. Tillie was the manager and chief cook who decided which foods should be served and how they would be prepared. She was quiet, an unassuming individual whose personality was of such a nature that she did not seek a great deal of recognition or acclaim. She let the results of her efforts seemingly speak for themselves. Every meal was an event of note as students and faculty alike recognized the quality and expertise that had been involved in all of the food which she prepared. It seems that when the meals are good, conversations at mealtimes are also more inviting. When memories of days at Waldorf are recited and recorded, much credit will be due Tillie for making dining such a gracious part of life at the college. My recollections of the privilege of enjoying the Waldorf dining room are all exceedingly pleasant.

Clifford Johnson

Clifford Johnson was reared in our rural neighborhood of Upsala, Minnesota. He acquired basic secretarial skills at a relatively early age which enabled him to accept employment in routine office settings. Eventually he obtained a job as an officer in the Men's Reformatory in St. Cloud. His assignment was to register prisoners who were committed to the institution for specified periods of time. While I was a student at St. Cloud State he and his family would invite me to dinners and picnics. I deeply appreciated all of the generosity they bestowed upon me. On one occasion, Clifford asked me to ride along after he agreed to bring Evelyn Jacobson back to her teaching assignment following a weekend in St. Cloud. A ways out of town we were forced to turn back due to the intensity of the blizzard which had developed over Minnesota. I rode along in case we got stuck in the snow. When I returned from nearly four years in the Army I was employed as a counselor at St. Cloud State. During my first Christmas as a civilian, Virginia and I invited Clifford and his wife to our apartment for holiday refreshments. During the course of the evening, while Virginia happened to stand under the mistletoe, Clifford gave her a big hug and kiss. From that time on, Freida, Clifford's wife, was cool to us—a case of unrequited jealousy.

Al Madden

I was well acquainted with Al when he lived in Minnesota, especially as a teacher in the Upsala Consolidated School. My acquaintance with Al was especially strengthened when he invited me along with Frieda and Marvin Bacon to accompany him on a trip to his parental home in southern Indiana.The tour occurred in August of 1937, previous to my enrolling at Gustavus for my senior year. Our first stop was in Chicago where my first impression of the city was made when I saw a man guarding a mail truck with a machine gun. Much more interesting was our tour of the big city at night. Some of the offices we visited in the downtown area were especially impressive. After breakfast the following morning, we drove through Gary, Indiana, where each stack was emitting a different color of smoke. Eventually we reached Al's home area. While in that part of the country, we toured parts of Kentucky with Al as our guide. I specifically remember the watermarks on many buildings, indicating how high the flood waters had gone in early 1937. On our way home we traveled through much of Illinois, including a stop at

Galena, General Grant's hometown. One interesting incident that happened in Illinois was when I ordered milk and fish in a restaurant. I was told that the combination was illegal, so consequently I ate an illegal lunch and survived.

Clair Gurwell

I met Clair Gurwell for the first time when we were students at the University of Denver. It was 1950, he was a graduate student in the English department, whereas I was studying for my doctorate in Educational Psychology. One morning he invited several of us, all graduate students, for a coffee hour in his family's Quonset hut. While there we met Lois Gurwell and Dennis, who after appropriate introductions passed a coffee cup around, in essence of asking for a contribution. All of us thought this was a humorous thing for him to do as the boy wanted attention more than money. In another year or so Lois prevailed upon Clair to seek a full-time teaching job rather than have him continue his work as a graduate student and assistant in the English department. Clair was subsequently employed as a member of the faculty in the Lusk, Wyoming school system. Virginia and I visited them there as part of our Black Hills tour in 1951. During a visit to Denver in 1952 we visited the Gurwells briefly. On that occasion I became the godfather for Douglas, whose baptism we attended. In 1956 we visited the family again but this time we renewed our friendship in Medford, Oregon, where Clair was a member of the high school faculty.

Ed Pfau

Ed Pfau was a student at the University of Denver, enrolled the same time I was involved in completing requirements for the doctorate during the 1950–51 school year. Ed lived in the same apartment facility as Virginia and I; in fact we were neighbors on the second floor of what at one time had been a private home. Ed was friendly and enjoyed warm discussions on a variety of topics. One day he came into our apartment laughing. For some reason he had returned to his apartment and almost immediately came to visit us. His laughter was motivated by the fact that he had so recently knocked on his own door. On another occasion he purchased all the ties in a men's store as a result of his liking one especially well. One evening, Virginia, Ed and I walked over to the campus to listen to an account offered by a refugee from Russia. We left after the main presentation was given so that we could listen to General MacArthur's farewell report to Congress. Ed felt so guilty about our leaving the campus early that he subsequently invited the speaker and another guest to our apartment for coffee the next evening without letting us know about the invitation. Virginia and I enjoyed visiting with our guests that evening while Ed spent most of that time in our apartment sleeping.

Easter: Denver

Easter morning, 1951, Virginia and I arose sufficiently early so we would arrive promptly at the Red Rock Theater west of Denver for sunrise services. Marco, a Chinese friend of ours, rode along with us so that he might share in the Easter inspiration. The morning was beautiful in the semi-darkness as we drove out to the theater. Marco wished to learn more about Christianity as we traveled along—he was a good student. Upon our arrival at the site for the service we soon determined that we were part of a large crowd in attendance that Sunday morning. Just as the sun rose, flooding the theater with light, the music began in all of its springtime resonance. The speaker was impressive but I cannot identify him at this late date. When the program was completed and as we left for our apartment complex, we felt that sacrificing some sleep and having Marco as a guest was all worthwhile as we considered the messages we received. As we entered our apartment after wishing Marco a good day, we decided to spend the rest of that Easter Sunday in reasonable solitude. As our "resting" began, we observed a family parked outside our apartment building. We immediately recognized them as Ortmanns, friends from Minnesota. Erwin, the father, was a student at Greeley, Colorado, where we earlier had found housing for them. We did enjoy their company as we spent the afternoon in City Park. The visit was in the nature of a social break, one appropriate for an Easter Sunday afternoon.

Marco

Marco was a student at the University of Denver in '50–'51 who was involved in the Nationalistic cause while he was living in China. In his homeland Marco was a member of a wealthy family, all living the "good life" previous to the Communistic takeover. He was the recipient of a student visa which gave him a fair amount of freedom as a student. His primary field was chemistry where he extended himself by preparing bird's nest soup and thousand year old eggs in the laboratory. Marco's chief hobby, nearly a vocation, was Chinese cooking. On one occasion while we were in a Denver restaurant serving Chinese food as part of its menu, Marco said the items on the menu were Americanized Chinese dishes. Marco's reputation as a cook became quite well known as a result of the banquets he and a Chinese friend were serving. They would "take over" a home, where the host and hostess lived, buy all the groceries, prepare a delicious dinner, one course at a time. When the cooking and serving were completed they would leave the home as they had found it. Marco moved eventually to an apartment near downtown Denver where on one occasion he invited Virginia and me along with other friends for the enjoyment of a real Chinese dinner. The dinner was deliciously prepared and served in a royal manner. Marco was at his gracious best when he could prepare and serve as he did for us.

Gurwells in Medford, Oregon

Virginia and I visited friends in Medford, Oregon, for the first time in the mid 1950s. When we entered the valley in which Medford is located, we saw the smoke of so many lumber mills that we thought we were entering the "Valley of a Thousand Smokes." Over the years and through pleasant visits with the Gurwells and Scotts, our friends in that locality, we gained the impression that Medford was a scenic and inviting place. The Gurwells' two boys, Dennis and Douglas and their parents, Clair and Lois, entertained us royally even to the extent of eating Oregon blackberries that grew wild in their neighborhood. Eventually, Clair accepted a teaching job in the Taft High School, Taft, California. Art and Betty Scott had no children; both made us feel very much at home as guests in Medford. During the visit in 1956 and in subsequent visits the Scotts, who continued to live in Medford, were our hosts at Crater Lake, a magnificent park especially in considering the natural beauty of the lake located in an extinct volcanic crater. We enjoyed the historical and "down home like" atmosphere of Jacksonville and its scenic environs, the natural beauty of the Medford area with its lakes and streams. The pear orchards, the peach crops and stately forests all appealed to us. During our most recent visit in Medford the air was sparkling clean and forests yet uncut appealed to us mightily. The Medford-Ashland area is one of our favorite locations in Oregon.

Harry Huls

Harry was born in a log cabin in central Minnesota. I was born in central Minnesota several years earlier. He was a member of a high school graduating class of seven; my class was somewhat larger, twenty one. Harry Huls was reared on a farm near Deer Creek; my home farm was situated near Upsala. Both of us attended St. Cloud State. I graduated from the two-year course in education; Harry earned a bachelor's degree in the same field. When he was an adolescent Harry was offered course work on a scholarship basis in engineering in a school in Milwaukee, Wisconsin, but parental approval for this opportunity was not available, consequently this offer was rejected. My friend continued his work in education as a classroom teacher and administrator. While he was superintendent of a suburban Minneapolis school district he earned a Ph.D. at the University of Minnesota. Following the earning of a doctorate, Dr. Huls became a member of the faculty of South Dakota State, and later, a professor at San Diego State University. His experience in the fields of math and reading enabled him to accept assignments in various schools in California as a counselor beyond his teaching load at SDSU. He used his computer potentials in developing lessons which brought his skills national recognition. Dr. Huls was in every sense a recognized professional.

Bjorn Karlsen

The first time I met Bjorn Karlsen was in September 1954 on the campus of what is currently San Diego State University. He and I shared an office in the Dept. of Ed. in a building that was then the Campus Lab School. The fact that we were both of Scandinavian ancestry helped in developing a close friendship early on. Bjorn was given an opportunity for early advancement when the "Johnny Can't Read" idea swept across the country. He refuted some of the claims of European progress in reading by stating that as a citizen of Norway he knew that Western Europe was having the same problems that existed in reading instruction that seemed to be typical in the U.S. His well stated impressions soothed away some local and national criticisms, much to the relief of American teachers. Bjorn's wife and three boys almost became family with Virginia and me. When Bjorn's parents from Norway visited in San Diego it seemed as though we were their relatives too. Dinners, picnics, camping trips were all on the social calendar for the Andersons and the Karlsens. Bjorn's future successes as a faculty member at the University of Minnesota and the family return to California (Cal State at Sonoma) strengthened Bjorn's professional status. We were content to stay in San Diego, especially as I eventually became a full professor at San Diego State. I still respect Bjorn even though our current associations are more distant.

Art Kartman

Art and Anita Kartman lived on 60th Street right across a communal driveway from our house. Art was a member of the faculty of the Economics Department at San Diego State. We learned to know them as a neat couple recently married. While the Kartmans lived on 60th Street, they announced the birth of their only child, Elizabeth. Anita had teaching assignments in the San Diego Public Schools and also participated as a member of the San Diego Chorale. Art's parents visited from Chicago on at least one occasion. Through friendly introductions, we became acquainted with them as well as with Anita's mother. Even though Art and Anita were neighbors, they sometimes seemed rather distant to us. Eventually they moved to Encinitas where they located in a new home as residents of North San Diego County. I would meet Art occasionally following their move. On one occasion Anita Anderson and I invited Elizabeth and her dad to go with us to a county fair in Vista. We all had an enjoyable time that day. As years went by, Art and I would have lunch together once a week during the school year. In recent times when Irene and I stayed at Irene's timeshare unit at Lawrence Welks, we always invite them over for dinner. Currently our relationships with the Kartmans has been one of warmth and understanding. Anita has finally accepted us as Art always did.

Cairns Family

The Cairns family lived across the street from us for a decade, 1954–64. Their three children "grew up" during the time the Andersons and the Cairns were neighbors. Betsy, the oldest of three children, graduated from San Diego State University as an elementary level teacher.

Freddie, the only son, was outstanding as a little league baseball player who eventually obtained an administrative position with the Pennzoil company. Jeanie was the youngest. One of the characteristics she displayed was a high level of curiosity. She enjoyed things of nature especially, almost every living creature that moved. She was a student at the Campus Lab School at San Diego State. She would at times during opportunities for silent reading, have a more interesting novel hidden within the larger text from which she should have been reading. Eventually she graduated from the University of Chicago, then became a faculty member on that campus. As a mother she encouraged her children to become skilled in the field of music. The most recent visit I had with Jeanie was at her father's memorial service, where I also met her husband. They now live in the Los Angeles area as very successful monetary experts.

Pastor Arne Christianson

Reverend Christianson served as pastor in 1958–1973 during a period of rapid growth and development at College Lutheran Church, San Diego. The qualities of his leadership encouraged members of all groups and committees to work together for a common purpose—the advancement of the Kingdom of Jesus Christ. I admired these characteristics as I observed how his leadership strengthened the congregation. His sermons were classical in the sense that they enabled the parishioners to more closely understand the teachings of Jesus as they applied to everyday problems and circumstances. In coffee break conferences with Virginia and me, he revealed how his life was guided by his Christian beliefs and convictions. Following our informal visits and church services every

Sunday I felt that growth had occurred in my spiritual life inasmuch as I became more patient in my relationships with all persons I encountered on a daily basis.

Trips to Mexico

On the basis of hints and suggestions by guests over the years revealing a real desire to visit across the border while visiting in San Diego with Virginia and me, we did venture into Mexico to insure their happiness. When Arthur Anderson was our guest he wanted to see the horse races in Tijuana. We won little, lost some, but what excited Arthur most was the bargain priced gasoline for his Cadillac. The Gurwell boys wanted to test their Spanish; with them, their folks and us, we went to the popular tourist center of Tijuana. The Ortmans along with their son, Paul, wanted to visit a Roman Catholic Church in Mexico. They expressed disgust as they viewed people ascending the church steps on their knees. Virginia, Anita, and I accompanied the Thoresons to Ensenada one afternoon for shopping. On our way home we stopped in the vicinity of Rosarita Beach where the Thoresons opened the trunk of their car, revealing a picnic lunch. Bjorn Karlsen's parents from Norway chose to see a bull fight which we viewed in the bullring in Tijuana. Oscar and Clarabelle, Virginia's aunt and uncle, then new residents of Chula Vista, wished to see the various booths displaying wares at a national fair in Tijuana. Each state in Mexico had a display on hand which reflected Mexican diversity. Other trips to Mexico were enjoyed, one with my parents, one with Virginia's mother, and another with my Aunt Ida. We also brought Jack and Marilyn, Virginia's sister and her husband from Santa Rosa, to Tijuana since they were searching for Mexican bargains. As residents near an international border, we did enjoy sharing the enthusiasm for Mexico that was expressed by relatives and friends.

A Relaxing Experience

Several years ago during the course of a warm summer's morning, Irene and I were invited to share a picnic with her sister, Vernia, and Vernia's husband, Russ. The four of us ventured into an area in east San Diego County known for its falls: Green Valley. As we relaxed in an beautiful wooded area among the oaks and coniferous trees, we proceeded to enjoy our picnic lunch. Above us large thunderheads were forming, reminding us of the possibility of rain showers. Amid the thunder and lightning a few drops fell, sufficient to refresh the air but not sufficiently heavy to interfere with our picnic. All of us relaxed in this marvelous setting with no interference from automobile traffic or telephones. Following our lunch we sauntered over to the area where the waterfalls were attracting a few visitors who with us admired the rocky layers that formed patterns for falling water. It was a great place, especially for children who might enjoy swimming in the location. As we strolled toward our vehicle, parked nearby, we continued to feel the warmth of fellowship and the grandeur of the scenic views spread before us.

Erik Palmgren

Both Irene and I learned to know Erik as an excellent teacher and refined gentleman as we were enrolled in one or more of his Swedish classes. He was born in Sweden, came to the United States to pursue employment as an engineer. His linguistic skills were well defined beyond English and Swedish. As a teacher he was well versed in regarding both planning and enrichment. His interest in student progress was well illustrated by the volumes of materials he brought to each class session. Erik encouraged members of his classes to select materials for home study at no charge. His expertise in grammatical instructions knew no peer as he made the content he employed useful and interesting. Reading assignments would focus on folk tales and humorous antics which made his classes more stimulating. Even an early involvement in his classes made Sweden seem like a second home with appropriate stress placed on government, including the royal family, history, the arts, and economics. Through discussions and pictorial reviews we would visit the Town Hall in Stockholm where the Nobel prizes were distributed. During the midtime break each evening (the classes met during evening hours) we shared refreshments which gave us a better sense regarding Swedish hospitality. Erik would invite students to his home, especially for Christmas parties. He was an outstanding host, a great teacher and a refined gentleman on all occasions.

II
THE FARM AND
COMMUNITY

THE FARM AND COMMUNITY
Table of Contents

THE FARM AND COMMUNITY

The Source of the Mississippi River

From an elevation of 1475 feet, the mighty Mississippi begins its course at Lake Itasca in northern Minnesota, flowing until it reaches the Gulf of Mexico. It's just a small stream as it begins its journey in a location where a few well placed stones enable tourists to walk across the river. The stream bed of the Mississippi meanders north and east through the Bemidji area, providing the sources and mouths for a series of lakes as it forms a large question mark on the map of the state. Its course is south through St. Cloud, then southeast into the Twin Cities with the river forming the boundary line between Minnesota and Wisconsin. It continues south, forming the boundary lines between several states. South of Little Falls the Blanchard Rapids Dam was constructed several decades ago. I had luck fishing for walleyed pike in the fast flowing water that came gushing over the dam with its gates open. In the St. Cloud area below the campus of St. Cloud State, there is a series of islands dividing the river into several park like areas. The Mississippi has provided many scenic attractions for me as I have viewed it in a variety of historical locations.

From Timber to Prairie

When the first pioneers entered the area which now encompasses the Upsala community, they made their way through miles of heavy timber, consisting mainly of beautiful hardwood trees. White oak, red oak, birch, maple, and elm were growing in large quantities in the area. The assumption early on was that farming was to be the chief occupation in central Minnesota, that trees were somewhat of a handicap for the plowing of the land. As the years went by more and more land was given over to the growing of grain crops and hay rather than trees. We had a beautiful woodlot on our farm with some trees reaching the century mark. My dad was always careful to cut only trees that were fading, with the thought that young saplings should be encouraged to grow. As a result there was an air of permanency regarding our trees. In various parts of the community more and more trees were cut down with no plan to replace the older crop with new growth. The kind of thinking that has produced timber depletion and has made the Upsala area a prairie with limited appreciations for trees, also caused obvious soil depletion. My feelings concerning this matter is not that I didn't like prairies, but rather how they were sometimes formed by cutting beautiful trees that help conserve soil and protect water supplies. On one occasion I visited an officer in St. Paul who was in charge of conservation in Minnesota, suggesting that a light tax benefit for saving woodlots would be acceptable. He disagreed, thus promoting the destruction of some of the beautiful woodlands of rural Minnesota.

Little Falls, Minnesota

This city is the county seat of Morrison County, the locale in which I was born. Little Falls is especially famous as the home of Charles A. Lindbergh, the community in which he spent his youth. The first train ride I ever had was out of Little Falls with St. Cloud as my destination. This experienced occurred in a November blizzard in 1934. In July of 1927 the confirmation pictures of our class at Gethsemane Lutheran Church, Upsala, were taken at the Nelson studio in Little Falls. In more recent times while my parents were with me, I checked my birth records at the court house. There were five errors in the document which subsequently were corrected. In the summer of 1952 I was assigned to teach in Little Falls as part of an extension program associated with St. Cloud State University. The primeval forest, the Mississippi River and Lindbergh's boyhood home are scenic and historical attractions in Little Falls. Our family has enjoyed birthday parties and family reunions in this community. My mother had a teaching assignment in an area nearby. I have always enjoyed the local attractions and genuine friendly feelings expressed by the citizens of Little Falls.

Work Schedule on the Farm

Our farm consisted of 100 acres of which approximately 40 acres were tillable. When the last snow drifts of winter had thawed and the dark soil in our fields appeared, the time had come for us to follow one of the working schedules on the farm. The fertilizer that had been accumulating in small piles during the winter on what would become a field of corn, was spread out evenly. Following this procedure the soil was plowed and dragged. (The dragging was done by equipment made up of small wooden or steel beams into which numerous spikelike metal pieces had been placed.) When dragging was done the surface of the field would be acceptably smoother. Following the winter freeze and spring thaw large rocks had risen to the surface, so the next job was to remove as many rocks as were reasonably removable. The seed grains were fanned so as to remove unwanted residue. When the grain was ready my Dad would put sacks of grain into a seeder; as the horses pulled the seeder the grain was planted in even rows. At corn planting time the horses would pull markers across the potential corn fields, leaving small depressed channels in the soil. The marker was first pulled north and south, then east and west, leaving numerous squares in the soil. In each cross section my Dad would plant a few seeds of corn. Optimism for good crops prevailed at this time of year. Then with good weather our wishes were realized.

Our Well

The most valuable natural resource on our farm was the cool, refreshing, clean and safe water available from our well. Originally it was dug by hand, to a depth of approximately 30 feet at which level we had a dependable supply of water. Our waterwitch expert, Mrs. Sundquist, had indicated how the water was flowing underground and thus we knew where to locate the well. During the exceptionally dry years of the 1930s, it was essential to us to deepen the well by several feet; this done, our effective water supply was assured. During the warmer months of the year the well served as a refrigerator for keeping our cream fresh. Twice the well was broken into, the lock severed and the cream stolen. Following the erection of a tent on our premises for more comfortable summer sleeping, with my brother Laurel and our dog Buster, and me sleeping outside our house, no more stealing of cream occurred. A hand pump enabled us to gain access to the water in the well. It was my job to fill the stock tank every day in addition to carrying pails of water to the house.

During colder weather the water in the stock tank would freeze so to make it more palatable, I would build a fire of wood in a cast iron stove positioned in the tank to thaw the ice. Pumping the water, carrying water to the kitchen and thawing water for the livestock all enabled me to retain a measure of physical fitness.

Rocks

For farmers living in parts of central and northern Minnesota, one involvement that was persistent and strenuous out of proportion to other jobs on the farm, was the matter of dealing with and getting rid of rocks. The big rocks which resisted moving had to be driven around when grass was being cut or ground cultivated. The smaller ones which varied in size from a few pounds to many, through strenuous labor were lifted and deposited in huge piles on farm property. As the frost and thawing of the colder season would force rocks to the surface, each year a new crop appeared. Where a glacial movement had been slowed down or stopped with a considerable amount of thawing, as part of a terminal moraine, piles of rocks would be deposited in that area. The glacial impact was very much in evidence in the soil of our farm with rock formations and depositions. In some areas of Minnesota and neighboring states, the top soil was several feet thick with few or no rock problems. The water from the melting glaciers and subsequent plant formations had blessed the farmers in these areas with freedom from the natural burden of intensive rock distribution.

Hazelnuts

The warmth of summer would be tapering off with shorter days and cooler nights. At this time of the year the hazelnut crops in our area was ready for harvesting. I would find a clump of hazelnut bushes and seclude myself in it, equipped with two handheld rocks. One was quite smooth and the other was in the nature of a hammer. At a time like this I would feel that I was detached from the world with a blue sky above and bushes all around me. The sounds of birds would break the quietude of the area in a soothing pleasant manner. I would always deliberately save a portion of my appetite for the feast at hand. The leafy cover of each nut would be removed, providing easy access to the meats within. Then the nuts would be ready for cracking with my hammer-like stone. One taste assured me that the nuts were adequately ripened to a peak of tastiness. My feast would continue until I felt I had adequately sampled one of nature's excellent gifts to the fullest. There were still enough nuts remaining for the squirrels as nature had provided so well for all of us.

Threshing

One of the biggest events on our farm occurred when the grain we had harvested was threshed. A steam engine pulling the threshing machine would station itself so it could furnish the mechanical power required to separate the grain from the straw and chaff. With the thresher parked between the stacks of grain which we had earlier put together, with the windstacker extended for the building of a good straw pile, and with the grain spouts ready to pour the fresh grain into cloth bags, the threshing process began. Members of the crew would pitch the bundles of grain into the extended arms of the thresher while a man receiving the grain as it was being threshed sacked the golden crop into bags at hand. Members of the crew were always fed excellent meals during their breaks at work and usually were considered as highly accepted farm workers. When the job was complete we had a well-rounded straw pile with bins full of grains harvested during the growing season. Threshing was truly one of the biggest events of the year on the farm.

Road Repairs

It was early in June, school was out and it was time to repair some of the damage the early spring thaws had done to the dirt roads in our area. The township office had allotted certain funds designated for road repair, money to be used to smoothen the ruts that so obviously developed each spring. Our neighbor, Carl Thies, hired me to drive a team of his horses and wagon involved in hauling gravel from a pit nearby to the places where the road repair work was being done. I'd drive the horses into the pit so we could position the wagon for loading the gravel. From the pit I would drive down a country lane to the road where the work was being done. Each time I would meet a driver returning his empty wagon, we would engage in a brief conversation. The visiting we did as we hauled the gravel or loaded or unloaded it was always interesting. The bond which existed between neighbors was always a factor in stimulating good relationships. That's why I relished the road work as a means of promoting basic friendships and making summer driving more comfortable, plus earning a few dollars for the work accomplished.

Weeds

A major problem with which every farmer in our area had to deal was spelled w-e-e-d-s. When the threshing was done not all of the weed seeds had been removed from the grain crops stored at the end of the harvest and threshing seasons. Consequently, my Dad would fan the grain each spring before planting in an attempt to remove the residual weed seeds. The wheat, barley, and oats grew in such a manner that they could choke a certain number of weeds, but not all. Since corn was planted in spaced rows, each hill would compete with the weed crop unless the corn was cultivated several times during the growing season. The weeds would grow rapidly unless cut or uprooted. One weed that we cut before the seeds would spread was Canadian thistle. Unless these weeds were cut by each farmer, hopefully to the point of eradication, the county would remove the crop, assessing the farmer for work accomplished. Another weed that we had to cut before it could do much damage, was the nettle, whose leaves would create a stinging rash. The quack grass had cancer-like characteristics—unless you dug out each root it would rapidly reestablish itself. Poison ivy was always a threat and had to be cut away. The identification of weeds could be done at great length and still not be completely covered. To keep a field or any area on the farm weed free was a continuous challenge.

Dogs

During the time I lived as a member of the family on our family farm, we had three dogs. One was part Collie, two were part Boston Terriers. Our first terrier did not survive very long but our other dogs experienced an effective longevity. The collie's name was Bob but for purposes of sophistication we added the name Harrington to our pet's given name, Bob. Bob was friendly but only to a certain point. He would growl and show his teeth quite readily but this assertiveness made him a good watch dog. Buster on the other had (his surname was Barrington) was generally quite friendly. He used to spend a bit of time indoors during cold weather and was especially pleased when my brother Laurel and I bought a tent where we comfortably slept each night during summers. His keen hearing and forceful bark alerted us to any intruders. Buster killed numerous rats and quickly made any stray livestock return to their home pastures. He was an excellent dog, a good friend and a serious loss at the time of his death.

One Barn + One Barn = One Barn

Not correct math, but for a project on our farm it worked out very well. In circa 1920, the neighbor to the south, Mr. Lawrence, sold his farm, including buildings such as his barn. This particular farm building had the same dimensions as our barn. A carpenter friend reasoned to the effect that if my Dad wanted a bigger barn, two barns could be put together. One afternoon as I was playing in our farm yard I saw a steam engine, the kind used in threshing, pulling this farm building down our road from the south, then eventually depositing the structure near our barn. Months of labor followed the positioning of the new barn against our old barn, now one. In the process the walls of the new barn were efficiently strengthened. I was amazed at how well the carpenters were doing their jobs. One day when they had taken a break in my presence, even offering me a drink of whatever they were enjoying—probably root beer. I was happy to join them. When my mother heard about my sampling she hoped that it would not develop an interest within me for something stronger. No need for her to worry! The last part of the barn building involvement was to place a cement brace on the west side of the barn. My Dad wrote the date in the fresh cement, 1920–21. I assumed all the work involved could easily have gone into two years. The last time I saw the "old home place" the 1+1=1 was still standing firm, doing its usual job effectively.

Economy on the Farm:
1914–1932 Income and Expenditures

There were definite guidelines that determined how the economy on our farm would function. One guide that functioned very efficiently was to the effect *"If you don't have the money, you don't buy it"* or *"If you don't really need it, don't buy it."* These were basic guidelines that tended to regulate business on our farm. As a result we were with the last to buy a car, and our family had no telephone and no radio and no daily newspapers. The eggs the chickens laid during the milder months paid for our groceries. Our little pig crop determined how large our orders to Sears, Roebuck and Montgomery Ward would be. The cream from our dairy herd helped pay our taxes and helped purchase supplies and equipment we might need, especially if an emergency arose. For awhile my Dad had health insurance, but the rest of the family did not have such personal protection. Fortunately no great medical bills confronted us. During the winters our kitchen stove and one heater kept us warm as we burned wood that was obtained from our large woodlot. Until we purchased a Model T Ford we used only kerosene for our lights in the house and for our lantern. We adjusted to our economy as a family, thankful for all the gifts we had—free of debt from time to time and healthy most of the time. Even though limited, life on our farm was great.

Auction Country Style

A source of excitement and at the same time one of regret had to do with the announcement that someone in our community was having an auction. There was excitement, brought about by being present in a big crowd and regret knowing that a good neighbor would be leaving our area. Auctions were usually scheduled for the springtime when all the crops had been planted or in the fall when the crops had been harvested. Since our area was primarily given over to dairying, the sale of livestock, grain and farm implements was in the inventory of things going for sale. The crowd of potential buyers would be on hand by nine o'clock in the morning when all chores were completed. At the outset some piece of equipment was offered. After a brief description of the item the bidding would begin with, *"How much am I offered for this—"* then the description again if necessary if the bids were not forthcoming. Then a bid was made, then another until the final chanting, *bid once, bid twice sold to—"*. This process continued all day for items to be sold. At lunch time the owner might furnish the food or a lunch wagon would be there to supply refreshments. The money for the sales would probably be collected by the local banker with the auctioneer receiving a percentage of the amount gained. When all financial transactions had been made the owner received the remaining amount. In "good" times with the sale of good items the amount would be substantial. During the depression sometimes the total would be only a few dollars. In this case a loan against

the property was settled by the bank before the farmer got
any money.

Chimney Fire

Early one beautiful spring evening while we were
enjoying our dinner, we heard a strange sound, like the
sound of wind blowing over a wooded landscape. For a
moment we could not discover the source of this strange
noise. Suddenly we realized that the strange sound was
that of a roaring fire in our chimney. Immediately my
Dad ran upstairs and rescued all the contents of a drawer
where important legal documents were stored. All of us
ran outside to see really what was happening as a bright
flame shot out through the top of the chimney. Sparks
were flying, showering the roof of our house with bright
flames. Smoke was pouring into our house since doors
and windows had been left open due to the effect of the
mild spring weather. Fortunately the metal covering the
roof of the house prevented any flames from penetrating
to wooden surfaces. The bricks which made up the chimney were not cracked or otherwise damaged. The odor of
the smoke had penetrated every stitch of our garments;
for days afterward people asked us how much damage
had been done.

Surprise: Skunk

Early one summer evening while the twilight was
deepening, my mother was out in the barn gathering eggs
and chickens that would "set" on the eggs and thus hatch
chicks and not lay any more eggs. My mother gathered
up one hen that seemed to be quite heavy but with a soft
underside like chickens have. She carried the eggs in a

basket with this fairly heavy "chicken" cuddled in her arm. When she stepped out of the door into the dim light she saw what kind of chicken she was carrying—a big fat skunk! She dropped the creature gently so as not to frighten it. Apparently the skunk didn't mind being held; upon its release it sauntered off in the direction of the woodpile. No skunk odor was emitted. Apparently skunks like to sample eggs that is why my mother found this creature in a chicken nest. We did have other skunks in our neighborhood and as noted, one evening as my Dad, brother Laurel and I were walking on a road through a meadow, we saw a mother skunk leading its brood across the road and then disappear into the tall grass on the other side. Displays such as this remind us of the beauty of nature and of the demands nature places upon its children.

Wood for Our Stoves

There was a considerable amount of effort involved in preparing our wood supply for fuel required for our kitchen stove and one or two heaters. First of all, our Dad would select the trees that would be cut into various sizes for convenient usage. His would be quite selective in his choices so that assurances of a self perpetuating woodlot would be very much in evidence. Dad, my brother Laurel and I were all involved in the second stage of our wood gathering procedure. Trees would be cut down, branches removed and the wood sawed into lengths for efficient handling. The third step involved in the fuel supplying process would include transporting the tree trunks to our farmyard and stacking them for the fourth step. This step was expedited with the assistance by a neighbor who transported his powered saw into our yard for the cutting of the trees into proper lengths. Two of us would move the tree trunks over to the saw for proper cutting as one person intercepted the chunks from the saw, now about a foot in length which then would be chopped into convenient pieces. The larger pieces would be used for heaters, the smaller pieces of wood would be used in the kitchen stove. Our Dad was also an expert at chopping and piling the wood, making it readily acceptable for future use. I still enjoy the smoke from a peaceful wood fire—it is a reminder of home.

Lilacs

A beauty of the spring season comes back to life in the form of lilac blossoms. The color and fragrance of this attractive floral harbinger is most welcome as is evidenced by the fact that displays of these gorgeous flowers grace the tables, windows, speaker's stands, and auditoriums where their appearance inspires and satisfies the desire for color and perfume existing in combination. In some of the ranches in the mountains east of San Diego these marvelous reminders of a new season grow gloriously. In downtown San Diego in what was then the Marston Store, the management would arrange to display grand bouquets of these flowers on the main floor and elsewhere. In my home town of Upsala and elsewhere in Minnesota, at graduation time and on Memorial Day, lilacs would grace the platforms of commencement speakers and add color and respect in local cemeteries. While on a tour in Nevada some years ago, Irene and I were very much impressed by the beautiful lilacs in Carson City. These gracious floral displays were much more inspiring than the flashing lights of the various casinos.

Life: Wild and Somewhat Wild

Due to the dry weather during the summers I worked for my Uncle and Grandfather, we were able to clear away some of the brush that had grown freely during years of greater rainfall. I was in the process of clearing away some of the growth when I heard a strange sound, like the buzzing of many bees combined with the noise of a truck. As I looked around a huge swarm of bees passed by led by the queen all searching for a new home for their comfort and convenience. On another occasion I was evaluating the condition of a fence line in a swampy area partially owned by a neighbor. As I continued checking the fence line I nearly stumbled upon a bull partially submerged in the swamp. Obviously I could do little to assist this valuable member of the neighbor's dairy herd. My uncle called the neighbors, reminding them of the accident that had befallen the helpless bull. It was finally rescued. Another creature that was made nearly helpless by wild emotions was one of my uncle's horses, named Pet. The horse, when harnessed, would rear up, dash ahead, try to run and in every way free itself from any restraints. All of this violent activity would cause sores to develop on its shoulders, thus making it disabled and limited it from basic employment.

Trees to Lumber

In our area of Central Minnesota, there were a few enterprising farmers with access to steam power who would operate saw mills for the convenience of anyone who wanted lumber made out of local hardwood trees. For some jobs my Dad would opt for homemade lumber as the local wooden product was called. First of all he would determine which hardwood trees, elm, oak or maple, would produce the kind of lumber he would choose for certain construction projects. Then he would select several large trees with no branches a few feet from the base of the tree. The timber was cut and made ready for the production of lumber at the sawmill. The logs from these trees would be loaded on our sleigh, then drawn by our team of horses to the proper location for sawing. At the mill each log in turn was put on a conveyance resembling a large table. The sawyer who ran the equipment made certain that the log being cut would be pushed against a circular saw several feet in diameter. The bark was cut off, then the log was cut into boards; 2 × 4, 1 × 4, ext. according to the dimensions of the lumber my Dad had requested. The resulting sawdust and bark that were cut off would be burned. Currently at large sawmills all the sawdust and bark are saved to be used in the construction of building materials—good conservation.

The Creamery

One of the busiest centers for social and economic activities in the Upsala community was the creamery. Each morning, Monday through Saturday, dairy farmers would bring fresh cream in metal cans to the platform door of the facility where the contents would be weighed and a sample taken to ascertain the amount of butterfat in each can of cream. Sometimes the cans would be returned empty to the waiting dairy farmer but on occasion a certain amount of buttermilk would be sent out to the farmers who patronized the creamery. Since our community was supported by the dairy industry, each herd of cows would be milked twice a day. The milk would be separated, the skim milk going into one container, the cream into another. The cream would be placed in some kind of cooler whereas the skim milk was fed to the hogs. I remember bringing cans of cream to town, having the weight of the contents determined and a report received that told us the butterfat content, and on occasion receiving in return a portion of buttermilk. Each trip to the creamery was also a social affair during which I would learn where the best fishing occurred that week, who were the school board candidates, who was about to be married, as well as an assessment of weather conditions. It was at the creamery that I learned that I had been selected to teach in the Upsala Consolidated Schools. This is where I heard about people moving into and out of the community, and how well Land 'O Lakes was dealing with our creamery.

Erosion

One of the massive problems faced by all tillers of the soil and all others who exploit the soil that covers this planet, is in regard to retaining this valuable resource. The covering can be many inches or feet thick, spread out over all areas not covered by water. The erosion of ponds, lakes, streams, oceans, all areas covered by water is known as pollution. In our community we had erosion concerns which were typical statewide or worldwide, wherever agricultural pursuits were supporting the lifestyles of the areas. Whenever the ground is plowed or loosened in some way, the valuable top soil might be carried from the plot of ground being cultivated by wind or water. Every reasonable method should be employed to prevent one of the world's richest resources, the top soil, from being carried away. My Dad tilled the soil on our farm in such a manner so that no steep exposure of ground was threatened by severe wind loss or water seepage. On one occasion, I noticed how severe rain showers had cut into one of our fields. I systematically built a small dam which over a period of time helped the field heal itself. Systematic tree planting, employing useful grasses to hold the soil in place and contour plowing all assisted in retaining valuable top soil. As the soil diminishes, so does the value of the land tilled by its owner.

Wild Flowers

Some of my favorite wild flowers that grew in abundance in the Upsala community make the growing seasons in our area more glorious. In recesses in some of the forest regions in Central Minnesota, we found moccasins (the state flower) growing. It is a member of the orchid family. In the wooded areas the jack-in-the-pulpit grew in lavish displays. The blossoms of wild fruit trees were also identified as some of my choice wild flowers: plum, thorn apple, Juneberry, and on the vines, the blackberry and raspberry blossoms. Along our country roads displays of clover and wild roses added color and fragrances to the landscape. It is still my opinion that the fragrance of wild roses is not surpassed anywhere in the plant kingdom. In our meadows tiger lilies and Indian paint brushes grew. The honeysuckle and daisies added much to our rural scenes. In lakes and ponds water lilies and buttercups grew in profusion. All the glorious floral displays that nature provided soothe and brighten my memories of spring and summer. The goldenrod and colored leaves added another dimension to the glories of nature during autumn. Even the most famous of work done in water colors or oils cannot surpass the beauty that nature has provided.

Fencing

On the farm this was not a kind of athletic activity; it had to do with securing our fields and pastures from our livestock so that there would be not breaking out of the pasture areas and onto cultivated fields. The total of all of our fencing was 3 miles, plus. My Dad would survey a given line of fencing to determine which posts would be replaced due to deterioration of the wood of which they were made. He would determine how many new posts would be required and how much barbed wire would be needed for the portion of a given fence that had to be repaired. The old posts would be removed and the wood used for kitchen fires. The length of wire estimated as wire at three levels on each post would be required. New post holes were dug, followed by the accurate placement of the new. Then the wire would be strung at three levels. A special piece of equipment for wire stringing was used for this purpose. With the posts in place and the first level of wire accurately positioned, my Dad and I would hammer staples over the wire and into the posts. We placed all wire levels inside the area we were fencing; outside placement would have enabled the livestock to eventually push the wire out and away from the posts. My Dad always wanted good fencing; some of our neighbors were less careful regarding their fences. Thus Dad always kept our cows and horses "at home." This was not universally true in our neighborhood.

Fruits and Nuts

On our farm in Central Minnesota, we harvested a bounty of fruits and nuts each summer even though we had not planted the trees and bushes that produced so lavishly. Nature had planted the crops which we so much enjoyed. In our woodlot, trees and bushes produced Juneberries, pin cherries, wild plums, raspberries, chockeberries and blackberries. On a portion of the farm that was used as pasture for our cattle during the summer we harvested gooseberries. Along the road north of our farm buildings we found hazelnut bushes which produced a delicious crop late in August. A portion of our meadow was covered with wild strawberry plants which provided us with a delicious type of berry which was sweeter than the domesticated kind. Of course we shared part of our bounty with the birds, which they truly appreciated with song and color.

Bees

One of our neighbors, Mr. Slagel, was very interested in bees and in honey. He did not have any hives of his own rather during the early weeks of the fall season would search for bee trees in some of the wood lots in our area. On one occasion he found a tree in a part of our farm that was used for summer pasture for our dairy herd. The tree was hollow with a large opening on one side where the bees could fly in and out at will. They must have been very busy during the summer considering the amount of honey they had deposited in the tree. In the rich deposit Mr. Slagel found honey in different colors, depending on the plants from which the bees had obtained their pollen. This was not the only bee tree our neighbor found since he was skilled in locating places where the bees decided to spend the summer. While he was visiting one fall evening he could hardly talk as the result of a bee stinging his tongue as he enjoyed a sample of the honey.

Cats

So many essentials comprised the need lists for those of us who have lived in rural areas and thus were accustomed to the requirements of life on the farm. Cats occupied prominent places on the need lists for farm life. We generally had several who occupied various stages of development—kitten to mature mother cat. I recall one mother cat in particular, colored gray, white and orange. Her name was simply "Snip." During summer months she was especially adept at finding gophers for her offspring, calling them each time she brought one home. There was the usual growling and snarling until the quarry was divided to the satisfaction of all concerned. We counted the number of gophers "Snip" caught one summer with the total up in the dozens. During cooler weather this ambitious cat kept the mouse population in check. At the end of a busy morning when the cows had been let out to pasture and chickens were involved in their daily routine, sometimes cat families found nice nests shaped to their comfort where they would experience socialized resting and sleeping. Later at milking time all mother cats and kittens were wide awake awaiting rations of fresh milk served in clean oblong shaped sardine cans. In the cool of the evening the kittens would frolic and play and enjoy the last of the meat that "Snip" had caught that day. Summertime was great, especially for the kittens. With the chill of autumn descending on our area we discovered that there were no more kittens around, only mature cats. During the winter they stayed indoors much of the time, assuming their friendly but somewhat detached behavior.

Trip to Royalton

This town is 14–15 miles east of our farm, located on the main line of what was at one time the Northern Pacific Railroad. A trip to the community in early June was a treat for one's vision and invigorating to the other senses as well. The songs of the birds, especially in the early morning hours, the fragrance of the many forms of vegetation were all inspiring. The wild roses along the highway offered a sweetness that hardly any other flowers of its kind could rival. The wild rose is not the neatest in its appearance but the delight of its fragrance is overwhelming. A variety of farm crops offered a blanket of color and fragrance all its own. The red clover about ready for its first harvesting of the year filled the air with a special delight. Honey bees are attracted to its color and nectar. A crop of buckwheat with its relatively light coloration promotes an air of prosperity. As the road executes a steep decline toward the Mississippi we pass an old mill, then cross an ancient bridge over the river. As we experience the crest on the opposite of this valley we enter the Mississippi flood plain, sandy and broad. In this area a colorful display of fields of rye attract the traveler. As the gentle breeze blows across the landscape, the tall rye stocks wave, reminding the observer of the movement of water on a lake. After the harshness of winter the colors and fragrances of June are like a visual paradise in this area.

Buildings I Recall and Loved

Near the end of the main street on a height of ground south of the business area in Upsala stands the Swedish Lutheran Church which holds many memories for me. It is not identified as a cathedral but as a country church that served its members as effectively as did more elaborate houses of worship. Early in its construction it was built with a board siding painted white. Subsequently a brick veneer was added to the exterior. The steeple houses a bell which announced the coming Sunday services each Saturday evening, it tolled mournfully at funeral services, called people to worship each Sunday and joyously rang out the old and in the new each New Year's Eve. The sanctuary with the pulpit to the left and the choir to the right with the altar between was an imposing arrangement which set the mood for various services. Both my Mother and Dad are buried in the churchyard near the exterior of the building, as well as many relatives and friends. I was confirmed in this church in 1927, spoke to the congregation or special groups on a variety of occasions. The structure has been replaced by a house of worship built for the appropriateness of the 21st century. Colored windows and a painting of Christ receiving Peter in the storm at sea were impressive in the old church. The spirit of the congregation seems to be still present in memories of the old structure.

Significant Buildings in My Life

I was a student in this building from 1921–1932, from my first day of school until my high school graduation in 1932. During the academic years 1935–1937, I was a teacher in the elementary department in this building. It is the original Upsala Consolidated School that opened in 1920. Structurally it was designed with all elementary classrooms on the east side of the building and the high school classrooms located on the west side. The exceptions involved the girls' Home. Ec. Classroom on the east side and the library on the west side with services available to the whole school. During the depression the floor of the gym was lowered several feet in order to expedite the basketball performances. The auditorium on the second floor was a high school study hall and community gathering place. In recent times a new elementary school building was dedicated in addition to a new gym–auditorium for the high school. Increased enrollments necessitated the building of the additions. All of my basic reading skill, skills in math, efficiencies in the use of the English language, and basic scientific skills were initially gained in this building. In effect, this school is a monument for all of the Anderson children, Evans, Laurel and Evodia, as they were educated in this building for effectiveness in the adult world.

Churches in Upsala, Minnesota

In the 1920s there were two leading churches in my hometown of Upsala. One was the Swedish Lutheran Church and the other was the Swedish Mission Convenant Church. Our family had relatives buried in the cemeteries of both churches even though we were active members of the Swedish Lutheran Church. From time to time, our friends who were members of the Mission Covenant Church, felt that something special should be done to deal with the sins that citizens in our community were committing. One occasion a Rev. Ost was invited to hold a series of revival meetings at the Mission Church. His appearance was well advertised so people came to hear him. On a Sunday morning he even had the church doors locked to seemingly make it easier for children to confess their sins. During the series of meetings, Rev. Ost conducted pressures that were so great that as a result, one person was committed to a mental hospital. I recall how on a Monday morning following Rev. Ost's appearance while I was at the creamery, someone in the crowd tore down the poster proclaiming the revival meetings. Pressure in the crowd at the creamery indicated that people did not want Rev. Ost to ever return to Upsala.

III
GROWING UP

GROWING UP
Table of Contents

GROWING UP

Upsala, Minnesota—My Home Town

With a population of less than 500 people, Upsala would be identified as a village. The early settlers in the area were Swedish, consequently naming the new community after Uppsala, Sweden, thus honoring the university city. Supplies for the village were brought from places like St. Cloud, 35+ miles distant. Journeys through the heavily wooded areas were slow and difficult. Roadways were constructed over a period of time, enabling settlers to use rail service offered by other communities within the county. No railroad was ever built into Upsala; the river flowing through the area was too narrow for any commercialized traffic. When I was enrolled in the Upsala Consolidated School, the village had a busy creamery serving the dairymen in the community. A printing shop, hardware store, a bank, grocery and clothing outlets were well established. Two Lutheran churches and a Mission Covenant church served the spiritual needs of the people. Medical and dental services were intermittent. Two barber shops, eventually one, were particularly for men. A telephone exchange and a limited drug store were available. During severe winter weather only horse drawn conveyances could be used in the community. Yet it was my hometown. Currently, retirement facilities are a fast growing business in Upsala.

Albany, Minnesota

During my youth at home on the farm, my address was Route 3, Box 46, Albany, Minnesota (no zip code). Upsala was my hometown but Albany was a place of influence for me, nevertheless. It was there in a restaurant on Main Street, along with my Dad, my brother Laurel, and Uncle Albert, that I enjoyed a mug of coffee and ham sandwiches in the early 1920s. Our family visited George Nelson in a small hospital in Albany following an accident in which he lost his arm. We purchased our 1930 Model A Ford through a dealer in Albany. It was in 1931 that Dr. Mahewald treated me, granting me relief from a case of hemorrhoids. Fall, 1933, my folks were there to meet me but Rev. Bergdahl misdirected my folks to Royalton instead. I walked the 13 miles from Albany home on that occasion. In the early 1940s a friend of mine, Oakley Ellickson, was to meet me in Albany, and I was to ride to Forest City, Iowa with him. He was delayed so I traveled to Iowa by bus and by rail instead. My memories of Albany are somewhat those of one passing through, arriving and leaving for good reasons.

Favorite Foods of My Youth

As I think back into my childhood and adolescent years, memories of a variety of gustatorial experiences come to mind. The chicken my mother roasted for my birthday and for our Thanksgiving dinners were unequaled by restaurant chefs. The dressing she used contained delicious raisins which added to the enjoyment of eating. The breads she baked and the rolls she prepared were always superb. Those baked items, fresh from the oven and saturated with our own homechurned butter, even now arouse a hunger pang within me. For desserts at home, raisin pie and chocolate pudding were my favorites. As the corn ripened in late summer, the fresh items from our new crop cooked and spread with butter and salt, were utterly delicious. At my grandmother Ryberg's house, the home made rye bread she baked was as delicious as the best of cakes; her rice pudding was fit for royalty. The meats my Dad would prepare each winter—the T-bone steaks, pork sausages, fried ham, would grace our kitchen table. From the store, liver sausage and pickled herring were great appetizers. Memories of our dining on the farm reflect upon the great meals we had, stimulating a feeling of kindliness and social harmony within our family circle.

A Man's Lunch

I must have been about 6 years of age when my brother Laurel, my Dad and Uncle Albert Ryberg planned to make a trip to the Paynesville area, approximately 35 miles south of our farm. My Dad was quite generous in allowing any one or all three of us children to go along on trips in which he was involved. As I recall it was a nice day, sometime during the late summer of 1920. The trip to our destination was through areas that are (at least were) quite typical of central Minnesota, with fields, meadows, woodlots, streams and lakes. When we arrived at the Henstrand home, our destination, we were warmly welcomed, reflecting typical Scandinavian hospitality. Shortly after our arrival my Dad, Albert and Edward Henstrand left to complete whatever errand that was the reason for our visit. Laurel and I stayed at the home, pleasantly watching Mrs. Henstrand bake cookies. It was well into the afternoon when we extended our good-byes.

On the way home we stopped in Albany for a late afternoon lunch. My Dad ordered for himself, Laurel and me:
a big ham sandwich and a cup of hot coffee for each of us.
I felt as though I was now definitely among adult peers, at
least as far as my order would provide the proper maturity. Of the events of the day, the refreshments in Albany
were a highlight. Any signs or events like this one seemed
to assure advancements into maturity.

Airplanes

It must have been about 1919 on a beautiful summer
morning that we heard a heavy droning and humming
sound overhead as we were working in our garden. Upon
looking up we saw a fleet of WWI vintage aircraft flying
in formation, approaching from the southeast and moving
in a northwesterly direction. The squadron or these
squadrons (I have no ideas as to the number) were flying
from Minneapolis to Fargo, North Dakota. I was thrilled
at the sight of seeing so many aircraft at one time. They
seemed to be flying in a relatively low altitude so our
view of the whole display was magnificent. The planes
even reappeared in my dreams. One afternoon many years
later we heard another humming sound of aircraft approaching. This time a single engine plane was flying in
clear weather through the chill of winter southeasterly
between Fargo and Minneapolis. This aircraft, the size
overall was larger than the Spirit of St. Louis, Lindbergh's
plane, belonged to Northwest Airlines. One night in the
thirties my dad wondered as to why there were people
in our south woods using flashlights at about sundown. A
subsequent explanation was to the effect that the federal
government had built a path of lights for nighttime flying.
Where red lights were flashing at that location, there

would be no landing field. A green light flashing identified an airport. A row of white lights flashing would mark an acceptable flight path. While on a fishing trip, my dad and I were near the path of a Northwest flight. The time was 4 P.M. We were signaled to leave the lake and go home to milk the cows. Even on our farm and in our area, we observed progress in aviation.

Walk Home from Upsala

In the fall of 1927, our teacher Mollie Wallburn, arranged for us to have a party after school. Each member of the class volunteered to bring something to eat for the occasion. I brought a box of ham sandwiches from home which I believed was adequate and appetizing. The party was quite sedate but the food was good. We played some games and thus socialized beyond our eating. Darkness had already fallen when the party was over, in fact, since the days were getting shorter, much of the party was held in the early evening darkness. Since I had not arranged for transportation home I began a solo hike across fields and meadows, into the woods and home. The trip at night assumed a structuring different than a hike by daylight. Strange sounds from denizens of the night increased my feelings of tension. An owl hooting, a frog croaking, a coyote whimpering, I almost stumbled over rocks and tree stumps. Occasionally a strange light would appear with no sound of burning. (These lights were activated by decaying material in an old stump or log.) Twice when I had crossed a fence into a pasture a monster arose immediately across my path. (A cow lying down had suddenly arisen from its resting position.) I arrived home safely but somewhat shaken. Our dog, Bob, was happy to see me, especially when he could enjoy the left over sandwiches.

The hike through early evening darkness was indeed a maturing experience.

Upsala Consolidated Schools—Christmas Seals

One of the activities in our school that became traditional involved the sale of Christmas seals. There seemed to be something compulsive about these sales since it was assumed that all students enrolled would sell these items. On the morning the sales began, the persons who went downtown for their lunches would claim sheets of stamps at $1.00 per sheet, assuming that they would be the first to contact the merchants doing business in our community. Within a day or two some of those "living in town" students would have sold $2.00 in stamps or more. Those of us who lived in the country had only limited access in selling Christmas seals. My folks did not want us to venture out in the cold to sell anything, much less seals. As a result, my brother and sister and I each sold ten seals right within the household. It's doubtful that these seals were used since our Christmas card list was quite brief. We never were oriented as to how the money obtained through these sales would be used, thus the sales had to stand on their own merits.

Our Tent

Summers in Minnesota can be very warm in intervals, especially in our house on the farm which was not air conditioned. My brother Laurel and I convinced our Dad that if we owned a nice tent which we could erect near some trees in our yard, that at least cooler nights would be assured. We sent an order, based on his consent, that we thought would be just the right size for us. Eventually we got a notice from the freight depot in Holdingford that our order had arrived. An early assignment reminded us that our tent was much larger than we had anticipated. We brought it home and immediately erected it. Mom allowed us to have comfortable blankets placed in boxes that Dad made for our convenience. Even our dog, Buster Barrington, was excited about the tent as we discovered when he insisted upon sleeping with us each night, either over or under the blankets. Laurel and I did sleep well in our tent as for us near to nature meant cooler nights. On occasions at night Buster would suddenly discover that some sound or movement would demand that he bark for the protection of all. Previous to the erection of our tent we had lost cream from our cooler but now with two of us, plus our dog nearby, potential thieves lost their courage. We would sleep in the tent till about the time of our first snowfall when getting dressed in the morning was a chilling experience. The fresh air, closeness to nature and comfortable sleeping all made the tenting experience a happy and healthy one.

Marbles

One evening during our dinner at home, my brother Laurel and I discussed what was going on at the Upsala School, much to my Dad's displeasure. The following day he had a conference with Supt. Olson who later called all boys in the school to a meeting. Gambling was the topic discussed, emphasized to the point that it must stop. It did that! It seemed as though the gaming started very mildly with someone bringing a few marbles to school. He'd sit down on a short stretch of sidewalk with his ankles about three feet apart, placing a glass marble between his outstretched knees, then invited another player to roll clay marbles in his direction in an attempt to hit his glass marble. If he did hit the glass marble, it would be his. In a few days more glass and clay marbles were brought to school and more straight line marble playing occurred. Some basic rules were established: if a clay marble hit the glass marble, the owner of the clay marble became the owner of the glassie, as glass marbles were called; the more valuable the glass marble, the greater distance for rolling the clay marble in order to capture it. In a matter of days the marble games were being played on sidewalks, in school cloak rooms, in the school gymnasium. Gaming for accuracy in shooting baskets could gain cash for the winners. In fact, the whole school was caught up in gaming, especially in the buying and selling of marbles.

Green Beans

One beautiful spring day another salesman stopped at our farm with what sounded like a good proposition. Plant green beans for our canning company in St. Cloud and reap a bountiful harvest, selling them the beans you grew. Sounded like a good idea, especially after our Dad approved the idea to the extent that he would let us have a ½ acre plot for the bean project. We went to Holdingford to get our seed at the same place where we would eventually sell our beans. The planting was a success, the cultivating required was not complicated so the bean plants prospered. The weather was favorable and no pests threatened the first crop. Laurel, my brother, found out that there would be no feast without a considerable amount of labor. We were surprised as to how our beans were graded with not enough identified as A-1. Finally the last bean had been picked, brought to Holdingford, and a check was presented to us. It bounced and so did my feelings as I wrote a stern letter to the company which eventually motivated the presentation of a good check. In our early teens, Laurel and I had earned another lesson subdivided into several parts.

Upsala High School, '32—A Clique

When our eighth grade class became the freshman class at Upsala High School in 1928, several girls from rural schools not in our district became freshmen with us. They were neatly dressed and mannerly. A clique of girls who had been together for several years in the Upsala School found it difficult to accept the new students who came from outside our district. There was "this clique" then several other groups at various levels of social acceptance, including groups of boys, formed groups. The boys were inclined to accept every member of our class but at different levels of friendliness. The girls in "the clique" were much more exclusive, preferring not to express a high degree of friendliness even outside their own class play in which "the clique" would have the major roles, the other girls rebelled to the extent that the teacher was forced to choose another play. Due to levels of acceptance very much in existence, class parties were rare occurrences. Our class was severely divided even through graduation in 1932.

Church Picnics

In addition to other traditions at Gethsemane Lutheran Church in Upsala, picnics were scheduled for the summer season. Ordinarily one would follow a two week session of Bible School which was on the calendar for a June date, another for July. The picnic in June would be held during the course of a Sunday afternoon following a program offered by the Bible School students. When the event was held at the church park, a part of the parsonage property, the food was served in what looked like a band stand surrounded by tables. The picnic menu was traditionally the work of wives and mothers, serving meats, vegetables, salads, breads, beverages and desserts, all tasting as though they had been prepared by master chefs. The social event in July was more on the order of an ice cream social, prepared and served by women's organizations in the church. On a hot night in July the ice cream and home made cakes were regarded as nothing short of fabulous. Another event not regarded as a picnic was the Thanksgiving feast served on that special day. Special events honoring or recognizing someone or scheduled monthly meetings when food was served seemed like picnics of a minor sort. The socializing and serving of food were special influences which strengthened the members of the congregation.

Confirmation

On July 3, 1927, our class was confirmed at Gethesemane Lutheran Church, Upsala, Minnesota. It was a cloudy day with a bit of drizzle which occasionally lent a gray shade to this glorious day. Our pastor, Rev. Bergdahl, had given each of us some verses from the Bible which we had memorized and repeated back as Pastor Bergdahl moved around the semicircle altar up front in an attempt to evaluate the degree to which we had learned at least portions of Holy Writ. Each of us received a new Bible and a certificate of confirmation. In each Bible, Rev.

Bergdahl had incripted verses which would be significant as guides through life's journey. The next day, July 4th, a big Independence Day observance occupied the crowds as people moved from booth to booth in downtown Upsala. The following day we all appeared for group and individualized pictures at a professional photo studio in Little Falls, Lindbergh's home town. Anna and Walter Mattson, good friends of mine and members of the class, planned to have pictures prepared for relatives in Sweden. My Dad, Marian, a member of the class from our neighborhood, and I rode in our 1925 Model T Ford that day. My Dad let me drive home, at least most of the way which was a real treat for me. Death has claimed a number of the members of the class by accident or other demanding incidents. Our pastor, Rev. Bergdahl, was called to our congregation due to the fact that he was born in Sweden and thus knew the language well. As a leader of young men and women his effectiveness was at another level—bless his soul.

Accident

Since my brother Laurel was a star basketball and baseball player as a student in the Upsala High School, my Dad arranged to have a basket placed in our haymow (upper story of the barn) as well as purchasing an expensive catcher's mitt and mask; he made the bat himself. The Thompson boys, Robert and Russell who lived on a farm nearby, were enthusiastic users of the basketball equipment as well as the baseball supplies. During the month of May, baseball fever had developed so it was not unusual for Robert and Russell to pay an athletic visit to our place. The incident which I refer to as the accident occurred in May, 1927. In a fit of enthusiasm, Russell began swinging the bag, traveling around and generally displaying a great deal of enthusiasm. At one point he released the bat which almost instantly hit my nose. I fell over, recovered from my fall but not from the pain involved in the accident. My Dad drove me to our community doctor's office, the same one who had removed my tonsils. Luckily, my nose was not seriously damaged so recovery was quite rapid except for a scar which remained as a reminder of what had happened. The fact that my 7th grade teacher, Mr. Bourne, chanced to meet my Dad and me as we left the doctor's office boosted my morale. His smile and greeting were good therapy.

Shopping: 1923–1933

During a ten year period our family, my Dad, Mother, Brother, Sister and I adjusted our shopping tour to fit the kind of transportation we had. In 1923–24 we shopped in Holdingford, six miles away to which we traveled by horse and buggy. When we got to town the horses were led into a livery stable where they stayed feeding on hay and oats while our shopping was being done. The family's main destination for the day was the Shuler Mercantile, a general store. We also had errands to Fink's Drug Store and at least one hardware store. I always chose to walk over to the Soo Line RR station so I could watch the trains come and go. In 1925 we purchased a Model T Ford which enabled us to expand our travel distance to the extent that we could go to Little Falls, the county seat, 25 miles away. There we were customers in a relatively large Penney store and a bakery nearby. Some window shopping was also included. In 1930 we purchased a Model A Ford, enabling us to extend our shopping by another ten miles. We would park our car away from Main Street so we could leave it in a spot for the entire day near the Stearns County Courthouse in St. Cloud. A day in a larger city with more stores made it possible to locate more bargains, especially in the clothing line, as at Sears and Penneys. In more recent times we continued to expand our territory but always in our memories the family shopping tours of 1923–33 conjure up warm recollections.

Treats

In the 1920s my Dad would make trips by horses and wagon to a feed mill located in Upsala, our hometown. Previous to making the trip he would fill several grain sacks with barley; the grain was to be ground up then soaked in a wooden barrel previous to being fed to our hogs. Always there would be visiting at the mill so my Dad would be updated concerning community news. After the barley was ground and placed back into the grain bags my Dad would shop at one or more of the stores in the downtown area. This would extend the family's knowledge of local news as always a trip to town was not complete without some news gathering in addition to information as to where certain fish might be biting that day. My Dad's shopping list included whatever my mother had ordered plus additional purchases of fruit and gifts for the three children. By the time all business had been taken care of in town it was time to make the trip back to the farm. All three of us kids anticipated our Dad's return to be close to noon so one or more of us would walk down the country line road for about three quarters of a mile to meet Dad. As we met him he would stop and help us up into the wagon for the ride home. Always he had special treats for us which made our meeting most enjoyable. Later in the 20s he would encourage one of more of us to go with him on the trip into town by wagon. This was fun but not as exciting as meeting him in earlier times.

Fishing with My Dad

June was one of the best fishing months in our part of Central Minnesota. After the morning chores, on a mild day, we'd go to a lake where rumor had it that "fish were biting." One of our favorite lakes was Little Birch Lake, a few miles west of Upsala. We had our bamboo poles ready, worms dug and my Dad's pipe ready. When we came to the lake of our choice ("we" could also include my brother Laurel) we'd rent a boat which came with oars and a can for dipping out excessive amounts of water. My Dad would row to a spot on the lake where sunfish, bass and crappies might be found. I'd drop the anchor, we'd cast out our lines and wait. Our lines had bobbers affixed to them so a strike by a fish would cause the bobber to bounce, even go under the water. At the end of a few hours, following attempts at fishing at several different spots on the lake with a few fish in our bucket, we'd head for shore and our drive home. Since time for the late afternoon milking of our cows coincided with time when fish would be most apt to bite, our catches were generally modest. The fun was in the catching, rowing on the lake and generally enjoying the scenery. We'd enjoy the fish as the main course for our evening meal, basically a real treat. Fishing with my Dad was always a highlight of my youth in Minnesota.

Spearing Fish

Although catching fish by this method is no longer legal under certain conditions and circumstances, during the spring season, circa 1929, such fishing could be done. On at least one occasion I had discussed spear fishing that my brother Laurel and I had done with my friend Walter Mattson. His interest in this type of activity was thus aroused to the extent that he would like to go with us next time we fished in this manner. We got our equipment ready, spears and rag balls soaked in kerosene. When these balls were ignited their light would brighten the entire bottom of the stream where we would fish. Walter said he would drive his family's Chevrolet, 1920 model, with the top down to our fishing location. The evening for our adventure had arrived, mild and clear. We parked near a stream just a few miles southeast of our farm, lit the first of our rag balls, then walked slowly along the banks of the stream. Luck was with us to the extent that we managed to spear several fish. On our way home we stopped at the Thompsons, the neighbors next to our farm. There was a bit of honking and shouting as we wanted them to come out to see our fish. They didn't. When we came to our place we still wanted them to see what we had speared. All quiet, lights out at the Thompsons. The next evening I went to town with my Dad for shopping and visiting. While we were gone the Thompsons visited at our farm, inquiring of my mother about three drunken men in an open car—us, but we were not drunk. My mother never told us what she told them.

Tonsillectomy

While I was a student in the Upsala, Minnesota Consolidated School, as a result of readings concerning health and hearing about the surgery involved, I felt that I needed a tonsillectomy. Our medical doctor, serving local patients, seemed to be of the same opinion. The day finally arrived when the surgery was to occur in his office. The injections and slicing were quite painful. Through the whole procedure I felt somewhat victimized. Finally it was over and my tonsils lay on a table nearby. My Dad came to the doctor's office to meet me and take me home. It took me several days to recover from that painful experience. Some years later while I was a prof at Waldorf College, a local physician, upon examining my throat told me that part of a tonsil was still within my system and that it would be well to have it removed. A second tonsillectomy followed. When I heard reports subsequently that the doctor in Upsala had been victimized by drugs, that the physician in Forest City had undergone treatments for ailing mental health, I wondered about threats to my survival. When I consider the experience my daughter, Anita, was exposed to when she had her tonsils removed, I felt that medical science had made great strides regarding that kind of surgery. Thoughts came to mind as to whether or not I should have suffered, even had my tonsils removed.

Lindbergh—August 1927

Lindbergh returned to Little Falls, Minnesota, in August of 1927 during his extended tour following the great flight of May 1927. The whole state of Minnesota was honoring him as a native son, a former resident of Little Falls. His home on the banks of the Mississippi River was such an attraction that the general public had almost decimated the house where he grew up, board by board. Later it was rebuilt as part of the Lindbergh State Park. The day that Lindbergh 'came back home' as an international hero was the day our uncles, Axel and Willie, had arranged for a big potato picking event with my brother Laurel and me invited as potato picking guests. There was some discussion, however, as to whether we should go to Little Falls to see Lindy, my hero, or work out in the potato patch. Laurel and I were too young to vote so when the decision was made, the adults had decided to do field work—our young opinions didn't count even though the big celebration was only 25 miles away. The last time Lindy came home to visit Little Falls was in September, 1973, the very same day of my mother's funeral not many miles away.

Rudy

One wintry night on the farm we had all retired for the night, there was a banging and rapping sound on the north door of our house. When my folks opened the door they discovered one of our neighbors in a state of near exhaustion. Our neighbor, Mrs. Nelson, told of the terror that had descended on their peaceful home that night. Their son, Rudy, had turned violent and had actually chased one of his brothers with an axe. Rudy loudly explained that he saw a strange, lighted face in the darkness that told him of a need to "get rid of his brother." This he had been motivated to do by a figment of his imagination. His mother, Mrs. Nelson, was almost beside herself explaining what had happened. My mother eventually calmed her, thus enabling her to return home in a state of recovery. Rudy was admitted into the state hospital in Fergus Falls, Minnesota, following his acts of violence. Some months later he came home to our neighborhood in a calm state of recovery. He did warn his parents, however, that he would let them know whenever he felt another spell approaching. Subsequently during the time

Rudy was in Minneapolis, he was restrained on occasions, but apparently was never a serious threat again.

Rosella

Our neighbors, the Slagels, had one son, Frank, and a daughter, Rosella. She was quite protected and closely sheltered by her mother. Near the Slagel home, a one room school had been built for the training of children in grades 1–8 who lived in that area. Traditionally one activity which helped raise funds for school activities was a basket social. This socializing activity called upon each young, single woman in the community to bring a basket to the social, a basket containing what was reputed to be an excellent meal to share with the young man who bought her basket. On the day scheduled for the event, Rosella, along with other young women, prepared her basket with a delicious lunch that she traditionally would share with a young man. At an appropriate time Rosella prepared to leave for the big event. In order to assure her safe passage from home to school, Mr. Slagel went with her. In the course of the evening the auction began, Mr. Slagel announced his offer for the basket which proved to be the highest bid. Thereupon Mr. Slagel shouted, "Rosella, it's time to go home!" Apparently the contents were enjoyed at the dinner table at home—and not with a possible suitor.

Saturday Night Radio

Occasionally on a Saturday night, my Dad and I would, at his invitation, share radio programs with our neighbor, Mr. Slagel. My brother Laurel would go along to visit at the Slagels but more often other attractions were available for him. Our good neighbor could read and write only in a very limited manner. He would make discerning marks on a pad near the radio, identifying programs that he would enjoy, especially those from WLS Chicago and WSN Nashville. When, as his guests, we were pleased with some of the Saturday night music he seemed to be enthused by our reactions. During the course of the evening while we were listening to radio music, Mrs. Slagel would serve light refreshments but would not in engage in any extensive conversations with my Dad and me. It seemed as though Mrs. S and daughter Rosella were subdued almost to the extent that their role was as servants in satisfying the needs of the male members of the family. The enjoyment which we manifested upon hearing Saturday night music overcame any feelings of social inequities, especially when Kinkade Bradley played his hound dog guitar and sang Barbara Allen—a great tradition.

Gypsies

On a beautiful summer afternoon this strange vehicle which looked like a painted covered wagon parked in one of our woodlots. My Dad gave the couple who were riding in the wagon permission to park there overnight. My curiosity concerning the people who came in this wagon was almost overbearing. I was brave enough to go up to the wagon and briefly view its contents. The woman inside was colorfully dressed displaying an assortment of beads around her neck. She invited me to come in, then asked me if she could buy some milk for their supper. I said "OK" even before I had asked my parents regarding the request. I got the milk and in exchange I received some dimes and nickels. The husband had gone to take care of the horses for the night so the wife was the only one present with whom I could converse. She told me of the fabulous places where they had visited and regarding some of the exciting towns that she and her husband were planning to visit. Next morning when I arose I planned to visit my gypsy friends again but they were gone. I envisioned that they had embarked on another exciting adventure which I could only visualize in my imagination.

Tobacco in My Face

During the mid 1920s, one of the relatively new scenic attractions in Central Minnesota was the New Blanchard Rapids Dam, built across the Mississippi River a few miles south of Little Falls. On a number of occasions we'd enjoy picnicing on the shores of the lake built by the dam. During one of these pleasant summer time experiences some of our relatives shared a pleasant afternoon with us at the lake which had become an enlarged Mississippi River. On our return trip to Upsala and the farm my Dad would be driving our new 1925 Model T Ford. I sat on the right side of the back seat immediately behind a very friendly tobacco-chewing relative who sat in front. We had just passed through the village of Elmdale when all of a sudden something hit my face. Whatever it was it made my eyes sting and my cheeks smart. A wad of chewing tobacco carried by the breeze from our relative in the front seat landed squarely on my face. I began wiping the debris that hit me as the gentleman sitting in front of me turned around and began to apologize. My Dad did not know what had happened so began to scold me for something he knew nothing about. When we finally arrived home the whole matter was clarified. Then I felt more comfortable with a clean face and what I eventually heard turned out to be an unmodified apology from my Dad.

Hired Man

When I was 16 my uncle Albert felt that he desperately needed the assistance of a hired man to help manage all of the field work that must be attended to during the summer months. Into the month of July my grandfather, who was in his 80s, could no longer offer the assistance required to help Albert. For milking the cows twice a day he could help but he was not able to meet the heavy requirements of the lifting that was essential in harvesting the hay and grain crops. Albert did not own the mechanical assists now available to many farmers for use in harvesting so much hand labor was required. It was on July 20, 1931, when I began helping Uncle Albert. During a period of about a month we had stacked most of the hay crop as well as the crops of oats, wheat and barley. Because Albert and I had truly extended ourselves physically and efficiently, our harvesting goals had been met. During the summers of '32–'35 I worked with Albert again, attaining a reasonable level of success as a hired man on grandpa's 200 acre farm in meeting harvesting requirements.

My Skis

In our area, skating was somewhat limited since access to lakes or ponds during winter months was difficult. We had no community facility for skaters so skiing proved to be a popular kind of replacement. Because no one in our immediate area was selling skis, I consulted with a Mr. Hagstrom to make a pair for me. It seemed that his production schedule was not easily hurried. It seemed to me that I would be missing out on part of the winter if I didn't obtain my new skis fairly soon. Finally I received a reminder that the skis were ready. I went to his home in downtown Upsala and there saw my prize for the first time. They were big, long and rather heavy. I paid $2.00 for them. My first trial with my new equipment was a 3 mile trip home. They were quite effectively made, the tips well bent, the bottoms smoothed, the straps held firm, but they were heavy. Over the years I received a good measure of exercise every time I went skiing. My dad reprimanded me on one occasion because he thought I was too slow in the wet snow. They were good for tobogganing, however, if they were held side by side. I did get some of the winter exercising I needed while skiing but not always an assurance of happiness.

Sunday Afternoons

During the milder months of the year and especially during the summers, I enjoyed many opportunities for fun and relaxation. Our community beach at Cedar Lake drew sizable crowds each Sunday afternoon. Opportunities for visiting with relatives and friends, in addition to diving and swimming were very much enjoyed. Then there were times for visiting at the farm homes of people I knew especially well. In addition to family get togethers at Grandpa Ryberg's and Axel and Willie Anderson's, I would spend Sunday afternoons at the Mattson home where we would play baseball and enjoy the sights and sounds that are quite normal in dairy farm homes and farm yards. Also a delicious lunch was one of the traditional attractions. Visits at the Biniek home, at Ed Nelson's, and to the Thompsons were also traditional. When

Upsala had a baseball team that belonged to an amateur league fans would gather at the ballpark to watch the excitement each Sunday when the team played at home. Another attraction available especially during the summer months was bass fishing. We had a choice of lakes for this activity which made prospects for a good catch much more a reality. The memories of Sunday afternoons spent at home when we hosted or in a variety of other places as guests are warm and most satisfying.

Quarantine

For a period of approximately two weeks, our whole family was quarantined as a result of a scarlet fever epidemic in the Upsala community. Almost half of the enrollment in the high school was absent due to the epidemic. I had a severe attack but recovered with no serious after effects. Nevertheless I was more ill than any other member of our family. When recovery was almost over for our family, we were quarantined, much to our dismay. We had no radio, no daily newspaper, but from time to time a neighbor would stop at our house so we could order groceries and hear the news. We did get some materials from school enabling my brother, sister, and me to study as well as to play basketball and during our winter confinement. There was wood to be chopped and our stock water tank to be filled by hand, all were part of our pattern of chores. In spite of difficulties the warmth of home and close family bonding were among the benefits we gained.

Swimming

During the long days of summer it was a delight to experience a refreshing swim. When we went to Cedar

Lake where the favorite local beach was located, it was relatively easy to feel that large crowds were delighted at that location. (I learned to swim at Gustavus Adolphus College as a freshman. If I had returned to the campus the following year I would have been a member of the swimming team.) The bath house was somewhat limited but it did not meet local standards for both men and women. The water in Cedar Lake was refreshingly cool and clear. A swim there was particularly invigorating. Another place within about three miles of our farm was a swimming hole in the river that began west of Upsala and finally emptied into the Mississippi. There were rock formations in this part of what people called Two River (there was a South Two River and a North Two River, so officially the name Twin Rivers was applied, geographically). My brother Laurel and I would walk to this spot, sometimes with friends. Occasionally someone did give us a ride. No matter how we got there we enjoyed the bathing—the area was too limited for much swimming but large enough to assure refreshing dips and plunges.

Walk from Albany

Albany was the location of our post office and convenient bus stop. Our farm was located about 13 miles north of Albany. In early September 1933, I planned to spend a weekend at home on the farm. I had told our pastor, Rev. Bergdahl, to inform my parents that they were to meet me in Albany the following Friday afternoon. When I arrived in Albany my parents were not at the bus stop as I had planned for them to be. The late afternoon was mild, the breezes light, so I decided to walk the 13 mile stretch back to our farm. As I walked along on the dusty graveled road I came to the Soo Line Railroad crossing, a few miles out of town. A freight train was approaching so as the train came I watched it go by. Farther along I walked past the Lutheran Church which had been dedicated a few years earlier. I recall how at a congregational dinner at the church I had only cole slaw to eat inasmuch as my bashfulness prevented me from asking for more. As the shadows of evening were lengthening, I strolled past a one room rural school where my brother Laurel would hold forth as teacher. As darkness began to fall I was in our old neighborhood and eventually home. Rev. Bergdahl had told my folks to meet me in Royalton.

First Train Ride

1934 was one of the driest and hottest years that the Upsala community had ever experienced. From early in May until late in November, hardly any rain or snow had fallen to provide even minimal moisture for any growing thing. On Thanksgiving Day, 1934, we had memorial services for Grandmother Ryberg at the Ryberg home followed by a service in the Swedish Lutheran Church in Upsala. On the Monday following Thanksgiving weekend, my Dad and a neighbor arranged to make a business trip to Little Falls. They agreed to allow me to ride with them so I could catch a train back to St. Cloud where I planned to enroll at St. Cloud State for the winter quarter. I boarded the train as scheduled. Before we left home for Little Falls it had started to snow heavily, but as the train proceeded on its way to St. Cloud we were caught in a November blizzard. I seated myself so I could see approaching trains, especially the North Coast Limited on a double track arrangement. As we met other traffic, all we saw was a blur. When we tried to view the landscape

111

along the Northern Pacific tracks all we saw was the severe whiteness of the storm. The towns of Rice, Sartell and Sauk Rapids were gooey blurs on the horizon as we passed through them. This was my first train ride, a memorable one. I remember the comforts in our coach and the persistent curtain of white on the world.

IV
EDUCATION

EDUCATION
Table of Contents

EDUCATION

Poetry

Previous to my entering the Upsala School at the first grade level, (we did not have kindergarten), my mother had taught me the basics involved in reading and writing English and Swedish. Eventually it proved to be interesting to write sentences as it seemed to be so easy to say them. I recall how it was fun to speak a sentence, write it down, then write another line below that in combination with the first line seemed to tell a brief story. This I wrote on an occasion when my mother was preparing the evening meal: "when the sun is setting, Mother's supper getting." From time to time during my academic tour through grades 1–6, I would compose some ideas that would rhyme. In grade seven, following Lindbergh's flight and some of the accidents that preceded and followed his classical performance, I was inspired to write a poem that was awarded a blue ribbon during a display of academic accomplishments that had occurred that school year. The last two lines of my poem were: "History will remember them, they tried and died while flying." I have written poems concerning the seasons, weather, family events and in offering personal greetings. Poetry effectively serves as a special means of honoring and evaluating people and events.

First Day of School

It was a bright, sunny day in September, my first day as a pupil in the new consolidated and constructed Upsala School. When I got off our bus with the other children who rode on route no. 5, I was somewhat confused. Fortunately a girl a few steps beyond grade one showed me where to go. I was greeted by the first grade teacher, Cora Sanderson, who directed me to a seat in our classroom. (There was no kindergarten in our school so the academics began at the first grade level.) Eventually, our schedule of activities got underway, including basic reading. Since my mother had taught me how to read early on, this kind of activity proved to be much to my liking. Then came the noon recess part of our daily schedule. Every child in our room strolled out the front door and onto the playground. Before I was fully aware of what was happening, several boys had lifted me and carried me to a slight depression in the playground. They wanted to bury me due in part to what I was wearing—white shorts and white shirt. With tears shed and bitterness arising in my thinking when I got home from school that day, no more white shorts but blue overalls like the other boys were wearing. One of the leaders in the group that was trying to bury me was Ray Nelson, who eventually became one of my best friends.

Upsala School

It was a beautiful day in September at 9:20 in the morning at Upsala School. Miss Ina T. Olson, our teacher, following the pledge of allegiance, had just begun to explain what the basic rules and regulations for the school year would be for us 4th graders. At that very moment something she was wearing, something heavy fell to the floor. At that instant Miss Olson dashed to the cloakroom, abandoning us for a few minutes. She returned shortly explaining that it was only a petticoat that had fallen to the floor. We thought she might have been falling apart! She was our teacher through grades four and five. Her attitudes at times were quite authoritarian and her punishments quite harsh. One day she tied a rope around the ankles of one of the girls who in Miss Olson's opinion was shuffling her feet too much. In June 1925 my dad and I were in Holdingford transacting business when I heard the passenger train on the Soo Line RR just leaving the station. As the train passed by the place where I was viewing its passing, I saw Miss Olson seated by one of the coach windows. Neither of us initiated recognition, although I could not mistake Miss Ina T. Olson for some other person. At that moment she had passed out of my life.

Miss Goss

Miss Goss was our 6th grade teacher in the Upsala Consolidated School. Early in the month of December, she thought it appropriate for each of us to draw the name of a pupil to whom we would give a Christmas gift. The price of the gift was to be no more than 25 cents. The rumor got around, however, that she had selected the name of one of the boys to be the recipient of the gift that she had chosen—cost $1.00. We had a tree in due time and a party the last day before what was then called Christmas vacation. I estimated that the gift I received cost 10 cents. When classes resumed early in January we were asked to write about our Christmas gifts, how many and what kind, with a thank you note about one gift. I wrote rather large and filled two sheets even though my

119

gift list was quite brief, but the envelope into which I placed my document seemed to be quite bulky. When Miss Goss saw my envelope as she was collecting them, she said it was as fat as me. The comment hurt. Some years later when I was a professor at St. Cloud State, I had her son in one of my classes. His friendly demeanor greatly softened the memory of his mother's comment—almost to the point of extinction.

Turning Point—Seventh Grade

I was promoted from grade one to grade three in the early 1920s. From my memories of grade 3, it seemed as though our teacher, Miss Youngberg, made life quite acceptable and learning opportunities quite reasonable. That was not necessarily so in grades 4 and 5 when our teacher was Miss Olson. Grade 6 was relatively uncomfortable with Miss Goss as our teacher. (This was the same Miss Goss who in marriage had a son who was in one of my classes at St. Cloud State. I enjoyed his company and through him I learned to appreciate Miss Goss.) At the beginning of grade 7 our teacher was Miss Kerns, but through marital plans could no longer be an employee of the Upsala School District. Subsequently, Kenneth Francis Bourne became our teacher, our first male instructor. In the course of events he gained considerable popularity among the pupils in our class. On one occasion, report card time, he announced who had gotten the best grades during the term just past. He said they fall to a boy and at that point it was announced that I was the recipient of the honor. The reassurances granted me on that occasion established a feeling of confidence within my being which had been lacking earlier in my life.

Kenneth Francis Bourne

As a student in the seventh grade at Upsala School, I was most fortunate to have Mr. Bourne as my teacher. Our entire class felt the same way about our first male instructor, a man whose sense of humor made learning more pleasant. One day when my friend Walter and I were visiting during a recess period, he greeted us by saying, "Ike and Mike, they look alike." On a special occasion when our class gave Mr. Bourne a bow tie, he showed us how that tie could do tricks as it was fastened to his shirt collar. When the end of the term arrived, that critical date when report cards were due, Mr. Bourne announced as he was distributing the reports that the highest marks fell to a boy. For a moment I wondered who among my classmates could be so fortunate, whereupon he identified me as the lucky recipient of good grades. K.F. Bourne was one of the best teachers I ever had. I learned from him that cheerfulness and optimism are critical factors involved in motivating good learning.

Teacher Tactics

During the course of my year in the eighth grade, our teacher, who was quite cool, distant and unfriendly, decided that we should have a citizenship club to make our classroom situation more friendly, more democratic. The teacher failed to realize that in order to make our classroom more friendly, she would have to change, which she did not do. Over a period of time students in our class became disenchanted by our citizenship club so we circulated a petition which was signed by all students except one. All of us but one girl withdrew from the club. When report cards came out a few days later, all of us got "D's" in citizenship, all except for the one girl who refused to sign our petition. Another incentive designed to promote reading by this teacher was a bulletin board with a pocket for each student. Each time a student read a book, a brief review of the volume was placed in the appropriate pocket. Some time later the pocket containing the greatest number of books read would have earned a prize. I happened to be a "front runner" with the most books read. Before the date set for the ending of the contest, the board with all the pockets disappeared. Miss Wallburn did not want me to win.

Agriculture

I was a pupil in the 8th grade at Upsala School in the fall of 1927. Because the girls were given the opportunity to study Home Ec., the question arose as to what would be offered to the boys beyond the traditional academic schedule. The school administrators decided to offer a course in agriculture for the boys. Molly Wallburn, our 8th grade teacher, would be in charge of the class. We had our first meeting in our school library, presided over by Miss Wallburn. After a few polite introductory remarks the question was raised as to the different kinds of farming, basically a good question with the intent of initiating an interesting discussion. Elroy, one of our fellow students, suggested that successful farming was one kind of agriculture. Upon hearing this response, Miss Wallburn stood up from her chair and ran through the library door out into the hallway, screaming. All of us sat there spell-bound. No one said anything until the comment was made to the fact that the class session was now ended. The class was never resumed—it was canceled.

Assembly Programs

Each day our high school was in session, the school day began with Bible reading with a different student each day reading a portion of scripture. One morning following the reading I had chosen, our superintendent provided a supplementary lecture, explaining what humility meant in everyday living. Mr. Amidon would lecture to us briefly almost every day on some aspect of morality. On occasions we had assembly programs with guest speakers. During one such program, the speaker requested that each of us produce a ruler to be used for measuring the contours of our heads in an attempt to determine our personalities and vocational prospects. Apparently he was a phrenologist. Whatever he was did not impress me very much. On another occasion our guest speaker was the Rev. Gilberg, pastor of the Mission Covenant Church in Upsala. I can recall one illustration that he included in his presentation: "As the young suitor escorted his date of the evening home, they paused at the garden gate. He kissed her hand, whereupon she responded, 'Aim higher.' " Over the years I have used this illustration in some of my speeches, as I believe that the motivational impact involved is quite significant.

Upsala High School Field Trip

During the month of May, 1929, our general science class in the Upsala School was the recipient of an interesting field trip. We were excused for the day but we did have to provide our own transportation. I rode in a 1927 Model T which was the John Lindstrom family car. Elmer was the driver, a position all of us who rode in the car envied. Our first stop was at the paper mill in Sartell, a short distance north of St. Cloud. There we saw coniferous logs about a foot in diameter piled high. They had been hauled into this location by the Northern Pacific Rail Road. Our class saw these logs crushed in a digester till they were the consistency of mashed potatoes. Eventually what had been logs with certain additives included were spun out in fresh sheets of paper, the end result of the process. Our second stop was at the St. Cloud Men's Reformatory, a penal institution run by the State of Minnesota. We viewed the cells where prisoners were kept while they were not working or exercising. Our tour included shops where clothing and selected pieces of furniture were made. When the tour was over no one opted to work in the facility.

Upsala High School Graduation '32 (112)

We were graduated from Upsala High School during the course of a pleasant evening on June 2, 1932. The fragrance of lilacs was everywhere, which made the occasion seem like a harbinger of summer. There were twenty-one of us—eight boys and thirteen girls, none of whom were pregnant. Such things were foreign to our community. All of us appeared on the stage of our high school auditorium, some all but slipping as the steps up to the stage were quite unstable. Our class motto was "We build the ladder by which we climb," did not seem to apply to the short ladder up to the platform. Miss Mollerstrom, pianist, had played effectively so our last march through the "halls of learning" would remain as a pleasant memory. Mr. Hellig, superintendent, master of ceremonies, provided an acceptable introduction of our guest speaker, who almost tripped over the feet of our class president, Walter Mattson. Elsie Shodeen was our top student and I was second so each of us added verbal wisdom and sentiment to the occasion. My family was in the audience in addition to my grandparents who only spoke Swedish. I should in respect to them, have offered a few words in that language. There was no party following the graduation to which all of the class might have been invited. Elsie became a rural school teacher and eventually, a farmer's wife. I returned to Upsala School within three years as an elementary teacher. Two of the boys became quite wealthy—Walter in construction and Elmer as a commercial fisherman. There were no star athletes, no one became a politician of note, yet our class left a reputation of solid scholarship and good citizenship. We became part of our nation's "greatest generation", maturing through the depression, drought and war. What we endured made us stronger, as my daughter Anita says.

Turning Point—High School Graduation

When I was graduated from the Upsala High School in 1932, futures for the members of our class seemed to be quite limited. The depression was on with its multiple of limitations and a severe drought was developing which would eventually affect our crops. As to my destiny, I knew I could work for my grandfather on his farm during the summer of '32 but beyond this possibility, things seemed to be quite limited. Shortly after graduation I had an involved discussion with my mother proposing that our Dad go to Rochester for a thorough physical checkup rather than that I should go on to college. As the top male student in our class, I was offered a small scholarship at Gustavus Adolphus College in St. Peter, Minnesota. My mother offered her reply to my suggestion regarding my Dad by stating that "He would live. I would go to college." And so it was that I did enter college as a freshman at Gustavus in 1932. This was the beginning of academic training beyond high school which extended through several campuses, eventually culminating in a doctoral degree. My Dad lived to be 86.

Men's Dorm

While I was a freshman at Gustavus Adolphus College, I was an occupant of the only men's' dorm on the campus in 1932–33. As with the other students in the dorm, we lived under certain restrictions but any limitations were modified by limited enforcement. Conrad and I were roommates, occupying a unit in the inner court, a fact that I regretted when I discovered an outer court unit on the east side of the building would have given me excellent views of the town of St. Peter and extended views of the beautiful Minnesota River Valley. Living in a dorm as I did gave me a very positive impression of what life at college really was. The men living in this spacious facility were given a great deal of freedom. Beyond our class schedules and campus programs, our lives were to be lived as responsible adults at a Christian college. I did my course work and visiting in such a way that I met academic and social obligations with a fair degree of effectiveness. Noise, shouting, lights on at all hours, leaving campus whenever you wished, some gambling, some card playing were all discernible in the dorm. I had never had so much personal freedom previously in my life. The enjoyment accompanied by a measure of academic success was very assuring to me.

An Impressive Building

The old main building on the Campus of Gustavus Adolphus College stands like a sentinel on a hill overlooking the Minnesota River and downtown St. Peter. It was constructed of native stones generations of students ago. Its impressive bell tower and massive stairs leading up to the main entry reflect upon an architectural plan of many years past. When I was a freshman on campus, 1932–33, our Biology class, English courses and Christianity class met in this sturdy old building. Our cafeteria served three meals a day in the basement of the facility which echoed with the laughter and cheers of many bygone collegiate activities scheduled in this structure. When I returned as a senior in 1937–38, I recalled pleasant memories of earlier days on the campus. Due to the fact that some of my senior program was scheduled for Old Main, I could relive and reflect upon experiences of earlier times in this place of hallowed halls and busy classrooms.

Math Class at SCTC

One of the courses which was required of those of us completing the two-year teacher training course at St. Cloud Teachers College was math methods, basically how to teach arithmetic. Our instructor was Cliff Bemis who had firm roots in Minnesota. At least that's the impression we got in this class because he often referred to Ashby, a small town in western Minnesota where he seemed to be well acquainted. He was outspoken at times. An impression of him as being inflexible was further demonstrated as I served with him on an executive committee when I eventually became a professor at St. Cloud State. One day in the session of our math methods course, Mr. Bemis came to class very much disturbed. Apparently he had been listening to a newscast at home before he left for the campus. He explosively stated that the announcer in giving the time, had said that it was exactly seven o'clock, a serious error because all measurements are approximate. The lecture he gave on the basis of this reaction was the most remembered by me of all in this math course.

Student Teaching at SCTC

My first teaching assignment was under the guidance of Miss Larson, who emphasized effective discipline including efficient practices in dealing with classroom routine, followed by Miss Perry who supervised student teaching in the field of American history. She insisted that each lesson plan include all of the questions and anticipated answers that would be involved in each class period. She would tell us what should be done; students were required to listen and follow her advice. Miss Cadwell, who supervised student teachers in the field of science, had the reputation of requiring promptness at all times. On the first day of my assignment under her supervision was the day that my old alarm clock failed me, so I was late for my first class session under her supervision. She forgave me. Miss Paull supervised students who were assigned to various classrooms in the St. Cloud City School system. At Riverview School on campus, our classes were small; in the City School system they were generally quite large. My math teaching assignment with

Miss Paull was one of my best in spite of the need to adjust to numerous students. All of the assignments I had as a student teacher at St. Cloud were at the grade levels that are now considered to be at the middle school level.

Miss Graves

During the time I was enrolled as a student at St. Cloud State Teachers College, one of my favorite faculty members was Miss Graves. She was continually optimistic, would smile optimistically at students and faculty. One of her primary interests focused on earth studies with special emphasis on geology. One beautiful spring day she arranged for our geology class to visit some granite formations north of St. Cloud, bordering the Mississippi River. In reality, these were large granite outcroppings which with other formations made St. Cloud the granite city of Central Minnesota. We enjoyed the tour with its scenic beauty and geological significance. One of the "additional treats" on our tour proved to be very satisfying. Miss Graves had ordered two freshly baked apple pies for us to share. These gustatory treats and emphasis in scientific displays make the day a memorable one.

Classes—1933–1935—SCTC

In Cliff Bemis' math experiences: when you use an "and" in reading numbers you're actually including a decimal point where one does not belong: 100 and 50. Measurement is approximate, counting done correctly is exact; 8:30 PM is not exact, 100 pennies in a dollar is exact.

In Al Brainerd's physical education class: always walk with your feet pointing straight forward, not off at an angle.

In Zeleny's sociology class: become involved socially with ethnic groups other than your own.

In Miss Budge's children's literature class: read numerous children's books if you choose to learn children's interests.

In Miss Hill's literature class: the world's greatest short story is the account of the Prodigal Son and his experiences.

In D. Brainerd's Minnesota history class: read the history of the state with a professional sense of humor.

In Miss Adkin's methods class: accumulate as many pictures of different subjects to motivate effective learning.

In Miss Graves' geology class: learn to identify rock formations that are of volcanic origin.

In Miss Penning's art class: how to develop artistic talents.

The impact of the composite of impressions from these and other classes at St. Cloud Teachers College was to learn how to apply the psychologies of learning in ordinary and extraordinary classroom situations.

My First College Graduation

In November of 1934 I had completed the basic academic requirements of the two year program at St. Cloud State which made me eligible for graduation and a Minnesota teaching credential for assignments in grades 1–8. This graduation preceded three more as I gained my doctorate in 1951. The fact that our graduation in St. Cloud was scheduled for the day before Thanksgiving made the occasion somewhat more solemn. We even sang a well known religious hymn as part of the exercises: "Lead On

Oh King Eternal". Back in the thirties the line of demarcation between church and state had not become as clearly drawn as seems to be the case currently. While the graduation program was offered, the remainder of our family was downtown shopping and appropriately preparing for Grandmother Ryberg's funeral which was held on Thanksgiving Day. On our drive home we had the misfortune of having a flat tire which was quite readily replaced due to the conveniences of owning a Model A Ford. At our graduation we were told of limited employment possibilities and low wages. Perhaps a flat tire at night on a deserted road was an omen that tied in with the theme of our graduation exercises—look beyond.

Turning Point—University of Minnesota

Another particularly critical time in my life developed about 09–01–38. I had received a B.A. degree from Gustavus Adolphus College and had applied for a number of jobs at the middle and secondary school levels but without success. The new school year was beginning but I was definitely not among the employed. Of course it would have been possible for me to have worked with my parents operating our farm, but I was not encouraged by them or anyone else to make that choice. My brother Laurel was beginning a new school year teaching in a one room rural school in our area. A friend of the family, Al Madden, was about to begin another year of teaching in Upsala. Through some miracle my brother offered to lend me money that would enable me to enroll in graduate work at the University of Minnesota. Al promised to drive me to Minneapolis and help me enroll in graduate school. I got my M.A. degree in 1939 which enabled me to accept employment at Waldorf College, Forest City, Iowa. Eventually Laurel was able to return to the University of Minnesota and earn a Ph.D. degree. Al Madden left teaching and became wealthy in real estate. Thus my brother initiated one of the most satisfying decisions for me. Eventually I returned to graduate school, enabling me to earn a doctorate at the University of Denver.

War of the Worlds

During the fall quarter of 1938, I was rooming with Earl Morrissette in a private home near the campus of the University of Minnesota. I had just begun my work on a schedule which would prepare me to function as a school administrator. One Sunday evening as I was doing homework in our room, Earl was listening to the radio with the family downstairs. The program that was attracting the group seemed to be especially loud as though an invading army was threatening the listeners. Suddenly Earl came dashing upstairs shouting, "they're invading, they're invading" as though violence and reality were being broadcast. My curiosity was aroused so I followed Earl back downstairs about the time a report was broadcast that some aliens had already attacked the Eastern seaboard. It all sounded real enough so I continued listening to the broadcast, not having heard the announcement earlier that "War of the Worlds," a story of H.G. Wells, was being featured on the Orson Welles program. This repeated reminder provided a calming effect but the impact of seeming reality did not suddenly disappear. The following Monday national recovery occurred, but slowly, as Orson Welles explained why he had chosen to broadcast the story that Sunday night.

Minneapolis

In September, 1938, I enrolled as a graduate student at the University of Minnesota. During the course of the year '38–'39, I earned my master's degree in the College of Education. Minneapolis was my home. Thanks to the assistance freely given by my friend, Al Madden, I became acquainted on the campus and in the city. One service that I truly appreciated and used regularly was provided by local street car traffic. For 10 cents it was possible to ride to any part of the area. As a student I discovered that excellent entertainment, musically, athletically, and theatrically, was available for very respectable prices. I love trains so every morning as I crossed the bridge from a main traffic thoroughfare, I could see steam powered trains passing beneath me. As I looked from my vantage point on the bridge I could see the Mississippi River and downtown Minneapolis with flour mills near at hand. Shopping in the city proved to be much more convenient than in a small town. The churches and schools from my involvement with them indicated that leadership in the city was highly effective in dealing with community matters. The lakes and parks in Minneapolis have gained national and international reputations. I have departed the city by bus, rail and air on numerous occasions; it always seemed to me upon my return to Minneapolis that I was being beckoned back to my second home.

Turning Point—University of Denver

While I was stationed at Camp Funston in Kansas, Virginia, who was staying in Manhattan, Kansas for awhile, decided that a military pass to Denver might brighten our spirits. We rode the train to Denver through wheat fields in western Kansas and ranching country in eastern Colorado until we arrived in Denver. We enjoyed Denver scenically and socially to the extent that I opted to continue graduate work at the University of Denver when I became a civilian. The first opportunity came in 1949 when I was a veteran and could be supported in part under the GI bill. During the summer of '49 I continued to work at the graduate level and returned to St. Cloud State for my school year teaching assignment. I was involved in a number of seminars in '49 at which time Dr. Roy Ivan Johnson of the College of Education, Denver University took an interest in me. In the fall of 1950 I had a leave of absence from St. Cloud State so I could continue my studies in Denver. During registration, 1950, Dr. Johnson offered me a part-time teaching assignment in the College of Ed. This was quite an honor for me, one which I had not anticipated. This offer supplemented my income so with the GI bill in addition, it was not necessary for me to borrow funds while I was working for my doctorate. I received my degree during the summer graduation exercises in August of 1951. It was the conclusion of a pleasant stay at the edge of the Rockies.

Outstanding Professors

Gustavus—1932–1933: Professor Youngdahl, skilled in the field of economics. His class sessions included lectures and discussions concerning ways and means whereby the great depression could be brought to a logical ending.

Gustavus—1937–1938: Dr. Peterson, an outstanding professor of modern and ancient history. His lectures made events and trends come alive. Dr. Peterson had a standing offer from Harvard to join the History Department of that campus.

University of Minnesota—1938–1939: Dr. Brueckner, a warm and extremely knowledgeable person. His expertise was in the field of curriculum building in education. His insights concerning educational psychology applied were outstanding. Educators would do well to accept his philosophies and designs in furthering effective basic learning.

University of Wisconsin—1943–1944: Dr. Becker was one of the faculty in Madison whose lectures were designed to prepare those of us in uniform for the eventual occupation of Western Europe. His knowledge of history and international politics made his lectures stimulating.

University of Denver—1950–1951: Dr. Roy Ivan Johnson was well versed in the workable aspects of a sound philosophy of education. His personal warmth and concerns for motivating young learners were superb.

It was this roster of faculty members who over the years encouraged me, among others, to continue my studies in Educational Psychology and to teach and counsel with greater effectiveness.

V
MILITARY

MILITARY
Table of Contents

MILITARY

Minneapolis to San Antonio

In September 1942, following my volunteering to enter the U.S. Army, I was accepted for an assignment at the Aviation Cadet Center in San Antonio, Texas, there to join a Psychological Testing Group. One evening following the testing and orientation at Fort Snelling, I was assigned to ride a sleeper to Kansas City, Missouri, on the Rock Island Rail Road. The following morning I transferred to a Twin Star Rocket for an all day ride to Fort Worth, Texas. The train glided through wheat fields in Kansas to grain and cattle raising parts of Oklahoma, through such cities as Enid, El Reno and Chickasha. As shadows of evening fell we transversed parts of Texas, eventually arriving at Fort Worth after dark. For the remainder of the journey I transferred to an overnight on the Katy Line. We continued south through rural Texas, viewing the countryside with homes revealing severe differences between "haves and have nots." Towns like Waco, Austin, San Marcos and New Braunfels reflected degrees of prosperity. Finally about noon I arrived in San Antonio for my first military assignment. The place seemed to be hot and busy with vehicles and people in uniform. I finally got a ride to the Cadet Center but the driver did not exactly know where I was assigned so he directed me to get off his vehicle in the area I was supposed to be housed. In the heat of the afternoon I was finally told where to go. I was glad to sit down, deposit my heavy barracks bag and accept the greetings offered.

San Antonio, Texas

I arrived in San Antonio by rail in September, 1942. My trip to this part of Texas had carried me all the way from Minneapolis to near the Mexican border. My first impressions of San Antonio were to the effect that it was busy and hot. After meeting some of my buddies and an assignment to a bunk, adjustment to my life as a GI had begun. Initial information regarding the city related to bus fares and hitchhiking techniques. During the year of my assignments in San Antonio, I ventured into selected parts of the city on numerous times. An early discovery as to the locations of the Lutheran Service Center and the USO was profitable. An initial desire on my part was to tour the Alamo which I discovered in the downtown area. The old mission transformed into a fort looms large in Texas history. I was very much impressed by the beauty of the river which flows through the business district. The local zoo proved to be another attraction with a great variety of plant and animal life. Architecturally and socially the Spanish influences are very much in evidence throughout the city. Military installations almost encircled the municipality in 1942. The kindly civilian influences that I felt warmly were expressed at a Methodist Church in North San Antonio and in the prominent Lutheran Service Center and church downtown. I still carry in my memory the history and thoughtfulness of the people residing there.

San Antonio Aviation Cadet Center

I was warmly received by the fellows in our barracks, followed by a bunk assignment and a reminder that it was time for dinner. My first impressions were to the effect that conditions in these facilities were indeed very comfortable with very good food. But circumstances would change shortly as we moved into a new barracks and a new dining room across the road from the Cadet Center. The new facilities had the appearance of pioneer housing units but early on we adjusted as good soldiers are expected to do. I was assigned to what is called a psychomotor unit. Our job in this part of the research unit was to assess the cadet's motor skills somewhat similar to the aptitudes required for flying aircraft. The potential pilots with whom we worked cooperated effectively if not optimistically as we tested them. In fact, one day a cousin from central Minnesota was part of my group, a Mr. Swanson who later proved to be an expert pilot under combat conditions. Every Friday afternoon our barracks were thoroughly cleaned in advance of "white glove" inspection which followed on Saturday. As an indication of ongoing buddyship, if anyone got a package from home, he would open it to an assortment of goodies which would be shared by everyone. I soon learned that the word 'buddy' was more than friendship—it was in the nature of a social plus.

San Antonio

We did have time off with passes and occasionally, furloughs. I spent a number of evenings and Sunday afternoons in the downtown area, frequenting the Lutheran Service Center and the USO facilities. Very enjoyable in terms of historic and scenic opportunities were visits to the Alamo, the zoo and walks along the San Antonio river. For Thanksgiving dinner a Methodist minister and his wife invited a small group of us to their home for a banquet served in Southern style. Occasionally friends would take us for rides in the hill country west of San Antonio and for tours of Austin and New Braunfels. On one occasion I was invited to speak at a convocation at Texas Lutheran College in Seguin, followed by a seminar and dinner at the home of the college president. The relatively intense heat of the hours of duty were relieved by the friendly evening breezes from the Gulf of Mexico. I learned to adjust to climatic extremes as this was part of the job of soldiering. Virginia visited me in San Antonio at Christmastime in 1942. The socializing we shared was a therapeutic relief from the service routines of barracks life. After about a year at the Cadet Center I was transferred to Texas A&M, there to wait for my next assignment. The Army had called for volunteers to serve in occupied countries following WWII. I was motivated to respond, motivated by the thought of serving in Norway.

Texas A&M

This university offers outstanding course work in agriculture and engineering in addition to general education opportunities, as well as supporting an active Marine Corps unit on campus. The atmosphere at A&M was one of acceptance and cooperation as I discovered when I inquired regarding library services. The librarian suggested that since I had graduate library privileges at the University of Minnesota, I might have the same opportunities at Texas A&M. When military duties were attended to and I had some free time to catch up on my reading, I again was the recipient of Texas hospitality. Virginia and I agreed to marry in Houston if my stay in south Texas was to continue for an extended period of time. This did not occur, however; we were married later in Iowa. One afternoon I had a pass for a sojourn to Bryan which was respectably close to A&M. It was there that I first viewed the film "Fantasia". As the fall season brought delightfully milder weather we enjoyed the color and football traditions of this part of the country. Especially interesting was the game pitting traditional rivals of Texas and Texas A&M against each other. As a railroad fan I viewed the Sunlite Special on the Southern Pacific R.R. running near the campus as it traveled between Dallas and Houston. With the arrival of December we knew that our stay in Texas was about to be concluded. My months in the Lone Star State had indeed been pleasant.

A Busy Rat

We were bivouacked in a hilly wooded area somewhere near a point where Oklahoma and Arkansas meet. Our outfit was conducting military maneuvers at that location one winter during World War II. Several of us who slept in a tent bedded down in our sleeping bags were marginally comfortable. One morning, quite early, we were awakened by the barrage of harsh words emitted by one of the sergeants who had been rudely aroused from slumber. During the course of the night, a pack rat had chewed a hole through the sleeve of his heavy overcoat and subsequently built a nest in a pocket of his garment. The intruder must have entered our tent early in the evening and almost noiselessly had prepared a comfortable home for itself. If it were possible to overlook the damage done, an observer might have admired the ambition this little creature had exhibited.

WWII: Texas to Wisconsin

The train ride from Texas to St. Louis was relatively uneventful through the early morning ride, but as we approached the Mississippi River it became quite scenic. In Missouri we boarded a train that would carry us into the Chicago area. It was our second night of travel that finally brought our group to Madison, Wisconsin. All of us who were in the ASTP program (Army Specialist Training for the occupancy of Europe especially) were conveniently settled in university dorms with dining facilities near at hand. It was on Christmas Eve, 1943, with Duke Ellington and band performing for campus guests (We were not overly inspired by his music although as a person the Duke was a very gracious individual). Our course work began before the holiday season was over with emphasis on every aspect of occupational duties: history, geography, economics, cultural aspects and linguistics were all included in our basic programs. We were well motivated, well treated and anxious to assume the new roles that we would be called upon to fill. All of the university faculty assigned to work with us were experts in their chosen fields. Our schedules at the University of Wisconsin were completed late in February so as we waited to journey to our next stations we had a few days of "freedom" with passes. It was during this time that Virginia and I were married, on March 7, 1944.

Madison to McCoy

Following a brief honeymoon in Madison and a very short trip back to Minnesota to visit my parents, we were all called back for a rail trip to Michigan. Following a short assignment near Battle Creek, we were called to serve at Camp McCoy, Wisconsin. During severe winter training we were taught how to kill and how not to be killed. All of our involvements were as severe and intense as the Wisconsin winter. Late in the spring of 1944, a new kind of duty was assigned to a group of us at Fort Riley, Camp Funston in Kansas. Our new jobs involved making and reading maps, a kind of pattern of skills involved in combat. For those of us who were trained at ASTP we were faced with the harsh reality that the skills we had gained academically could hardly be applied until military action had secured an acceptable peace. Eventually I was assigned to the combat engineers as an expert in personnel matters. This kind of duty prevailed until I was discharged in 02–46, following months overseas, especially in the Philippines. During all of the tours of duty in which I was involved in the Army, I learned much about myself and about other people with whom I interacted. I learned that "buddy" meant more than "friend"—in the service the definition of "buddy" refers to ongoing life or death situations, survival or not.

Manhattan, Kansas

While I was stationed at Camp Funston, part of the Fort Riley complex in Kansas, I found it convenient to relax and refresh myself in Manhattan, a city of some 28,000 people. (Part of my refreshing was gained by enjoying a steak dinner for $1.50.) Kansas State University is located here, where for sometime, a member of the Eisenhower family was president. Following the earning of a Ph.D. at the University of Minnesota, my brother Laurel received an appointment to the faculty at Kansas State.

While I was in the service I had library privileges on this campus. A friendly civilian invited Virginia to reside at her house, an offer which was very much appreciated. On Mother's Day I had the privilege of being invited to preach a sermon honoring mothers in a Lutheran Church located near the campus. Following the Allies victory in Germany, General Eisenhower visited this area as the honored guest of the local community. Agriculturally the growing of excellent crops of wheat was a long standing tradition in this and many other parts of Kansas. The 'home town' friendliness in Manhattan created a lasting impression of good will for all members of the Anderson family who had the privilege of living here.

WWII Engineers

My assignment with the engineers involved record keeping, personnel work and counseling. In addition, all members of our headquarters company were required to develop expertise in handling arms of various kinds, explosives and basic building skills applied in the construction of bridges and sanitary facilities. In war, training provides for physical fitness and efficient tactics for building up as well as for destroying. We were trained in the arts of construction and obliterating. At Camp Funston in the Fort Riley complex we were neighbors to friendly citizens in Manhattan, particularly due in part to the fact that the Kansas State University campus was located there. Again, as at Texas A&M, I had library privileges on campus, which I enjoyed greatly. For a matter of weeks Virginia stayed at a private home in Manhattan which made the community seem socially warmer. On Mother's Day 1945, I preached a sermon in the local Swedish Lutheran Church in honor of the occasion. On

Sundays when I was somewhat alone, following a dinner for $1.50 in downtown Manhattan, I would ride the train or hitchhike to Topeka for the afternoon. During a three day weekend I would take the train to Kansas City for a change of pace and scenery. As in Texas and Wisconsin, I found people in Kansas to be very friendly and cooperative, substantially strengthening my morale.

Camp Funston to San Francisco to the Pacific Ocean

With the assistance of German POWs we loaded a U.P. train for our trip to San Francisco and subsequent boarding of the merchant troop ship, the Sea Witch. Our unit included some 600 men so transportation in passenger and baggage cars was arranged more for efficiency than comfort. We traveled through western Kansas, eastern Colorado, Wyoming, Utah, Nevada and finally into California where the personnel of our outfit along with our equipment were unloaded. We were stationed in Antioch area for a few days at the eastern end of the San Francisco Bay area. Eventually orders were issued to the effect that we were to board ship in the downtown part of the Bay area. The loading of the ship with our supplies and equipment went very smoothly so as the late afternoon shadows lengthened, we sailed under the Golden Gate Bridge into waters unknown to most of us. This was in early July but the chill brought on by the cold ocean waters necessitated that we wear winter style overcoats. The emotional impact involved in sailing under the bridge with our futures uncertain, completely in God's hands, revived memories like a rerun of the first day in school when so much uncertainty lay ahead.

WWII: Pacific Ocean

A few days out of San Francisco we were in warmer, calmer waters. As the days passed more and more of our group opted to spend more time on the deck of the ship, especially at night since the air above board was comfortably cool. We were informed by the ship's radio of current events at home and worldwide as the days wore on. Our craft was quite definitely in tropical waters as we began to observe the presence of flying fish with their gossamer appearance. With the appearance of more birds and sea traffic we were aware, after many days, that land was in sight. Our first landfall in the Philippines was in the vicinity of Tacloban on the island of Leyte. Our unit was permitted to go ashore for a brief respite following so many days at sea. (I would return to Tacloban again within a few months to board a ship for the journey home, following the surrender of the Imperial Japanese military.) Next landfall for us was in the harbor at Iloilo on the island of Panay. We disembarked following sentimental best wishes for the crew of the Sea Witch. From the harbor area in Iloilo we were transported to our bivouac area several miles inland along the coast of the island beyond Iloilo. It was a new world for almost all of us, thus requiring readjustment and adaptation skills.

Philippines—Unloading at Panay

On the day that we anchored in the harbor at Iloilo, Panay, we were transported to a bivouac area inland, located within a grove of palm trees, some of which must have been 60 feet tall. As we unloaded the GI trucks that brought us to the area, a number of local citizens gathered to "look on" to see what was going on as we raised our tents and set up our kitchen. One woman who appeared to be in her early thirties attracted more attention than all of the other natives who came to observe the new arrival of American troops. She was somewhat wrinkled, sober in appearance but keen as an observer. She held a large banana leaf with a roasted chicken in it in one hand, and held a young child in her other hand while smoking a sizable black cigar. Later during our stay in this area, some of the smokers in our outfit said that those cigars were quite satisfying.

Within the bivouac area, a stand of coconut palms had apparently been cultivated and maintained for many years. Almost every afternoon one or two natives would come to pick nuts but would come mainly to collect the juice that flowed from stems, growing out of the trunks of the coconut palm trees. The juice was naturally produced to support the nuts, but the natives intercepted it with their bamboo containers. The juice was fermented, then served as a form of liquor for native drinkers. (I never heard any of my buddies express a desire for this kind of beverage although the coconuts were generally regarded as tasty.) Fortunately no one within our outfit was ever injured by a heavy coconut falling 60 feet from the top of the stately palms that graced our area. Whenever we rescued a fallen nut we enjoyed a treat as we opened this great fruit. These palms and their delicious nuts reminded us of the fact that we were indeed living in the tropics near the equator and adjusting to the demands of the area.

WWII: Panay

Shortly after our occupation of the Iloilo area on Panay, a small detachment set up a radio station so selected music and news could be broadcast to our men and others who might be listening. Harold Rocklitz was chief engineer of our broadcasting facility and I was the newscaster. After we signed off for the day (well into the evening) we would open a can of prepared turkey for our snack. We had our "private" jeep and as we drove back to the barracks we were amazed as to how many rats were scampering around us. When free time allowed, a small group of us toured more primitive and very scenic parts of the island. We would find cinnamon bark in large sheets lying out on the road drying. There were reptiles in some areas that would be longer than segments of them stretched across the road. We saw termite hills ten feet high in some of the fields we crossed. For lunch at one stop we bought 25 cents worth of bananas which filled our jeep with the fruit. Harold was an excellent driver, always navigating around the worst of the roadway but always bringing us back to the barracks on time. One evening a native invited me to sail over to another island in his outrigger canoe. It was a wonderfully moonlit occasion. The brilliance of the moonlight in a tropical setting was almost hypnotically beautiful.

Philippines—Giving Treats

Early during the time our engineer outfit was bivouacked on the island of Panay in the Philippines, we learned that the children in our area had developed a keen sense of and interest in American candy bars. They seemed to realize that each of us would receive an allotment from time to time, and that friendliness to American GIs would enable them to share the candy with us. Their enthusiasm and excitement were great enough so that each member of a small group of children would almost tear your shirt off until each got a bar if the treats were distributed informally. What I would do when a small group appeared with their loud requests for treats was to have them stand a short distance away from me, show them how many bars I had, have them line up, six bars for six children in the lineup and they all went away satisfied and happy with the treats.

Philippines

There were so many children in the neighborhood of our area of Panay that it seemed as though the war had not decimated the population. On many occasions they would play running games on the street that ran through our area, using dried puffer fish as balls. One day I was visiting a friendly native near a cemetery in the area when a little girl, obviously his daughter, began to cry bitterly. Upon inquiring why she was crying, the father said that it was in this area that the Japanese had killed her mother. Early in our stay on Panay, we established a water point for safe water for cooking and drinking. Soon some of the native mothers would ask for some of our water for their children. The death rate for infants and young children was reduced drastically as the native mothers continued to share our water supply.

Becoming a Civilian Again

We were transported to Angel Island in the San Francisco Bay area following debarkation from the Afoundria. The accommodations on the island were pleasant indeed, as no duty was required of us, allowing much time for relaxation. The food was good, especially following meals served on troop ships. Following a relatively brief stay at Angel Island we were transported by excursion craft to the dock area in Oakland where we paused to wait for rail transportation to various sections of the United States. Following at least one transfer, I along with other G.I.'s were unloaded at La Crosse, Wisconsin, there to receive bus transportation to Camp McCoy. We had returned to the chill of winter but there was no chill in the manner in which we were treated. All old uniforms barracks bags, etc. were turned in for new uniforms suitable for Wisconsin weather. When all documentation had been completed we were given money for tickets which enabled us to return to the places of enlistment. Instead of returning to Minneapolis where I had enlisted, I went by bus to Forest City, Iowa, where Virginia was living with her mother. Even though I arrived in Forest City at a late hour, I received a reception that was warmly overwhelming. I was emphatically assured that becoming a civilian again was most rewarding.

Adjustments

The days in Forest City in late winter of 1946 were days of leisure. Both Virginia and her mother were employed so I was left alone in our upstairs apartment for much of each day, Monday through Friday. I tried to catch up on my reading and on current events. One significant duty which I was obligated to fulfill was to keep an appointment with the president of Waldorf College, regarding the status of my employment on campus. We had a pleasant chat which early on indicated that my old job was not waiting for me. President Nielson maintained that he could not request the person now identified as Director of Teacher Training to resign from the job. I was offered employment, however, as a field representative of the campus, which meant that I was to recruit new students. I didn't have a car for this kind of employment and if I had owned one, I would not have accepted this job. Days of leisure continued during which time I received unemployment checks, made a trip to Des Moines and had my final official dental checkup, thanks to the military. As the early days of spring approached I decided that I would enroll as a student at the University of Minnesota. About the time of the beginning of the Spring Quarter I boarded a bus for the trip to Minneapolis. When I reached the campus the whole place sounded like a veterans' reunion. Friendliness abounded but crowded classrooms, a shortage of books and supplies created problems for everybody at the University of Minnesota.

A Veteran's Counseling Center at St. Cloud State

Very early in my employment at the counseling center I became impressed at the efficient functioning of our organization. The primary and official objective of our work was to scientifically ascertain what each veteran was prepared to do vocationally. When this objective was met the veteran would have determined how most effectively he/she could function as a well adjusted citizen and effective member of the community of which he/she was a member. Upon entering the center, the veteran was interviewed in an attempt to determine his personal qualities on the basis of earlier civilian experiences—vocationally and academically, his assignments and training in military service, his hobbies and his current interests. Following the initial interview a series of tests was administered to determine the applicant's level of intelligence, his interests, possible vocational skills and personality patterns, particularly in regard to his/her levels of maturity. When all tests results were available, another interview was scheduled at which time vocational choices were considered in view of interests, level of intelligence and potential vocational skills. For some veterans, levels of college training were outlined, for others vocational training on the job was offered. When choices were made that in effect suited the applicant, financial support for essential training was assured. Any physical or emotional limitation was taken into account. As a counselor in this program, my optimism for its success was well established.

Counselors at St. Cloud State Veteran's Center

The persons employed at the Veteran's Center were all professionally prepared to meet the needs of veterans who recently had become private citizens, especially in regard to their vocational futures. Bob Warnken, Charley Emery, Ralph Sorenson and I were assigned to be chief counselors in the St. Cloud Center. As veterans appeared for counseling, they were assigned to us, one counselee at a time for each of us. We would conduct initial interviews, request testing and schedule concluding interviews. During the months we worked together we functioned as somewhat of a team in sharing problems and prospects in addition to being involved socially with each other and our families. The four of us would have coffee breaks and occasional lunches and dinner parties together. When Virginia and I were searching for a house that might be available near the campus we purchased the Sorenson house as they were moving to a new location nearby. We learned to know spouses, children and children's problems quite well (Virginia and I had no children at this time so we learned about what other parents had to contend with). Following about a year in the center I was invited to become a full-time member of the Psychology Department at St. Cloud State. Charles Emery became Director of Placements and Ralph Sorenson accepted an appointment as chief counselor at Technical High School in St. Cloud. Bob Warnken was assigned to do counseling work in the Minneapolis-St. Paul area. Overall my adjustment to civilian life was effectively promoted by the contacts and assignments received in St. Cloud.

VI
FAMILY LIFE

FAMILY LIFE
Table of Contents

FAMILY LIFE

Summer, 1946

During the first summer following my return to civilian status,Virginia and I rented a house not far from Tech High School in St. Cloud. The walk from this location was a source of early morning exercise as I enjoyed my hike through some of the finest neighborhoods in the city on my way to work. From time to time my parents would conveniently let us use their Model A Ford for shopping excursions and trips to some of the lakes in the area. During part of the summer Tommy Graham, one of Virginia's youngest cousins, stayed with us, enabling him to appreciate a Minnesota vacation. In fact he was the first person to enjoy a swim in the new municipal pool just dedicated for the youth of St. Cloud. Walt and Irma Person with their two young boys were welcome visitors at our house one evening. The Person family was living in Albany for the summer previous to moving to Sioux Falls, South Dakota, where Walt would hold a professorship at Augustana College. Irma was involved in writing Sunday School and other church materials for the Augsburg Publishing House, Minneapolis. The entire summer of 1946 proved to be very pleasant, excellent for my adjustments back to life as a civilian.

Eden Valley: Memorial Day

This community is southwest of St. Cloud in one of the very scenic areas of Central Minnesota. I was invited to give the Memorial Day address at a community gathering in this place. Virginia and I did not own or rent a car at this time inasmuch as used and new vehicles were hard to find. We were all adjusting to shortages following World War II. This was May, 1946. My folks shared their Model A Ford with us on this and other occasions so they arranged to be with us on this day and furnish transportation. It was a beautiful day with spring colors and reds, whites and blues in profusion. The program went well as all of us felt a surge of patriotism following the conclusion of victories identified in recent bitter warfare. When the program was over we decided to have lunch in another locality so we could enjoy more of the sights and scenery in this colorful part of the state. We continued our tour well into the afternoon, riding in the comforts of the family Model A. Visits of this nature gave Virginia opportunities to learn more about my parents' likes and dislikes and to learn more about Minnesota which would be her home state until 1954.

Social Events

While Virginia and I rented most of a house (all except for a small apartment upstairs) we contacted many of the residents in St. Cloud who had formerly lived in Upsala to a party one evening. We had a great time playing games, telling Upsala stories, relating accounts of days, even years when Upsala was our home town. The evening's entertainment was concluded as we enjoyed desserts that Virginia had prepared. On another occasion in Minneapolis, Irene and I were invited to a high school reunion at the home of one of the graduates who lived in a pleasant home in a very upscale neighborhood. Some of the students who were in my 5th and 6th grade class arrangement when I taught in Upsala in 1935–36, were now high school graduates enjoying this reunion as Irene and I were. We reminisced over good food and fond memories of years past. Subsequently Irene and I were invited to a Reinertson wedding anniversary in the Minneapolis area where James and his wife were currently residing. I was the only member of their wedding party at this reunion, other than the bride and groom. When some of the Reinertson relatives and friends learned that I had been born and reared on a farm, my friendship with them became even more obvious. On both of these occasions we enjoyed ourselves immensely. The stream of memories which flowed through all of our visiting was especially ingratiating.

Crosby, Minnesota

On a beautiful day in late September, Virginia and I opted for a weekend of fishing in Northern Minnesota. We drove up to Brainerd from St. Cloud, then over to near Crosby where we found a lake that looked attractive in the brilliance of a colorful autumn afternoon. Fishing was fairly good as we caught several northerns, none of which would have won a prize for size. As darkness descended we drove back to Crosby where we rented a room in a modest hotel. (The manager agreed to keep our catch of northerns in a freezer as part of the guest service we obtained.) The next day we drove out to the same lake and anchored in a colorful and quiet bay. Fishing was leisurely until suddenly something big struck Virginia's bait. I said "easy, easy" as fate played its role - a fish line devoid of its former lure. We returned to St. Cloud by way of Upsala, stopping to share our catch with my parents. Their reaction was to the effect that we had caught the best - a bigger fish story.

Fishing in Pine Lake

Early one June evening Virginia and I thought it would be interesting for us to try our luck fishing in Pine Lake, in the 'lake region' west of Upsala. On the east side of Pine Lake there was a beautiful grove of stately pine trees which added to the scenic beauty of the area. We rented a boat at the shoreline of the lake and proceeded to row out to an area near the north end of the lake which looked like a good spot for fishing. We would like to catch sunfish and a northern or two. When the anchor of the boat was dropped we relaxed in the calm beauty of a perfect Minnesota summer evening. Little did we notice that there was a cloud forming above the shoreline behind us only a few yards away. Suddenly the cloud descended upon us, a large cloud of mosquitoes. They attacked us without mercy with their buzzing and stinging, apparently trying to enjoy an evening meal. We lifted the anchor and rowed to the landing where we had gotten the boat. As we left the boat and raced up the embankment and into the pines, we left the mosquitoes behind us. It was a beautiful evening.

Fishing along the Canadian Border

It was late in the spring of 1949 when nine of us, mostly faculty from St. Cloud State, rented a cabin on the shores of Lake Kabatogema for a week of fishing. We brought three boats and motors with us, thus enabling us to enjoy comfortable boating out on the lake each day. We organized our group of nine into three groups: housekeeping, cooking and fish preparation. All routine matters were dealt with at high level of efficiency. At about 9 AM we were out on the lake and continued fishing until about 5 PM. Each day we caught our limits of northerns and walleyed pike. When we'd cast into shallow levels of the lake we would catch northerns, while casting into deeper waters we'd locate schools of walleyed pike. All the fish were delicious since all we landed were caught in water that had until recently been frozen solidly. The fish we did not enjoy on site we sent frozen by express, first to Duluth and then to St. Cloud where the catch had been placed in storage lockers waiting our return to St. Cloud. This had been a great but altogether too brief vacation. The scenery, the solitude, the fellowship had been at its best. I even won a prize as the person who landed the biggest fish.

Apartment and Housing in St. Cloud

Our living accommodations in St. Cloud during the time I was a member of the faculty at St. Cloud State University varied from limited apartments to the greater part of a house. One of our better accommodations was on college property at the estate that had been given to the campus. Part of the property arrangement included the apartment built over a multi-vehicle garage; this we rented with space for our Pontiac. The facility met all of our needs in regard to price and conveniences. Another time we lived in the top apartment of a multi-storied home with the inconvenience of climbing several flights of stairs with little fire protection. It was at this place that we fed seventeen gray squirrels with unsalted nuts and water. Virginia and I lived for a year or more in a ground floor apartment immediately across from the campus. There one of our neighbors had a white dog that would beg for and get a carrot each time the vegetable truck stopped in our area. For most of another school year we rented a house with the exception of a small apartment rented to a couple on the top floor. It was at this house that we had ice delivery service for a real old fashioned ice box. The last apartment we rented in St. Cloud was a two bedroom facility, upstairs, with a separate garage arrangement. It was there at −30 degrees one day when I started the car; three connecting rods were damaged in the process. In June of 1954 we purchased a two storied dwelling for $7200. During the course of the summer I signed a contract for a professorship at San Diego State University. Our next purchase was for a house in California which has now been in the family for 47 years with my daughter as present owner.

St.Cloud, Minnesota

It was in the mid 1920s that my dad decided to make a one day trip to St. Cloud as a kind of vacation. This was the beginning of a long series of shopping trips to the city. Many additional trips were made to St. Cloud when my brother Laurel and I were students at St. Cloud State. In September of 1933 I enrolled at State for my sophomore year following my freshman year at Gustavus Adolphus. September of 1934 is the date of my graduation from the two year course, followed by completion of my junior year at State. I returned to St. Cloud as a result of being employed as a veteran's counselor at State in 1946. During the fall term of 1947 I was accepted as a tenured member of the Psychology Department until September 1954 when I joined the faculty at San Diego State. As citizens of St. Cloud, Virginia and I had a variety of apartment addresses until we finally purchased our first home there. We were active members of Salem Lutheran Church; I had memberships in the American Legion, several fraternities and the Kiwanis Club. During our years in the city we purchased two 'used' cars and two new. Virginia and I were well acquainted with officers in the state reformatory; on one occasion we accepted a dinner invitation to the home of the chief executive officer. As a result of church and brotherhood involvement, I became very friendly with Arthur Anderson, the manager of the local Penney store. St. Cloud to us was both friendly and accommodating, a great city.

The East Side of St.Cloud

In the late 1940s following my return to St. Cloud as a faculty member at St. Cloud State, Virginia and I were the recipients of a good housing offer. A Mrs. Jenson, a widow and member of Salem Lutheran Church where we were members, offered to rent her house to us at a very reasonable rate. We were to use the entire downstairs and a bedroom upstairs. The small apartment upstairs which was separate from the house would not affect us except for the loud sounds that arose at night from an asthma patient who lived there with his wife. Mrs. Jenson would stay in California for at least a year, visiting with her son while we occupied most of the property. Early on we became adjusted to the old refrigerator which required one or two deliveries of ice each week. My walk to the campus now became several blocks longer and meant more wintry chills such as happened when I walked to the campus over the Main Street Bridge at 30 degrees below zero. When spring arrived our healthy tomato plants were deprived of much of their leafy bounty by our neighbor's boys who wanted the greens for their gardening story. (Later in the season the tomato plants really thrived.) We enjoyed Thanksgiving and Christmas at Mrs. Jenson's in addition to the parties we hosted. Then one day Mrs. Jenson returned early much to our surprise. She compromised our arrangements which meant an early departure for us but with many fond memories of our stay in E. St. Cloud.

Squirrels

In 1951 following a leave of absence from St. Cloud State University, we rented an apartment on the third floor of a large house in south St. Cloud. One day we noticed a grey squirrel high up on one of the branches of a nearby tree. Virginia and I thought that he might enjoy a treat since it seems as though we had become neighbors. Consequently we placed a few nutmeats on the window ledge right outside our bedroom window. To our surprise the squirrel came down from the tree, ran over to our window ledge and helped himself to the treats we had deposited. We then made it a regular thing depositing unsalted nutmeats on our window ledge with a small container of water at the end of the nut display. Within a few days several grey squirrels were regular customers at our window. One day we noticed that an especially large customer would grab nuts, lift a shingle and deposit nuts there for storage purposes. If we didn't put nuts out early in the day, our friends would tap on our window, telling us to cooperate.

Car Trouble

It was somewhere in the 1950s that Virginia and I were about to seat ourselves and enjoy a steak dinner. The phone rang that moment with an urgent message from my San Diego State office mate, Bjorn Karlsen. He and his family were stalled in Oceanside due to car trouble. Sensing the urgency of the situation I promised I'd be in Oceanside as soon as possible. When I arrived at the place where Bjorn and his family were waiting, they all released a loud cheer. Mrs. Karlsen, her parents, Bjorn and their three young boys literally scampered into my car and off we went. Destination: San Diego. Upon returning to San Diego the Karlsens invited Virginia and me to share fresh strawberries they had purchased on a tour through our local back country. It was reassuring that the trip for the day had ended reasonably well with all of us enjoying strawberries. As we sat at Karlsen's kitchen table, I suddenly felt a sharp bite through the jacket I was wearing. Young Johnnie K. had just expressed himself with a pliers, revealing his not so warm feelings toward me. But I forgave him.

Apartment in Denver

During the summer of 1949 I roomed in a private home within walking distance of the Denver University campus. One of the neighbors understood that my wife and I were searching for housing for the 1950–51 year at Denver U. The offer she made was to the effect that we could rent her house for a year while she was involved elsewhere. When we arrived in Denver in the summer of 1950 we were told that she had changed her plans but that she would share the house with us for the period involved in the initial agreement. This was not satisfactory so I arranged for us to live in a basement apartment for the summer with the understanding that we would have a very acceptable apartment on the second floor in September. Virginia and I survived the summer in the basement apartment; in September we moved into the apartment promised us upstairs. During the course of our stay at 1939 E. Evans Avenue, Denver, we became acquainted with Ed Pfau, graduate student, three faculty members (I as a parttime faculty member that made the total four), several Chinese students who were in the Chinese Nationalist Army, a Norwegian, Arne, jack of all trades was a resident also, as was the son of the chief of police in Paris. Mr. Peterson, the manager, used to make pancakes for himself from very mature batter which filled the structure with unusual breakfast odors. The shark fin delicacies of our Chinese friends also added to the smells of the place as did the odor of glue used for patching. In a very real sense there were few dull moments in this place. We really enjoyed living there.

A Great Tour

During our visits with Laurel and Dorothy in an area where they have their summer home, we have enjoyed the attractions of Pelican Rapids and many other localities in Minnesota, including Moorhead in Minnesota and Fargo in North Dakota. A historical attraction in Moorhead-Fargo was the Scandinavian festival at which Dorothy displayed and sold some of her artistic creations. I was fascinated as I observed a spinning wheel operator take some fresh wool and produce new yarn. In a city park we boarded a Norwegian sailing vessel that had been constructed in this area, had sailed to Norway and then put on display locally for all to see. It was pleasant on one occasion to visit with Mr. Rendahl who interviewed and accepted me for my first college job. Our touring brought us to several of the college campuses that flourish in this area; Concordia and Moorhead State in Moorhead and North Dakota State in Fargo. In addition to experiencing life styles in several municipalities we also viewed the rural scenes of prosperous fields and meadows, saw displays of farm machinery, old and new. The entire tour was a great learning experience set in rural and urban beauty.

Summer Home

My sister Evodia and husband Wilfred own a wooded acreage in the vicinity of Grand Rapids, Northern Minnesota. Their property includes a portion of a lake which at times is frequented by water fowl. In this part of the state it is not unusual to discover huge mounds of tailings built up by the mining of iron ore. For decades the rich deposits in this part of the state supplied high grade ore for the blast furnaces of the eastern United States. The land following mining operations is healing to the degree that wild life, the quality of the water and new growths of trees are all very much in evidence. The cabin my sister and her husband lived in for about six months of the year is comfortable and serviceable in all kinds of weather. Gardening as a hobby is very satisfying to both of them. Visitations by bear and deer are not uncommon with the deer, uninvited, sample some of the wealth of the garden. Irene and I have explored their holdings, fished in the lake and enjoyed the hospitality of their cabin. The seclusion and next-to-nature style of living is stimulating for residents of this area.

Birth Certificate

Circa 1964 when we were in Little Falls, Minnesota, the seat of the county in which I was born, while my parents, Virginia, Anita and I were attending to whatever our errands of the day might have been, I suggested that we visit the courthouse to check on my birth certificate. Due to the fact that my folks were accompanying us they could completely accept or verify the need for any changes on the certificate. They certified to the effect that there were five errors in the document, all of which could be corrected by my Dad and Mother. Sometime later I received updated copies of my certificate from appropriate offices in St. Paul. On occasions when documents like mine are prepared, the pronunciation of names is not always effective, nor is the writing of certain statistics very clear. These kinds of inadequacies are apt to be widespread in places where many immigrants are involved. At least I feel that I am more adequately protected legally and also that I have a basis for suggesting that other people have their records checked.

The Summer of 1954

As a result of not hearing from San Diego State regarding a professorship, Virginia and I purchased a house on 9th Street in St. Cloud. Ralph and Elma Sorenson sold the house to us (two bedrooms—$7200) as they prepared to move across the alley to their "new" house. They were in total agreement that the move was excellent for all of us. During the first summer session at St. Cloud State I had an off-campus assignment at Anoka, Minnesota, near the Twin Cities. Another faculty member had an assignment at Stillwater, another Twin cities suburb. Each morning we drove a campus vehicle to our respective jobs. One morning a complete eclipse of the sun immersed the entire landscape in momentary darkness. Another afternoon a severe hail storm hit south of St. Cloud which damaged both our house and car—we had left the car in front, not anticipating such a severe storm. On another occasion Cousin Luther and his wife were visiting us, then due to the hot weather we went to a drive-in for refreshments. When Luther lifted his glass of root beer, the whole bottom fell out. The sticky contents covered his trousers and some of the upholstery in the car. During a heavy thunder storm in late June our phone rang, conveying the message that I had been accepted by San Diego State. As a result we were now planning to sell the house that we had so recently occupied. No better people could have purchased it than my cousin Martin and his wife Myrtle.

More Summer of 1954

During my first communication with authorities at San Diego State following my appointment we could not quite agree concerning salary arrangements but during subsequent discussions a slight increase was offered so I signed the contract for a professorship. I had a teaching assignment on campus at St. Cloud State during the second summer session in completing professional obligations on campus, culminating in my resignation. Our final weeks in St. Cloud during the summer of 1954 were at least borderline hectic. Decisions as to what to sell, what to bring with us to our new location, a long series of "good-byes" were all parts of a busy schedule. As we neared the end of August we felt that arrangements made locally in St. Cloud and distantly in California were quite acceptable. On the crucial day of our departure from Minnesota, our '51 Pontiac was loaded and we were ready to depart for scenes only partially known. On our way to San Diego we visited with Virginia's sister Marylyn and family in San Francisco, stopped overnight at Santa Maria, arrived in San Diego for the first time in our lives during the Labor Day weekend. We had made no reservations for housing but managed to engage facilities in a motel in La Mesa. A long series of adjustments to California had begun.

San Diego

Virginia and I arrived in San Diego on Saturday of the Labor Day weekend, 1954. It was a beautiful sunny afternoon with the crush of holiday traffic immediately at hand. Our first objective was to locate San Diego State where I was a member of the faculty from 1954–84. Our second objective was to find a place to stay. Following a number of inquiries along El Cajon Boulevard we finally located a vacancy in a motel in La Mesa. It is still in business. Virginia and I experienced a rural touch each morning as we were awakened by a rooster doing his proper duty. From this beginning and for 47 plus years I have observed San Diego become a large metropolitan center. In 1960 the first large shopping mall, College Grove, was opened, followed in rapid succession by several more and numerous mini-malls. During the decades of my residency a trolley successfully initiated and a new University of California constructed. Medical facilities have been extended with Alvarado Hospital opening and Sharp Hospital considerably expanded. Early during our lives in San Diego we heard discussions regarding a new airport and a new central library. They are still in the offing. The prices of homes have doubled a number of times with some advantages of home ownership brought about by Proposition 13. The infrastructure needs substantial improvements. But San Diego is my home. A new airport will happen someday.

First Day in San Diego

It was a bright and sunny morning that greeted us as we arose to our first day in San Diego. Earlier a rooster at a nearby chicken farm has awakened us, giving us the impression that our motel must be located in a rural area. As we left our temporary quarters that morning, our search for a restaurant for breakfast led us to a place that we would frequent on many occasions in years following. The College Restaurant always proved to be a friendly place, serving excellent food. The whole area in and near the campus gave us a small town feeling as at an early date we began looking for our new home. We had paid $7200 for a two bedroom house in St. Cloud, in San Diego comparable property would be three times as expensive. Nevertheless we were glad to be in southern California, particularly in San Diego. Virginia and I continued to explore our first day in town by including the zoo and La Jolla on our itinerary. In addition we viewed some of the beach areas which proved to be inviting and expensive. During our searching that first day we discovered apartments for rent conveniently close to the campus. As members of Salem Lutheran Church in St. Cloud, we also noted that there were Lutheran churches in the campus area. Our first full day had been a busy one but as we returned to our motel we were pleased with our discoveries.

College Restaurant

It was not associated with any campus, but was an attraction in the vicinity of San Diego State. On Sunday morning during the Labor Day weekend, 1954, Virginia and I had our first meal, a breakfast, in the facility. In days and in years to come we returned numerous times.

On many occasions we'd get the feeling that each time in the restaurant was in the nature of a family gathering, inasmuch as we knew so many people who enjoyed the food and sociability there. Their breakfasts were hotcakes, toast, sausages, orange juice and more if you liked a bigger variety. Lunches with salads, sandwiches, desserts and more, satisfied everybody's taste for good food. Afternoon coffee breaks were popular with beverages and freshly baked pie. The dinners in the College Restaurant with chicken and steak specials were outstanding. Mr. Shirts, the manager, supervised the work involved in preparing the food and serving it to assure levels of perfection. Twice he invited the men who usually came to lunch, to a Padre baseball game, and on another occasion, gave Virginia and me tickets to a ball game that he could not attend. Over the years we learned to know all members of his family; visiting with them was always a delight.

Sunday Breakfasts

During the early 1960s, Virginia, Anita and I would attend early morning services at College Lutheran Church, followed by breakfast at one of the new hotels or motels in the San Diego beach areas or in Mission Valley. Since we would enjoy a late morning meal generally our appetites were quite vigorous. We would choose a different facility each time, one probably new to us and also relatively new to the area. Due to the fact that Anita was with us enabled us to receive special services, almost always on the positive side. The quality of food in most places was quite satisfactory although I learned that there are many ways in which cream of wheat can be prepared, that raisin toast must be prepared with great caution lest it be burned. Also the quality of coffee served can vary considerably. Eventually we found ourselves returning more often to one restaurant. There was a waiter at the Town and Country Cafe who was especially attentive to Anita as well as to Virginia and my wishes. The breakfast plan which we followed for quite some time enabled us to learn more about San Diego and how it was developing.

Excellent Eateries

During the summers of 1961–1964–1966, I was a member of the faculty at Wisconsin State University at Superior. One of the enjoyable adventures Virginia, Anita and I shared while living in Duluth-Superior area was that of good eating. I would usually have an early morning class on my schedule, so following this part of my involvement on the campus, I would meet Virginia and Anita at Donnaly's for their fabulous breakfast rolls. They must have had a reputation that spread over most of Northern Wisconsin. When we chose to eat lunch out, the Patio Cafe served delicious meals as well as did the East Side Cafe. Some of my students alerted me to the East Side facility which had cole slaw and steaks fit for royalty and at very reasonable prices. In fact their entire menu was exceedingly appealing. If our wishes tended towards pancakes the Perkins facility in Duluth was conveniently available. Their assortment was excellent, their variety appealing. During evening strolls we'd stop at the Land 'O Lakes ice cream store where all of their dairy products were of the best. Anita discovered that Red Owl grocery store in our area served free coffee in a small cup, mainly filled with cream, she would have her samples there for the day along with her parents. The food, the sociability, the climate all promoted great appetites for great food: we had it all.

Rube's Country Store

One of the big attractions in Escondido in former years was Rube's Country Store. Each time Virginia, Anita and I visited this place we were reminded of bygone days. The sights, the smells and even the sounds which were created when Rube would thresh his oat crop on the premises were reminders of the past. Upon entering the store we were drawn to a small restaurant in one corner of the facility where we enjoyed refreshments. Then the three of us would walk down the aisles where canned and packaged goods were on sale at reasonable prices. The fresh vegetables and fruits on display were always tempting to the palate, especially the fresh strawberries. His meat department always displayed fresh products for pork and beef lovers. One display that I viewed as especially interesting was his display of auto service items, usually selling at excellent prices. I would purchase socks in his clothing area in addition to hats appropriate for the season. On our way out of the store we would stop in the bakery department and buy sticky bread which was saturated in some kind of delicious coating. It was also a treat to visit with Rube who appeared in the store like a farmer, appropriately dressed and as a business man sensitive to the needs of his customers.

Descanso

While Irene's sister, Vernia, and her husband, Russ, were living in Descanso, they would invite us to join them in some of the festivities at the Methodist Church of which they were members. There was a harvest festival during autumn and a luau during the warmer season of the year. The special occasion held each fall involved a dinner and displays of items that the members of the

congregation had made, particularly as the result of interests in hobbies. During this event we enjoyed the activities, especially visiting with members of the community.
The Hawaiian luau was a big event scheduled as a warm
weather attraction, thus enabling performers to wear
lighter garments while engaged in dances seemingly im-
ported from the islands. Roasted pig was a primary item
in the bill of fare at this event. The pleasures shared as
Russ and Vernia's guests on these occasions were always
anticipated, enabling us to enjoy good food and the
warmth of fellowship in a traditional manner. Following
these events and at other times, we would visit in their
delightful home, situated in a scenic forested area nearby.

Summer Cottage

My brother Laurel and his wife own a cottage in the
lake region of western Minnesota. Detroit Lakes, Fergus
Falls and Moorhead are traffic centers in this area. It's
easy to get the impression while traversing the roadways
of this area that there is a lake around almost every bend
in the road. Many elaborate homes have been constructed
on selected lake shores. Laurel and Dorothy's very comfortable summer home is on a very scenic lake shore with
a dock near at hand for launching of their grand motor
boat. In addition to an economy based on tourism, much
of the income locally is earned by the farmers who are in
the dairying business with crops of corn, soy beans,
wheat, barley, and sunflowers. Poultry processing also
provides employment in the area. My brother and his
family enjoy the refreshing coolness of this region when
contrasted with the intense heat of their home in Columbia in central Missouri. Irene and I have always enjoyed
delightful visits in this scenic and prosperous section of

central Minnesota. The hospitality we experience enable Irene and me to recall warm visits to this gracious summer home.

St. Louis

Irene and I were enjoying a restful and exceedingly pleasant visit with Dorothy and Laurel in their attractive home in Columbia, Missouri, when they invited us to share a day with them in St. Louis. On the drive to the city, we enjoyed scenic views of the countryside with brilliant scenes of crops growing in profusion. Upon entering the downtown area we saw reminders of the fame Lindbergh brought to St. Louis with his Spirit of St. Louis which landed in Paris in 1927. A considerable amount of our allotted time was spent in a city park with fabulous displays of flowers, beautiful shade trees, shrubs and gorgeous blossoms on vines and trellises. Set among the scenic beauty of the park were homes of great historical significance. Much could be learned regarding the history of the city by reading accounts on displays in the attractive homes. Due to my interest in steam power we drove to another park where engines of another era were on display. I especially enjoyed some of the exhibits displaying some of the greatest power that earlier had propelled traffic on the Union Pacific and the New York Central R.R.

We had a great day in St. Louis, thanks to Dorothy and Laurel's generosity in sharing their time and interests with us.

A Relaxing Experience

Several years ago during the course of a warm summer's morning, Irene and I were invited to share a picnic with her sister, Vernia, and Vernia's husband, Russ. The four of us ventured into the area in east San Diego County known for its falls: Green Valley. As we relaxed in a beautifully wooded area among the oaks and coniferous trees, we proceeded to enjoy our picnic lunch. Above us large thunderheads were forming, reminding us of the possibility of rain showers. Amid the lightning and thunder a few drops fell, sufficient to refresh the air but not sufficiently heavy to interfere with our picnic. All of us relaxed in this marvelous setting with no interference from automobile traffic or telephone. Following our lunch we sauntered over to the area where the water falls were attracting a few visitors, who with us, admired the rocky layers that formed patterns for falling water. It was a great place, especially for children who might enjoy swimming in this location. As we strolled toward our vehicle, parked nearby, we continued to feel the warmth of fellowship and the grandeur of the scenic views spread before us.

VII
PROFESSION

PROFESSION
Table of Contents

PROFESSION

Time Keeper

While I was a teacher in the Elementary Department of the Upsala School System, one of my assignments was to serve as time keeper for our boys high school basketball team. The only equipment I had for the performance of my duties was a stop watch and a small pistol that shot blanks. As I reflect back over those years, 1936–37, the basketball team had a good record in the win column. I would ride along to help officiate at out-of-town games as well as during games at home. The visiting team would also have its time keeper so we would work together. We set our watches as each game began, kept track of time outs and signaled when time for the game had run out. At that time I would shoot the pistol and the game ended. To the best of my knowledge it was the only gun in the school—would even a timer's pistol be tolerated today?

Upsala Elementary School: 1935–1937

Following graduation from the two-year teacher training course at St. Cloud State, I was hired to be a teacher in the Upsala School. My assignment extended over a two year period, '35–'37. I resigned in 1937 so that I would be able to earn my B.A. degree in an additional year at college. The teaching experiences I had in my home community were invigorating and satisfying. My first year I was assigned to teach fifth grade and a representative group of sixth graders. The second year's assignment was exclusively dedicated to working with a fifth grade. Some of the experiences I had enabled me to gain maturity as a teacher as well as a human being. A professional positive response to each contribution a student made was basically essential. Instead of oral reprimands if some behavior was inappropriate I would write the pupil's name on the chalkboard. Another offense would mean the name plus one check mark; behavior corrected, the chalk mark would be erased. I attempted to give all assignments, assured of complete group attention and with understandable illustrations. Childlike behavior was generally accepted with few deviations. There were people in class whose deviant behavior meant stronger measures, however. Johnny's loud talking and short attention span were examples of inadequate behavior. His challenge to me made me a better teacher.

Curriculum

As a teacher in the elementary department of Upsala, Minnesota Consolidated School, I was very much involved in a well structured curriculum. In reading the emphasis was on phonics and vocabulary development involving both silent and oral activities. Math was taught with much emphasis on the basics with so-called thought problems employed in order to make the basics seem practical and efficient. History classes employed the effective use of biographies and trends enabling students to gain insight into current developments. P.E. stressed the use of exercises which strengthened the whole body. Basic tactics as to the fundamentals in traditional sports were stressed as well as the significance of fair play. Music, handwriting skills and spelling taught appreciation and respect for correct and essential word usage. Elementary scientific facts and understandings were included. For the week ahead I would have my lesson plan workbook laid out on my desk so the superintendent could note that I had identified the sections of the state curriculum guide that I would be following, the content including the page identifications in the texts I would be using and objectives that served as lesson guides.

Punishment

In a variety or classroom settings the threat of punishment seemingly promotes more effective discipline. This philosophy has serious shortcomings, as I have observed as a teacher and as a school psychologist. Let me identify several examples of punishment which I feel had a negative effect on students involved.

1) Have a student go to the chalkboard and draw a circle by placing his/her nose on the board. "Keep your nose in the circle you created until further notice."

2) A student was heard using violent and in every way undesirable language according to the school's moral code. At the end of the recess period in which the language was heard, the guilty person who used the language was asked to step to the front of the classroom. There her mouth was washed out with soap and water.

3) Students whose behavior was not acceptable were asked to step out into the hallway and stay there until further notice.

4) A student's legs were tied to the legs of her desk so as to discourage her from shuffling her feet.

5) Spell downs tend to punish poor spellers while they offer little by way of effective drill for brighter students. This type of learning experience has inherent negative influences on classroom learning.

Only for Men
During the brief tenure I experienced at the Upsala School, I especially enjoyed the early fall and late spring social events scheduled for our athletic district in Central Minnesota. This district was organized in such a manner that the two social events provided opportunities for athletic coaches to discuss and arrange for schedules in various sports for upcoming seasons. All men in the area identified as "the district" were invited to attend. Fellowship and good conversation were always in evidence at these events. I especially enjoyed meeting people who were friends of mine at college but now were teaching full time. Discussions would vary from salaries to most effective teaching techniques. One fact that was subtly called to my attention was that I was the only elementary teacher in the group. Possibly that's one reason I decided to return to college following two years of teaching experience in grades five, five and six. I wanted my academic goals range substantially enlarged.

Field Trips: SCSU
While I was a faculty member of the Psychology Department at St. Cloud State, I helped introduce a course in Applied Psychology. In order to acquaint the students more effectively with Psych. Applied in the real world, we'd invite speakers to share with us. We would also go on field trips, especially to Minneapolis and St. Paul. On

one occasion we visited the plant where products such as scotch tape were developed. There was one area within the factory we visited where only desks and chairs were on display. We were informed that this was a "think tank" where many new ideas developed. Another tour brought us to the Ford assembly line and a glass manufacturing plant where new cars were prepared for a relatively large area in the Midwest. The routine assignments involved in jobs on the assembly line did not seem to appeal to our students. We were warmly welcomed at each place where we had been scheduled to appear. This was definitely the case at the Minneapolis Honeywell plant where at the time of our visit, thermostats were being produced in large quantities. A visit with a somewhat different kind of motivation was a stop at a large grocery warehouse. At this location it was interesting to see how food projects were prepared for wide distribution. At each place of our visitation it was necessary to note how the students reacted to the busy world of which they were a part—a world in which they would be motivated and where they must make adjustments.

Forest City, Iowa

Early in the 20th century, Forest City had two hotels, each designed and furnished with fine accommodations. Carriage services to and from the train depot were available for potential guests. When visitors arrived to visit relatives and friends, family homes would generally open to those guests. Others who arrived were salesmen, government officials, shoppers from smaller communities and land speculators. Competition along with factors relative to the economy resulted in the closure of the hotels.

One of the main structures was purchased by the Norwegian Lutheran Church to serve as the main building of the Christian College, eventually identified as Waldorf. Into the middle and latter parts of the 20th century, Waldorf prospered with students enrolling, especially from Minnesota and Iowa. A Mr. Hanson who earlier was a Forest City merchant, developed a professional interest in recreational vehicles. From a modest beginning he organized a company that has become internationally known—the Winnebago line. As his company grew, prosperity assumed new levels within the community with several employees gaining levels of considerable wealth. Yet there is a quiet modesty about Forest City. When the harbingers of autumn spread color and sound over the area, the rural influence had a calming effect on the souls who are willing to share.

Waldorf College: Site and Location

Waldorf College, at the time of my assignments there, was a two-year institution supported by the Norwegian Lutheran Church. Today, it is in restructuring, functioning as a four-year liberal arts college. In 1939 when I was appointed to serve as professor at the institution, on the map of Forest City, Iowa, the school was physically located between the county courthouse and the jail. When I roomed in one of the multipurpose buildings on campus, I could look into the jail from one of my windows. Elvina, Virginia's mother, and later my mother-in-law, was county recorder in an office that faced our main building. Occasionally she could see me walking over to one of my classes. Another contact with the county office arrangement was that once a year I had a conference with the superintendent of country schools in Winnebago

County regarding the placement of student teachers in rural schools for sessions of practice teaching which I helped supervise. Of impressions and incidents in the courthouse, Elvina had county maps which I would study to see who owned certain properties. It was amazing back in the very early 1940s to see how much land was owned by insurance companies. As seasons changed the landscape of Winnebago County it was interesting to observe changing colors and seasonal harvests. The rural, moderately urban nature of this part of northern Iowa provided interesting studies for my sociology class.

Waldorf College: Summer of 1939

During the summer of 1939, at about the time I received my master's degree from the University of Minnesota, I was accepted as a member of the faculty at Waldorf College in Forest City, Iowa. My appointment identified me as the Director of Teacher Training and my salary for a nine month's period would be $1600. My teaching assignments were in the areas of methodology and school administration. In addition I visited selected public schools where we had placed students in practice teaching assignments. I did some supervising work within these schools as did the full-time teachers. The teachers and I evaluated the quality of work that students displayed. With one part-time secretary, I was also responsible for our teacher placement bureau. To a degree my responsibilities included coaching our debate team and setting up a schedule for their appearances. We also had a brief radio program broadcast through KGLO, Mason City, Iowa. If we were to have anything done in the field of dramatics, that was also my responsibility. On special occasions I would speak at our chapel services, appear as speaker at high school assembly programs, give commencement addresses at high school graduations and on the basis of congregational requests, give Sunday sermons. During the summers of 1940 and 1941 I worked in central Iowa in a program that was designed to recruit students for Waldorf. My schedule was filled to overflowing all school year. In addition, I introduced a course in sociology one year, so I also became the sociology department at Waldorf. My tenure at Waldorf was interrupted during World War II. While in uniform, Virginia and I were married at Immanuel Lutheran, the campus church for Waldorf students and faculty. During the course of the ceremony the choir sang for us, a contribution we much appreciated. Following my discharge from the service in 1946 I requested that my old job at Waldorf be returned to me as I had anticipated. Instead, a job of recruiting students for Waldorf was made available to me. I did not accept the offer but returned as a student at the University of Minnesota, intent upon working for my doctorate.

The Interview at San Diego State

Following my graduation from the University of Denver with my doctorate I returned to St. Cloud State to resume my teaching duties in the Psychology Department. After a warm "welcome back" reception on the campus I continued with my academic assignments. During the course of the 1951–52 school year, Dr. Headly, our highly esteemed president, resigned following his acceptance of new duties as president of South Dakota State at Brookings. This change was not in the interest of our faculty and certainly not when Dr. Budd became our new president. In academic circles among colleges and university faculties in Minnesota the opinion expressed in evaluating Dr. Budd was to the effect that St. Cloud State was being dealt with as though it were a kindergarten. Consequently my thoughts as to my future were to the effect that I might be happier in a new situation on another campus. As a result I brought my status up to date in the Office of Placement, University of Minnesota. One of the better possibilities for a change came from a contact I had made with San Diego State. In March of 1954 I met Dr. Schrupp of San Diego State University on the University of Minnesota for an interview. While I was visiting with Dr. Schrupp, Virginia and her mother were shopping in downtown Minneapolis. We had agreed to meet for lunch, at which time I told them about my interview with Dr. Schrupp. My optimism regarding the prospects for a move to San Diego seemed to be very encouraging. In September 1954 I began teaching in the Department of Education at San Diego State.

SDSU Fall Term

During my thirty years at State, my professional involvements were on campus, out in the community, and out of state. My teaching load at State totaled 12 hours but added to that schedule were conferences with students, committee meetings, departmental and campus meetings for the entire faculty with some time (limited) for writing and research. There was some flexibility regarding courses to be taught due to the fact that generally one was assigned to classes of choice. Early during the fall semester when I was being oriented regarding these possibilities and obligations, Virginia and I had the additional responsibilities such as finding a house that we could purchase within the reach of our financial resources, register our Pontiac with the State of California and obtain our driver's licenses. We searched for a Lutheran Church that would satisfy our religious needs and information regarding shopping and medical and dental services. There were kindly faculty who assisted us as well as realtors and merchants who wanted our business. We also wished to keep relatives and friends in Minnesota and Iowa informed regarding our involvements. By the time the holidays of December had arrived we had purchased a house and attended to all the privileges and obligations involved in house ownership. We were beginning to feel more and more like Californians.

Teaching Assignments

Much of the work involved in my instructional schedule related to teacher training. One course which generally occupied part of my assignment was entitled Child Growth and Development. The various aspects concerning child development included physical growth with some emphasis on nutrition and exercise. Social and emotional phases of children's adjustment patterns were emphasized. Parental and academic influences were considered as well. Lectures, films and student reports occupied much of the time allocated to classroom activities. Educational Psychology was another course included in my schedule. Learning theory, social and emotional influences in classroom settings, home and community effectiveness were evaluated in addition to the use of scientific testing with respect to goals and levels of learning. A graduate course in thesis development was traditionally part of my schedule. Effectiveness in regard to library usage, statistical assessments, form and style in thesis writing, with stress placed on adequate structuring employed in basic sentence and paragraph construction. Those enrolled in Child Growth and Development were student teachers earning their credentials. The graduate classes in thesis development were comprised of teachers who were full time employees of various districts in our area. I did enjoy the course work to which I was assigned while sensing social and emotional growth as I did my teaching.

Supervision of Student Teachers

One of my traditional assignments involved the supervision of student teachers; the number would vary from term to term. During a given semester I might have eight students but the number could be as high as ten or more. I would organize my group into a functional committee, the chairman was responsible for reporting to me each Friday, identifying which school each student was assigned to and which class he/she would choose to have me visit and the time and place of the class session. (I preferred to have each student identify the experiences for each week that revealed his/her area of greatest competency.) On Monday morning I would make out my schedule for the week identifying the schools, in San Diego City or elsewhere in the county that I would visit and the times of my visit with each student. Earlier in the semester I would have contacted each school where I would be observing, acquaint myself with the principal of the school and learn to know each full time teacher who would be working with the student teacher (I met a large number of professional people through student teacher assignments.) Following each classroom visit I would conference with the student on the basis of his/her lesson planning so I could help the new teacher determine his/her level of proficiency on the basis of the following questions: When you asked a question did you call for an answer only after each pupil knew your question? Did you use praise deliberately and with discrimination? Seldom used the expression "OK" and varied your evaluations? Gave all directions clearly? Noted student improvement? Had a cheerful attitude? Answered children's questions professionally?

Other Professional Involvements

In addition to my regular class schedule I was involved in other professional opportunities on and off campus. I spoke to PTA groups on numerous occasions, employing the topic "Growing Up With Your Children." I conducted extension classes for SDSU and UCSD in late afternoons and Saturday morning sessions with special emphasis on the psychology of learning. For a period of several years I was a part-time school psychologist for Chula Vista School District and for a period of ten years I would travel to the Imperial Valley once a week on a similar assignment. I would hold seminars for Sunday School teachers and other church workers, emphasizing the nature of effective learning as I worked with these groups. During the course of ten summers I had assignments teaching in the fields of Education and Psychology at Western State, Gunnison, Colorado, Wisconsin State at Superior and California State at Los Angeles. I very much appreciated all of the professional contacts I made in San Diego County, elsewhere in California, in the Rocky Mountain area and the Midwest. Changes in locations as well as scenic attractions brought a variety of pleasant contacts and opinions into my evaluations as to what people in different settings and locations were thinking and doing. I enjoyed the stimulation I received in all the professional opportunities which I was privileged to share.

PTA

As a professor in the College of Education at San Diego State, I was invited to share some of my professional thoughts with parents and teachers at PTA meetings. A subject which I had selected for my entry into our speaker's bureau roster was, "Growing Up With Your Children," which proved to be most popular of the topics I offered. The emphasis on the process of growing had to do with the increasing skills which parents and teachers must develop relative to interests that children have and how adults must learn about these interests. Have you ever tried to play soccer or learn at least by reading what desires children do have? As an adult you must learn to be an effective counselor, mentor and leader. All of the skills involved in these categories must be learned if you are to keep abreast or ahead of the children and adolescents as they continue growing and developing. How to reward accomplishments in an effective manner so that success truly motivates the learning process is especially significant. Above all, parents and teachers must develop high level listening skills which involve effectively teaching children how to evaluate when questions are asked so they will "make sense", thus promote the learning process. Are you assessing your growth patterns so efficiently that both you and your children can note successful growth in all mutual activities? Then you have earned an "A".

Psychology Applied

When I worked with teachers in training some of the methodology I would teach was in regard to the use of basic psychological principles applied. When a question was asked in guiding a recitation period, a pupil was called upon only after the teacher believed that everyone had an opportunity to think of an answer—no calling the name of a student, then asking the question. Whenever a member of a class of students offered a response to a question or volunteered to perform a duty the teacher would respond in a positive manner as to whatever was offered. In evaluating the students' contributions, the expression "OK" was sparingly used. Evaluations worded in the following manner were far more acceptable: "that's great, a real improvement, now you're trying, keep up the good work"—a list of good responses was made available. Spelling bees were not recommended which gave more training to spelling to those who needed it least; Valentine's Day was not observed as a popularity contest with favorite students receiving most of the cards. Disciplining was generally a relatively silent matter: name on the chalk board for misbehavior, check marker following name if behavior is not corrected, both check mark and name erased when behavior was corrected. When these psychological principles are applied the teacher then, as a professional person, experiences a higher level of friendliness and determination that assures effective learning.

VIII
SEASONS AND WEATHER

SEASONS AND WEATHER
Table of Contents

WEATHER AND SEASONS

Drought

Beginning in the early 1930s the weather patterns in Central Minnesota began to change from an anticipated amount of rainfall to an amount substantially less. Through the middle thirties, this change was particularly devastating. We could feel the intensity of the hot, dry winds coming from the southwest, tainted with a bit of red coloration, dust flown from as far south as Oklahoma and Texas. Field and hay crops began to wither under the intensity of the noonday sun. In St. Cloud, where the soil is quite sandy, the auditorium at St. Cloud State was coated with dust. Our water supply for the farm, from a dug well, began to dry up, making it necessary for us to dig the well deeper. Some farmers herded their dairy cattle to areas farther north in our county where areas for grazing were not so badly damaged as those farther south. Some of our beautiful trees, like red oak, succumbed to the intensity of the heat, being exposed to inadequate supplies of water. Swarms of grasshoppers descended on our area. Their voracious appetites caused them to attack anything fibrous, including wooden fence posts and kitchen curtains. The lakes in Minnesota became smaller and smaller with only limited fishing. We still enjoyed swimming in places like Cedar Lake where the water was quite warm. As the 30s moved on there were signs of recovery, especially as the anticipated rains returned. The 2 DDs still conjure up unpleasant memories in my thinking-drought and depression—a heavy combination.

January and February

In central Minnesota, these generally are two of the harshest months of the year. When we lived in St. Cloud the white sales in the department stores didn't make the months seem any more inviting. Snow in the streets between heavy storms would turn from gray to black from soot deposited from coal burning furnaces. On the farm the livestock would have daily feedings of corn and forkfuls of hay. My job after arriving home from school was to fill the stock tank with water and carry in pailsful of water for household usage. Early in the next day I would build a fire in a stove placed near the stock tank to make the water drinkable. Particularly on Saturdays my brother and I would clean our barn (our dad did the job while we were in school) but on Saturdays we would haul manure out to what would be the corn field the next growing season. We would heap the fertilizer in piles for spreading in April. Another weekend job would involve cutting down trees to be used as firewood. Sometimes with cross-cut saw and in our shirt sleeves, my brother Laurel and I would cut logs into convenient pieces. During these cold months some of the earlier holiday cheer would tend to wear off but if all members of our family were well and healthy, we did adjust quite effectively to the storms of winter.

March and April

March was a wild month with intermittent blizzards and occasionally, days of bright sunshine when some of the wintry deposits of snow would melt. During these days between winter and the glory of spring a crop of newborns would appear: calves, chickens, and pigs. If our little pig crop was fairly large then the late summer orders to Sears Roebuck and Montgomery Ward would be larger. In late March and early April our seed grains, barley, wheat and oats were mechanically fanned to remove weed, seeds, and debris before planting in April. The corn field for the new year would be covered with the fertilizer we had spread during the winter and covered over as our plow pulled by two horses would cut neat furrows into the soil. Choruses of music would brighten the early spring with the arrival of flocks of new birds. Trees, shrubs and grasses would send out new shoots and leaves. In our garden a crop of horseradish became available. I wondered if horses liked this kind of vegetable so I offered generous portions to each of our two horses. They enjoyed a sampling of what I called a fiery root, hence the name.

May and June

These are two of the loveliest months of the year in central Minnesota. By early in May the garden would be planted. In June we could harvest peas and potatoes. The carrots, yellow beans, tomatoes, corn, melons, squash, etc., would be available during the weeks to follow. Strawberries and rhubarb ripened in late May and subsequently during much of the summer. Field corn had been sown in a well fertilized, checkered field where at each corner of the squares seed corn would be planted by hand operated equipment. The square arrangement would enable us to cultivate the corn north-south and east-west.

During June especially, and into July certain grasses, domesticated and otherwise, would be harvested for hay. The birds would be busy caring for their young as would the chickens who were responsible for broods of chicks. By June 21st almost all native fish could be legally caught in the lakes in our area. We had nearly several dozen lakes in a four county area where we could fish. The catching was fun, the eating delicious. Memories of late spring and early summer in Minnesota are especially precious.

July and August

These were the warmest months during each calendar year. July and August were the months when ripening and harvesting were at or near peak activities. Our garden produced an abundance of root and bush crops while in other parts of the farm hay crops and grain crops were available for cutting and harvesting. The hay was cut by a mowing machine pulled by a team of horses. The grass would become hay as it ripened under the summer sun. When dried this crop would be raked by another machine driven by horsepower "on the hoof." The crop would then be piled into small haystacks, later to be transported to a site where hay was stacked into piles that looked like loaves of bread or be hauled into the haymow of the barn for more convenient feeding of livestock. The grain was cut by a machine that tied the stocks into bundles. These bundles would be shocked, then later piled into stacks that looked like ice cream cones turned upside down with the large ice cream cup at the bottom of the heap. There was little time for fishing. Care of the livestock, especially milking the cows, was a two times a day job. Occasionally we could take time for a swim at Cedar Lake; our community beach was located there. Good crops, good times = a good old summertime.

September and October

These months seemed to have a calming effect on nature as we observed and understood the moods of the changing seasons. Many of the crops had been harvested, put into stacks, the haymow or granary. Before going off to college in early September I would have done much of our fall plowing. The job entailed walking behind the metal plow that cut into the moist soil as our two horses provided the power for movement. To me a well plowed field was a work of art. In early September or October we harvested the remaining root crops—potatoes, carrots, rutabagas and beets. The potatoes and carrots were stored in the cellar beneath our house. Flocks of birds would fly overhead in the direction of warmer climates farther south. Storm windows were put into place, the foundation of the house was banked and our car was winterized for colder weather. A thin sheet of ice would cover the tank where the horses and cattle obtained their water. The farm implements which had been faithful in their performances were put into sheds for the long, cold months ahead. Effectiveness of work done during the past few months would assure a comfortable winter. With our wood piles shaped for efficient availability and with enough kerosene on hand, our fuel supply was assured.

November and December

One of the most festive seasons of the year with Thanksgiving and Christmas dates occupying conspicuous places on the calendar. By early November all crops had been harvested and were safely in storage. Chores were still on our schedule: cleaning the barn and feeding the livestock, feeding the pigs and chickens were daily chores. I filled the stock tank each day after school while my brother Laurel carried in the wood. At least one snow storm could be anticipated. On Thanksgiving Day we attended services at our Lutheran Church, followed by a big Thanksgiving dinner. When the dinner had been served an auction followed at which time "fancy" items the women at the church had made were sold to provide funds for various church activities. Christmas was ushered in as school closed for a two weeks vacation. Trees decorated, gifts bought and distributed were all parts of the Christmas picture. A highlight of the seasonal festivities was the Sunday School Christmas program at our church. Children would repeat selections they had memorized, which were occasionally offered with dramatic effect. As we drove home from the program at church, we knew that soon all roads would be closed to vehicular traffic with sleds and horses taking over basic transportation. The heavy snow drifts make this change happen. Concluding the old year with festive activities in November and December always seemed so highly appropriate.

Snow

I am very well acquainted with snow. From my earliest days on our farm in Central Minnesota, I learned that it was white and cold and also that it was seasonal. Some years the first snowfall came during the early weeks of autumn but the amount that arrived in late September or early October would melt away quickly. As the days and nights of November became progressively colder we could be assured of heavier and more durable amounts of snow. An autumnal snowfall was usually very quiet and gentle blanketing the landscape with a new, white cover. This reminder of the approach of winter comforted us with memories of summer just past and the potential of winter fun soon to occur. Some of the realities of winter beyond the fun anticipated were weather reports indicating that a huge snow storm, a blizzard, was sweeping across Montana and soon would enter the Dakotas. Next in its path, Minnesota, and beyond to the east. A severe blizzard would stall traffic of all kinds, close schools and make walking very difficult. On November 11, 1940, a crippling blizzard blanketed the Upper Midwest. When the storm subsided and the sun broke through we beheld a winter wonderland, glistening and sparkling in the brilliant sunshine. Now was the time for heavy overcoats and overshoes, heavy mittens for all those who were involved in the great out-of-doors for fun and for work.

Blizzard: November 1940

Early in the morning of November 11th, 1940, I was on my way from Waldorf College in Forest City to the high school in Northwood, IA. I was scheduled to give an address at a meeting of the high school in recognition of Armistice Day. The audience was cooperative, the speech went well in recognition of the ending of WWI. As I began driving back to Forest City I couldn't help but enjoy the mild fall weather we were having in northern Iowa. There was a heavy cloud cover, a light drizzle was falling. As I neared Forest City the light drizzle became a snowstorm with large, heavy snow flakes falling faster and faster. Within about a mile of Forest City I became aware of the fact that a monumental blizzard had descended upon the area. The wind was driving clouds of snow flakes at a dizzying pace. Large snow drifts were beginning to form. When I reached a point two blocks from the Waldorf campus I became stuck in a huge snow drift, I walked a block to the nearest service station, caught my breath and stumbled another block to the campus. Because it was unanticipated, many turkey farmers lost numerous birds just before Thanksgiving. Some duck hunters lost their lives. When I review this experience, I thank God that I didn't lose mine.

Road Repairs

It was early in June, school was out and it was time to repair some of the damage the early spring thaws had done to the dirt roads in our area. The township office had allotted certain funds designated for road repair, money to be used to smoothen the ruts that so obviously developed each spring. Our neighbor, Carl Thies, hired me to drive a team of his horses and wagon involved in hauling gravel from a pit nearby to the places where the road repair work was being done. I'd drive the horses into the pit so we could position the wagon for loading the gravel. From the pit I would drive down a country lane to the road where the work was being done. Each time I would meet a driver returning his empty wagon to the gravel pit, we would engage in a brief conversation. The visiting we did as we hauled the gravel or loaded or unloaded it was always interesting. The bond which existed between neighbors was always a factor in stimulating good relationships. That's why I relished this road work as a means of promoting basic friendships and making summer driving more comfortable, plus earning a few dollars for the work accomplished.

Winter 1936

During the winter of 1936, for a period of one month, the temperature never climbed above the zero level. It was during this time that Marvin Bacon and I rented a room near the Upsala School where we were both members of the faculty. One night the local feed mill caught fire with not much help for stopping the conflagration. A plane that flew over the area to warn people of the current danger helped break the silence of a threatening winter's night. In the mornings the water in our wash stand was frozen, and as we tried to wash ourselves in ice water, we heard melodious tones of *"Nobody's Darling But Mine"* being played over WDAY, Fargo, North Dakota. When we finally were dressed we walked to the Johnson restaurant for our breakfast. Not often as we walked along did we escape a bit of ice forming on our ears and the tips of our noses. Fortunately neither of us caught severe colds or suffered permanent damage to our extremities. The winter of 1936 was, however, a real challenge for both Marvin and me.

Storms

I have lived through a considerable number of storms from near life threatening to somewhat milder threats. In my earlier years on the farm, we would have severe rainstorms with lightning, wind and pouring gusts of water. On occasions my Dad would escort the family into our cellar if the wind continued to produce evermore intensive squeaking sounds in the timbers of our house. Reports following particularly heavy storms would give accounts of the damage done to some farm buildings which would be substantial, with pouring rain causing severe erosion on some hillsides. During a trip in Arizona

215

we saw a heavy rain cloud threatening us as we traveled near Gila Bend. With a sudden burst the cloud released millions of gallons of water on the heated pavement. With rain pelting down and the steam rising from the highway, driving became especially hazardous. In northeastern Wyoming we had a similar experience one summer that compelled us to stop beside the road as visibility became zero. While traveling through the deserts of Imperial County, California, I encountered dust storms which did serious damage to my car. The flying debris made up of sand and small sharp pebbles posed a serious danger to any motorist who was unfortunate enough to be caught in the crossfire. On at least one occasion, Virginia, Anita and I found ourselves exposed to the fury of Lake Superior while traveling from Isle Royal to Minnesota. The craft in which we were riding proved to be safe but the pounding of the huge choppy waves gave us moments of discomfort. Another type of storm which by way of its intensity posed very real threats to those of us who lived through winters in the Midwest were the blizzards with blinding snow and bitter cold. These storms were always life threatening.

Sailing on the Ice

While I was a student on special assignment at the University of Wisconsin during one of my special orders of WWII, I was invited to go sailing on a lake that bordered the campus. The ice was smooth and reasonably thick, so activities on the lake were fast and numerous. A buddy of mine had access to a sled that was made of board large enough to hold two people. It was shaped in the form of a triangle with one skate out front and one at each side of the wide part of the triangle, making up the rear with a sail in about the middle of the boat. When we ventured out on the lake the wind was brisk, assuring us of a pleasant ride. With the sail let out completely we skimmed along on the surface of the lake at a remarkable rate of speed. My friend managed to keep the boat on an even keel with no chance of our toppling over. When we came back to shore, which in reality was the location of the student union, he maintained that ice boats could go 80 miles per hour—could I doubt him following the completion of our ride of 80 miles per hour?

Hail Storms

This kind of storm can become quite savage. On the day when rain storms are forecast, this kind of weather pattern can occur. One of the worst of its kind descended upon Virginia and me as we lived in our newly purchased home in St. Cloud in the summer of 1954. We had recently returned from a trip to the downtown area and left our '51 Pontiac out on the street. As rain showers began to pelt roofs and cars in our area, we thought nothing serious was happening until we heard some hard objects being dashed against our house and all of the outdoors. Before we were aware as to what was really occurring, a massive hail storm had descended upon our neighborhood. The sky was black, the rain was coming down in torrents along with hailstones the size of baseballs. It was too late for me to dash out to drive the car into the garage. The sounds of the storm were loud and threatening with damage occurring every second. Eventually the storm tapered off into the bright sunshine so we ventured out to assess the damage. There were little depressions on the body of the car where the hail had lashed the vehicle and pieces of wood had been ripped away from the siding of our house. It proved to be a million dollar plus storm, but strangely it had been limited to neighborhoods south of Main Street. North St. Cloud had escaped the damage completely.

Colorado Weather

During the summer of 1949 while I lived in Denver as a student I was fascinated by two experiences I had in dealing with the weather. Each afternoon while I was studying in the Denver University campus library, an ominous pattern of rain clouds would form in the western sky, threatening a seasonal downpour. The storm would descend upon the city with torrents of rain at about 3:30 PM. At 4:30 PM the sun would be out again, welcoming all of us to a gorgeous evening. I am not sure how persistent this phenomenon in the weather might be but during the summer of 1949 this occurrence was very predictable. Again in this same location I was reading one evening by the light of lightning flashes. What was in evidence was a display referred to as sheet lightning, another interesting phenomenon. In the summer of 1950, Virginia and I were invited to attend a Psychology fraternity picnic in the mountains west of Denver. On this occasion a thunder storm developed with little rain but a reverberating sound pattern developed as the thunder from each cloud would echo and re-echo among the boulders and mountain peaks. The sound was that of a continuous artillery barrage, interesting and exciting.

Sun Bathing

During the summer of 1949 while I was a student at the University of Denver, the American Sunbathing Assn.

held its convention in the mountains west of Denver. The only wearing apparel that the delegates at the convention were allowed to wear was socks for carrying their cigarettes. (Too bad that any of them smoked.) This convention aroused a variety of feelings and expressions on the part of the citizens of Denver. Sunday morning sermons assessed the impact of the convention in negative evaluations. Pilots from a nearby airbase were evidently changing their flight plans as information was circulated as to the location of the convention. From reports emanating from the conventioneers, lotions for treating sunburn were in great demand as some vacationers did not realize that at 8000 feet the rays of the sun would be more intense. Services by dermatologists possibly were much in demand. When the convention ended, I did not recall that the Association had planned to have its next convention near Denver. Perhaps the next gathering of this sort might rather be scheduled in the Midwest.

Northern Lights: Aurora Borealis

The sight of brilliant lights displaying the colors of the rainbow always thrilled me with excitement. On more than one occasion while I was driving home from Upsala at night I would stop at the side of the road on a hilltop so I could enjoy the celestial display. The shooting of brilliant rays of light, the dancing of multiple colors, fascinated me. My imagination would run wild as I reacted to the brilliance before me. It was as though the earth was drawing additional strength from the sun (which had already set) to make such a marvelous display possible. While we were on a tour in Alaska in 1969, Virginia, Anita and I observed a brilliant display from our motel window near the base of Mt. McKinley. The colors, the streaking, the dancing of the brilliant lights were all part of the performance we enjoyed that night. Sometimes the Northern Lights would be in the nature of a harbinger predicting a change in the weather. There were times when the lights appear so close to us that some of the brilliant action descended into our front yard. In our current location the appearance of the Aurora Borealis is almost never a possibility. I must reflect back in my memories as to how many times I was inspired and entertained by the Northern Lights. Their color and dancing have created indelible impressions that will last forever.

Snow Storm: SDSU

During my years as a faculty member at San Diego State University, we seldom had what might be called a phenomenon, a snow storm. One day, however, when the clouds were dark and the wind was on the chilly side, some people on campus thought we might get some snow, locally. As morning hours unfolded with a threatening weather pattern, my child psychology class gathered for its regularly scheduled class session. Shortly after class discussions got underway what had been dark and gloomy turned into something lighter and brighter. It had begun to snow. All members of the class, including myself, focused on the falling white substance—genuine snow. I suggested that we all go over to the windows of the classroom and look at the falling brightness. Some people said it was unbelievable that snow would fall on our campus considering the mildness of our winters. Yet on this occasion as we all beheld the snowstorm, we said weather history was in the making.

Balboa Park—Evenings

Occasionally in the 1960s I would teach an evening class in the vicinity of Balboa Park which was part of the SDSU extension schedule. I would leave home about ½ to 2 hours earlier so I would have time to explore the park before my class began. As the evening shadows lengthened with the chiming of the bells in the California tower it would seem as though it was being welcomed in a modern day paradise. The fragrances emitted by numerous blossoms, the fresh scent of the eucalyptus trees, the floral displays and the silence of small groves of tropical and semitropical trees were mystical. As I strolled through corridors and passageways a hint of old Spain and more recently, the centennials seemed to spell out the history of architecture and construction. The feeling that the park was mine, even for a moment, was nothing short of thrilling. The winding pathways in the international village conjured up memories of pleasant Sunday afternoons when Virginia and I would visit the area. The offbeat tours into the canyons, adjacent to, yet detached from the main concourse stimulated thoughts of exploration and discovery as I traveled through relatively unknown areas. I discovered another even more fascinating park—Balboa in the shadows and the sounds of early evening.

IX
VEHICLES

VEHICLES
Table of Contents

VEHICLES

Wagons

In preschool years, my brother Laurel and I each had a small wagon, made with steel boxes and wheels. We would coast down a small hill in our farm yard but what was more exciting happened when our mother would pull each wagon enthusiastically through the yard. Our neighbors whose farm bordered ours to the east, initiated another interesting idea relative to wagons for children. When they relinquished their buggy at the time they bought their first car, they had their old conveyance made into a wagon for their three children. The Thompsons had taken their buggy to a special shop where the wheels and the body of the vehicle were made childsize. What these children had was the envy of the neighborhood. On a day when my Dad had driven to town with our horses pulling our lumber wagon with at least two of us children as passengers, he suggested we go into a certain store where he wanted "to show us something." It was a play wagon made mostly of wood painted in blues and yellows. The excitement and fun upon learning that it was ours never quite abated. We made a circular track for the wagons near our garden where even the family dog enjoyed the trips around the enclosure. We coasted downhill, took turns pushing pulling our wagon. This proved to be one of the most interesting toys we ever owned.

Toys

Since my interests were guided by the rural environment in which I lived as a child, I desired to construct a sitting farm. (Sitting because that described the postural form I needed for operating the farm.) I built roads, my Dad built a structure that was an all purpose farm building, and I received a toy Fordson tractor which might power selected pieces of equipment. But my main interest centered on my plan for constructing a grain threshing outfit. I made it mostly of wood with a few metal pieces to lend strength to the equipment. The steam engine looked like the real thing even though it never operated on steam. The threshing machine was quite like the real thing, even to including details like a windstacker. While I sat and ran my farm, the threshing equipment and the Fordson tractor were at my bidding. In my imagination it was all great fun. Over the years I also received an engine and tender, a pull-type freight train and a couple windup toys. It wasn't until adulthood that some of my fondest desires were realized: electrically operated steam freight and passenger trains. My railroad hobby has brought a sense of accomplishment into my life as current "toy" action is very close to my heart.

Brother's Bicycle

During my days on the farm, and even into my days at college, I never had the privilege of owning a bicycle. My brother, Laurel bought one while our family was still functioning as a unit in doing work on the farm. Since he was liberal in letting me use his new, shiny, red and white bike, I did learn to ride and thoroughly enjoy it. We had a hill on the road south of our house which was not paved and not very smooth, but I would ride it to the full length of our farm with speeds that were beyond the limits of safety. I did acquire a few bumps and scratches but bike riding was worth all of them. On one occasion when my sister, Evodia, was riding on the handle bar brace, we hit a soft, sandy spot which caused half of the front wheel to go east with the other half facing north. With the wheel repaired the momentary unhappiness was almost forgotten. Any bike riding skills I ever learned to enjoy must be credited to my brother.

Winter Bus

When the severe winter storms of November and December blocked our narrow country roads with drifts of snow several feet high, we, along with our neighbors, would store our cars for a period of several months. During these wintry months, the Upsala Consolidated School would store its fleet of motor buses and activate the horse-drawn sled buses. These buses were made with canvas tops set atop sets of sleighs. The so-called horse buses were each pulled by a team of horses and looked almost like the prairie schooners of Oregon trail days. The horse buses put into service in the earlier days were heated by kerosene stoves; these were replaced by coal burning heaters. When we were still in the "kerosene stove" era I remember how our sandwiches were iced and tasted like the fuel that barely kept us warm. Since the bus trips were several miles in length, some students would spend considerably over an hour a day riding to and from school. These trips were not dull, especially when my cousin Milo was our driver. Singing, laughing, socializing were all part of each trip. Those days of hilarity will not be forgotten.

Cars

Our first family car was a 1925 Model T Ford. Until then we had been members of the horse and buggy set. Early on my Dad thought it would be a good idea to teach my brother Laurel and me how to drive. My sister Evodia would learn some years later. My mother never did learn how to drive. Initial lessons in driving concentrated on smooth backing and parking. With the three pedals, reverse, drive and brake, much basic foot action was critical. At age eleven my Dad's confidence in my driving had reached a reasonably high level so he let me try driving alone with my sister as passenger. The car was of the touring variety and with the top down on a warm summer day, the drive was fun. It was one of my best trips. (For our first driver's licenses in Minnesota we invested 25 cents for each license issued from headquarters in St. Paul.)

Model A Ford

On Saturday, the day before Easter Sunday, 1930, we purchased our new Model A Ford. It was blue, had two doors, two seats in front and a seat that would accommodate three persons in back. The person with whom we dealt was Carl Erickson who about five years earlier had sold our family the Model T Ford. We claimed the new car (which had been on display) in Albany, about 13 miles south of our farm. My brother Laurel drove the car home, enjoying the convenience of the stick shift and self starter equipment. In the Model T with no battery, we had to crank the car to get it into action. The "T" had three pedals, no stick shift. Its headlights varied in intensity according to the speed at which we drove. With our new car we were brought into an era of driving comfort and convenience. When we returned to the farm our old Model T was delivered by me to the Carl Erickson dealership in Upsala. I was the last one to drive the "T" so the trip to town was in the nature of a sentimental journey. The "T" had served us well as did the "A", which was the last car that my Dad ever purchased.

More Cars

The first car I owned was a Chevrolet coupe, green in color and old in regard to performance. I purchased it from a dealer who came out to the farm to show me a "good deal"; his definition of a "good deal" was not quite the same as mine. I drove it to Forest City, Iowa in the spring of 1940. It was the car that I used while soliciting students for Waldorf in the summer of that year. I traded the "Hornet" for a '39 Plymouth coach which didn't like cold weather. Also the gas tank was rusted. Until the tank was replaced, the gas controls were the source of trouble, intermittently. I sold this car to my sister, Evodia, who used it for her rounds in northern Minnesota as a public health nurse. In 1942–46 in military service, no car ownership. My first car as a civilian is described in an article entitled "A Trying Weekend." This Chevrolet was replaced by a 60 horsepower Ford which we named "Poke-Along-and-Haunt-Us"—we could not think of a better name. A '49 Chevrolet, two door, replacing "Poke-along and-Haunt-Us", was traded for a '51 black Pontiac sedan, purchased in St. Cloud upon our return from Denver. This excellent car was traded for a '59 Chevrolet sedan which we drove to Superior, Wisconsin, and earlier to Gunnison, Colorado for summer assignments and during all local California travel. This great car was replaced by a '66 Pontiac station wagon which I owned for 33 years. When

Anita became a student it was essential for our family to own two cars due to the driving Virginia did for Anita and my requirements for professional assignments. During the years circa '63–'80, we owned two Ford Falcons and one Ford Maverick as second cars. Currently I lease Anita's Baretta while she drives her new Chevrolet. During the years '40–'99, my years of car ownership, I ran the gamut of love-hate-love concerning car ownership.

Painful Plymouth

The second car in my inventory of vehicles that I have owned and driven was a used 1939 Plymouth sedan. It was one of the Plymouth models that had limited trunk space inasmuch as its back sloped directly down to the rear bumpers. I traded my old Chev, the Green Hornet, in a deal for this more modern vehicle. Early in the fall season, when the leaves began to turn color and frost settled over the landscape, it was then that I learned that my vehicle was allergic to cold weather. When the temperature dipped down below freezing the car wished for a home in the tropics. It refused to start in the chill of Iowa. Following a night in a heated garage, the car would start but if left out of doors in cold weather, I was compelled to park it on the crest of a hill for an eventual push down hill that was vigorous enough to get the car going. It would run smoothly for a while then choke to a stop. This embarrassing action was both dangerous and frustrating. An alert mechanic discovered that the gas tank was rusting and that small pieces of rust were clogging the carburetor. Another little trick that the car would engage in was to release the ball in a ball-joint connection for shifting. On one occasion I was compelled to crawl under the car and reconnect parts of the transmission involving the ball joint. This happened on one of the busy streets in downtown St. Paul. When I entered the service in 1942 I sold this car to my sister, Evodia. Apparently, according to reports, the car liked the new owner better than me.

A Trying Weekend

In 1946 Virginia and I, while living in St. Cloud, were a car-less couple being deprived of some of the luxuries and freedoms of ownership. In answer to our then current hardship, we purchased a 1934 blue Chevrolet sedan for $900. It seemed to perform satisfactorily on trips in town and on short tours around the community on rural roads. Since confidence in our new found freedom was increasing, we decided to drive to Forest City, Iowa, one weekend to visit Virginia's mother. We chose to make the trip on a beautiful sunny Saturday. The trip began almost effortlessly but while Virginia was driving she crossed a busy mainline railroad track without looking both ways. I asked her why she didn't brake to a stop to see whether or not a train might be approaching, she said, "We don't have any brakes." From then on the tour was a nightmare as we tried to drive with unusual care. When we arrived in Forest City (on a Saturday afternoon) the local garage mechanics said they would and did somehow repair the brakes. The visit to Forest City was by two nervous wrecks; eventually the drive home proved to be equally exhausting. On Monday I brought the car back to the place of purchase and got a refund of $900. The luck and enjoyment we had with the car might be summarized in identifying the good fortune of obtaining the $900 refund.

And More Cars

Between 1946–2000 I drove in what seemed like a moderate parade of cars, some old (used), some new, some good and others not so good. A '49 Chev that Virginia and I drove while we lived in Denver was good for mountain driving and street use. The 1951 Pontiac which we bought on a trade for our '49 Chev was one of the best cars we ever owned. A straight eight motor, a good body and ease of handling made it very dependable; even its body style was appealing. In 1959 we traded the Pontiac in a deal for a new Chevrolet sedan. This car proved to be one of the best cars we ever owned. A V8 with a shining white body built for racing, the vehicle provided us with thoroughly effective transportation to Colorado and Wisconsin where I held several summer professorships. On Christmas of 1999 we sold our '66 Pontiac station wagon, which had given us excellent service in comfort and safety. This 33 year-old car may have been the best of all the cars owned in the passing parade, 1946–2000.

X
TRAVEL

TRAVEL
Table of Contents

TRAVEL

A Trip to South Dakota

Because Albert and I were able to finish the harvesting and stacking of hay and grain crops before the last week in August, Albert decided that a trip to South Dakota was in order. My mother, my sister, Evodia, Albert and I were involved in the tour. Albert drove his top heavy 1927 Model T Ford on the trip. During the winter of 1930–31, Albert had hitched a team of horses to start the car but instead of going ahead on one occasion, the car backed into a tree which left an unsightly bump on the top of the car. Our trip started out comfortably in beautiful late summer weather. We stopped in Alexandria to say "hello" to the Peterson family. While driving through the downtown section of the city, the car began to shake and shimmy—I guess it was nervous since it was more accustomed to rural travel and embarrassed by the bump on its top. We stopped for lunch in a beautiful, shaded park in Brown's Valley, then crossed the Minnesota border into South Dakota. At first we encountered hilly terrain in the Sisseton area and later wide open stretches of fertile prairie land. During our stay in South Dakota we visited three different locations, including Aberdeen. It was my first trip outside my home state of Minnesota.

Northern Minnesota—A Snowy Trip

It was the first heavy snowfall of the season which very well served as a reminder that winter was at hand, even in November, 1937. I was a member of a team designated to visit Lutheran churches in the Iron Range country of Northern Minnesota. Our group left the Gustavus Adolphus campus in St. Peter early Saturday morning, continuing north into the Minneapolis area. The radio in the car was tuned so we could determine how the University of Minnesota football team was fairing. The snowfall was so intense that at times the announcer covering the game could not see the playing field. We continued to drive on northward, eventually arriving in downtown Duluth. As we viewed the city from the comforts of our vehicle we could only see forms of multistoried buildings through the storm. From Duluth we traveled into the Mesabi Iron Range, one of the most productive sources of iron ore in the United States. The drive from Duluth was somewhat barren due to the deforestation wrought by lumber barons of an earlier age. Our delegation received a warm reception, particularly in regard to overnight accommodations. The following day we took part in Lutheran services, departing the community in the early afternoon. On our way back to St. Peter we crossed the Mississippi River in Grand Rapids, eventually reaching Milaca where we stopped for another service. When we arrived in St. Peter, the heavy snow which had fallen for at least two days made the whole Minnesota landscape resemble a winter wonderland. The more intense chill of winter would follow but for now, in a sense, the weather was a soft, snowy inspiration.

Laredo

During my tour of duty in WWII while stationed in San Antonio, Texas, the desire to cross the border into Mexico became apparent at times since we were only an hour's drive from Nuevo Laredo. With weekend passes in hand, four of us decided to spend at least part of that time in Mexico. We lined up along the highway headed south in such a manner that if one of our group got a ride, he would ask the driver to stop as well to pick up his buddies. The man who gave us a ride to Laredo invited us to stay at his house for dinner and to sleep at his place overnight. The following morning he told us he would take each of us to the church of our choice and pick us up later so we could cross the border at Nuevo Laredo. Then he would meet us again for lunch (on him). Following lunch he brought us out to the main highway leading to San Antonio, flagged down cars and made sure that we all got rides. He was not a spy nor was he inclined to take advantage of us in any way. He was manifesting real Texas hospitality.

Manhattan, Kansas

While I was stationed at Camp Funston, part of the Fort Riley complex in Kansas, I found it convenient to relax and refresh myself in Manhattan, a city of some 28,000 people. (Part of my refreshing was gained occasionally by enjoying a steak dinner for $1.50.) Kansas State University is located here, where for sometime, a member of the Eisenhower family was president. Following the earning of a Ph.D at the University of Minnesota, my brother Laurel received an appointment to the faculty at Kansas State. While I was in the service I had library privileges on this campus. A friendly civilian invited Virginia to reside at her house, an offer which was very much appreciated. On Mother's Day I had the privilege of being invited to preach a sermon honoring mothers in a Lutheran Church located near the campus. Following the Allies victory in Germany, General Eisenhower visited this area as the honored guest of the local community. Agriculturally, the growing of excellent crops of wheat was a long standing tradition of this and many other parts of Kansas. The 'home town' friendliness in Manhattan created a lasting impression of good will for all members of the Anderson family who had the privilege of living there.

Visit to Denver

While I was stationed in the Manhattan, Kansas, area, Virginia was living in a private home for a few weeks. During this time I received a pass which enabled us to enjoy a short "vacation" which included a trip by rail to Denver. We traveled through miles of wheat fields in western Kansas and the grain and cattle raising areas of eastern Colorado, finally arriving in downtown Denver. We arranged for hotel accommodations and eventually rented a car for a short trip out to the mountains. As we enjoyed the fresh mountain air and the views of the snow capped peaks to the west, we agreed that someday we would come to Denver to live. The return to Denver happened in the summer of 1949 when I returned to the city to continue graduate work at the University of Denver. I had rented a room for the summer session while Virginia and her mother did some traveling. The course work, the friendly professional atmosphere on campus encouraged me to return to Denver to complete my work toward a doctorate. This goal was reached during my leave of absence from St. Cloud State. In '50–'51 Virginia and I enjoyed apartment living in the campus area. The memories we retain concerning tours, parties and campus events strengthened the warm impressions we gained during our time in Denver.

The Wisconsin Dells

One afternoon while I was stationed in Wisconsin during WWII, I arranged a tour of the Wisconsin Dells. Virginia and her mother were visiting me so it seemed appropriate for us to schedule a tour of the area where this scenic feature is located. We rode a bus to the Dells where we boarded a boat for a trip through this attraction on the banks of the Wisconsin River. The river cruise was enjoyable that warm summer afternoon. The timber growing near the water's edge, the fresh, cool water flowing in the river channel enhanced our enjoyment of the scene through which we were passing. We experienced the sensational part of the tour as we passed through a gorge with huge rock formations on both sides of the fast flowing stream. Our guide who was steering the boat told us that in this area the river was flowing at a depth of 100 feet. The narrow river bed at this point compresses the water, making the stream swift and more exciting. The experience involved in seeing the Dells was both scenic and refreshing, making the tour a grand adventure. We also learned that the nearby community of Baraboo was the locale for the beginning of the Ringling Brothers, Barnum and Bailey Circus.

San Francisco

Some people refer to San Francisco as 'Bagdad by the Bay'. Its history and its wealth, its ethnic diversity and economic aggressiveness may have, over a period of years, earned this identification. I have seen this attractive city from almost all possible angles, from its hills to Golden Gate Park, to the crossing of its bridges and to business involvements in the down town area. The days of the Flower Children in Golden Gate Park with their immature evaluations of the basics in life to the gay influence which promotes dangerous living in questionable life styles have all left their impressions. The pleasantness of Angel Island following debarking in San Francisco Bay following WWII assignments in the South Pacific, a plus in the military over our earlier bleak July departure, then the victorious return to the area has left indelible impressions on my thinking. The somber appearance of Alcatraz as I enjoyed fish dinners in harborside restaurants is another memory. Our visits with Jack and Marilyn always stimulated conversations relative to the greatness and near greatness of the city. A drive across the Golden Gate Bridge says much about the brilliance of planning and architectural skills of the city. May its history guide this great city into greater heights of future achievements.

Winnipeg

October 1946, the time of my first vacation as a civilian, following my tour of duty in WWII, Virginia and I decided at that time to make our vacation trip, a Canadian tour, our destination, Winnipeg. From St. Cloud, Minnesota, to this neighbor in the north, we had excellent rail connections to Winnipeg. It was an all day trip as we traveled through central and northwestern Minnesota into Manitoba, arriving at our destination at night. Visitors' services in Winnipeg obtained an elaborate facility for us the first night. The following nights we stayed in private homes. Our vacation included a round trip to the Lake of the Woods, a scenic location east of Winnipeg. We dined on 90 cent steak dinners except for any day that was meatless. Our shopping, particularly at the Hudson Bay Store, enabled Virginia and me to finally determine which silverware pattern we liked best—it was the only one they had in the store but we were impressed by the artistry in the Rose Point pattern by Wallace so this finally became our choice. We were impressed by Canadian hospitality as they joked with us, saying that they had ten months of winter and two of poor sliding. Our train trip back to St. Cloud enabled us to enjoy a beautiful October ride through parts of Manitoba and Minnesota. We have visited Canada on a number of occasions since then and were always much impressed by the scenery and the friendliness of the people during each tour across the border.

Duluth

During the summer of 1947 I was a graduate student at the University of Minnesota, preparing for a professorship at St. Cloud State. Virginia was living with her mother in Forest City, Iowa at the time. During the course of the summer she came to Minneapolis for a visit which included a trip to Duluth and the North Shore drive of Lake Superior. We began our tour on a beautiful sunny afternoon as we rode in a Soo Line passenger train through beautiful sections of eastern Minnesota, into the beauties of western Wisconsin, and on to Superior and Duluth. When we arrived in the twin ports area we were surprised at the chill in the weather with many people wearing heavy winter garments. Our hotel in Duluth was comfortable, adequate for our needs. The following morning after breakfast we arranged to take a bus trip to Two Harbors, another port city along the western shore of Lake Superior. Scenically, the tour was worth our while as we enjoyed north woods landscapes. That evening in Duluth, following dinner, we enjoyed a cool cruise on Lake Superior. Early Sunday afternoon we boarded a Soo Line train for a pleasant return to Minneapolis. This mini-vacation was scenic and refreshing—it provided therapy which both of us could enjoy.

North Shore Drive

One of the famous scenic attractions in Minnesota is the North Shore Drive. Beginning in Duluth it stretches northeast until it reaches the Canadian border. On occasions we would decide to enjoy some of the smoked fish available at restaurants along the North Shore Drive. We would leave our summer home in Superior where I was a summer faculty member at Wisconsin State University, continue through downtown Duluth then into an area of wealthy homes along the shores of Lake Superior. During the summer season the vegetation, the beautiful lawns and stately trees made this part of North East Duluth a virtual paradise. Upon leaving Duluth we continued along the lake shore past more attractive homes and north wood's type scenery with stately pines and hardwood trees. When we arrived at a restaurant of our choice we ordered select smoked fish, recently caught in Lake Superior. We had brought special crackers with us to enjoy in addition to the fish and orange drink. This kind of indoor picnic was always satisfying as was the fish treat we brought home for our gray kitty, Grolle.

Minnesota State Fair

In August 1947, following the completion of my work as a summer school student at the University of Minnesota, I arranged for Virginia, her mother and me to stay at a place in St. Paul near the fairgrounds so that we could enjoy this "late in the summer" spectacular. The Minnesota fair was regarded as one of the best in the nation with all of the attractions it offered for persons of all ages, levels and interests. The fruits and vegetables on display from many gardens statewide were fascinating considering how much in these categories could be grown in the upper Midwest, especially in Minnesota. Due to the fact that we were in a dairy state it might be assumed that dairy cattle would be a source of fascination. They were. The fact that so many different breeds were on display with statistics revealing milk production totals made the dairying industry feature seem even more interesting. The displays of various grains like oats, wheat, corn, rye, soybeans and buckwheat, gave us better ideas regarding basic sources of the food we eat. Also important as well are the hay crops like clover and alfalfa. Several acres of new farm machinery were also on display revealing how less manpower could cultivate more acres in less time. Displays of hobbies, various rides, nighttime displays in outdoor programs and fireworks concluded each day's activities. The Minnesota state fair taught lessons in conservation, good economics and good health. It was a great learning experience for all of us. I attended the fair a number of times over the years and always enjoyed it as an event which in a sense, concluded my summers.

Exciting Train Ride: Cloquet to DMIR

In northeastern Minnesota, not far from Duluth, we discovered Cloquet with its exciting short line railroad.

It ran from Cloquet north to where it met the mainline of the DMIR railroad. At least once each day during certain days of the week, the short line railroad would make a round trip business tour from Cloquet and return. When we learned of this railroad we decided to sample its comforts. Virginia, Anita and I bought tickets a number of times for rides in the caboose, attached to the end of the train. The ride was scenic, the train crew friendly. I managed to shoot movies as the train crew would do its switching at the DMIR. The colorful scenes on our trip are well recorded on film. On one occasion while the Carlsons, Myrtle and Martin, close relatives of ours, were visiting us in the Duluth-Superior area, we decided to ride the short line with them on its nearly daily round trip. The engine crew invited Martin and me to ride in the cab of the steam locomotive on part of the trip. The cab was noisy, smoky and warm. Each time the whistle was blown our ears would ring. Once or twice we were compelled to stop to help put out fires started by sparks from the engine. Nevertheless this was one of the most exciting visits we ever shared with the Carlsons. The memories of all of our visits with Myrtle and Martin over the years are some our brightest and best.

Washington Church Convention

The Augustana Synod of which Virginia and I were members, held its national convention in Washington in 1950. As delegates we made arrangements for housing and travel with the help of a faculty member at St. Cloud State Teachers College. Our train ride from Chicago to Washington provided a variety of scenic views; we finally arrived at Union Station, Washington, D.C. All sessions of the convention were inspirational, including the delegates' visit to the Swedish Ambassador's home. One afternoon there was a rather strange mood established as the president's official guards took seats in the church's sanctuary. At that point President Truman appeared, wearing his usual businessman's apparel. His talk provided a strong assessment as to the greatness of F.D.R. There was time for sightseeing during recess periods scheduled for the conference. We toured Arlington, the Smithsonian where I saw Lindbergh's plane, Mount Vernon, the National Cathedral, impressive memorials, and even had the freedom of touring the Capitol, groupwise and independently. Virginia and I saw the then Washington Senators play a night baseball game. Our friends, the Chells (he was our pastor), visited the roof garden of our hotel one evening, the evening of Johnny Chell's birthday. We enjoyed ourselves as Johnny's mother pointed out that the light on the top of the Washington Monument was the candle on an imaginary birthday cake. We all accepted the appropriateness of this patriotic reminder.

Colorado to Texas

In December, 1950, when I had gathered the basic statistics from two high schools in Denver for my thesis: "The Relationship Between Mental Health and Academic Achievement in Adolescents" and our winter vacation was continuing, so Virginia and I decided to use a certain fund for a trip as far south as the money available would allow us to travel. The first day we drove through towns in Southern Colorado, such as Colorado Springs and Pueblo, until late in the afternoon at 3:30 PM we drove into New Mexico, and eventually into Santa Fe where we spent the night. The following morning we had breakfast in Albuquerque, then on to Las Cruses and into El Paso. We stayed there two days and two nights, enjoying West Texas and Juarez, Mexico. On our return trip to Denver we spent a second night (Christmas Eve) in Santa Fe, in the midst of luminarias, the colored lights and holiday music. We returned to Denver on Christmas Day.

Barkers: A Sunday Afternoon Drive

It was late in the summer of 1953, possibly early September, that Virginia and I visited the Barker home in St. Cloud, Minnesota, when Hugh Barker suggested that we go out for a ride in their comfortable Nash sedan. The afternoon of our visit was perfect for travel, with a clear blue sky, a few white clouds, and a light wind. We continued east from St. Cloud across Highway 10, a main route to Minneapolis, driving on a quiet country road in Sherburne County, past several lakes surrounded by well-maintained cottages, possibly some of them belonging to members of the St. Cloud State faculty. We continued through a game preserve with was situated in a beautiful woodland area. The farm homes we passed reflected the fact that this region is part of the Central Minnesota dairyland. Another attraction that proved to be of interest to all of us was the sand dune display situated in a state forest. Eventually we arrived at Elk River, the county seat of Sherburne County. There we entered a main highway leading back to St. Cloud. For Hugh, Dorothy, Virginia and me this was in the nature of a farewell gesture for summer previous to the appearance of the chill of early fall.

Lake Superior: Isle Royale

We made trips to Isle Royale from the landing at Grand Portage, Minnesota over to the island. The beauty and warmth of the cruise among rock outcroppings and lapping waves was stimulating. Our destination at Isle Royale was Windigo Bay on the west side of this scenic national park. We'd begin our journey in Superior, Wisconsin, drive along the north shore of Lake Superior to our destination for an overnight stay at Grand Marais. The following morning we arrived at Grand Portage, so named as a point of landing for French fur traders. The craft that would take us to our destination was relatively small but quite comfortable. Upon our arrival at Windigo, we were served lunch, followed by a walking tour of part of the island. The tall pines, oaks and maple trees growing along the lakes of the island added to the north woods effect of the area. Decades ago an attempt was made to make copper mining a great success in this part of Michigan. The hypnotic beauty of this area far surpasses the wealth that copper may have brought to the region. A relatively severe Great Lakes storm tossed our boat on the return trip to Grand Portage in Minnesota, which added excitement to our trip. Tours like this one to Isle Royale are truly rewarding, storm or no storm.

Cedar Island Lodge

One day at Wisconsin State University-Superior, a student gave me a package of fresh fish with the invitation to visit Cedar Island Lodge at our convenience. This incident introduced my family and me to one of the most scenic attractions anywhere within the state as we discovered when we visited the facility. The lodge was comprised of several structures, the most elaborate of which was a guest house built to accommodate royalty. Somewhat beyond this building on the banks of the Brule River was a type of cabin, large and attractive, which housed canoes and fishing equipment. It was covered with cedar bark, surrounded by cedars, located on an island in the river, hence the name. When guests would seat themselves in the canoes, including presidents, a large door would open and the canoes would glide gently into the river. On one occasion my brother and his family joined the three of us for a hiking tour of the area. The river, the forests, including the largest pine trees in Wisconsin, a fish hatchery and the lodge were all included as we comfortably hiked, enjoying ourselves. Each time Virginia, Anita and I visited the lodge we felt that we experienced a great communion with nature. As to whether the Cedar Island Lodge will become a state park is conjectural. Whoever owns it is indeed indebted to preserve it. Proximity to Lake Superior makes this location all the more attractive.

On Our Way to the Fair, 1962

In March of 1962 we received information regarding the prospects of housing at the Seattle's World Fair to the effect that reservations must be made early. We did. At the conclusion of my summer term assignment at Wisconsin State University, Superior, we traveled to Forest City, Iowa, to meet Virginia's mother, Elvina, who would go with us to the fair. Late in August Virginia, Elvina, Anita and I left Iowa for the fair. We stopped in Sioux Falls, South Dakota, to visit the Thoresons, then continued on to the Black Hills. Our tour extended into Montana at which point the car began to complain. We limped into Broadus, checked into a motel and left the car in the local garage. Three days later the car was ready. While we were waiting for the repair job to be completed, we decided to have coffee in a local restaurant one afternoon. While there we noted that a car from Washington pulling a trailer, stopping at a local park. To our surprise and theirs, it was the Johnson family, pausing in Broadus on their way to Illinois for a new job for Dr. Johnson, an army buddy of mine. We had a great visit with them before they left Broadus. Our trip was solemnly enlightened as shortly after leaving Broadus, we visited the Custer Battlefield at the Little Big Horn. Following this inspirational stop we traveled on through several notable locations in Montana. Billings, Butte, Missoula, and finally entered Idaho with a scenic overnight stop in beautiful Coeur d'Alene. Perhaps Broadus, Montana, is not very notable or scenic, nevertheless this location left an indelible impression in our memories.

World's Fair—Seattle, 1962

After a pleasant evening in Coeur d'Alene, Idaho, which included a visit to the lake and dinner in an excellent restaurant, we continued our journey to Spokane, Washington. Beyond Spokane we stopped at the Grand Coulee Dam, a marvel of engineering skill. We became aware of the wonderful apple orchards producing some of the best fruit of its kind in the Wenatchee area. Following a peaceful and restful night in this part of Washington we were prepared for another day's drive. This plan was rudely interrupted by a severe spasm in my back. A few miles west of Wenatchee we found it necessary to engage a motel facility for the day and the following night. During the course of the day I showered frequently inasmuch as the hot water provided me with a sense of relief to the extent that I could comfortably drive the remainder of the distance into Seattle and enjoy attractions at the fair. Each day we drove about two miles into downtown Seattle from our rented facility. Memories of the fair tend to focus on displays such as John Glenn's space vehicle, a display of a million silver dollars and displays from a number of foreign countries. The artistics displayed projecting us into the 21st century, were impressive. The space needle and displays of ethnic foods appealed to us as we strolled about the fair grounds. Upon our departure from Seattle we counted pleasant memories of the city and the fair. During subsequent visits to this area I have always been impressed by its scenic beauty and the friendliness of its people.

Central City, Colorado

Central City is an old mining town located in the mountains west of Denver. During its heyday it was the center of entertainment and miners' supplies, serving a large mountain area. One artistic symbol of the glory days of the community is the face on the barroom floor. As to the emotions and history of this painting, there are conflicting stories regarding the painter and the motivations concerning his work of art. In modern times students from local universities, especially the U of Denver, staged performances reflecting the history and wealth of Central City. Nearby, according to reports, it is possible to find Madame Curie's radium mine, along with other mining sites located on various mountain sides. There is still mineral wealth located in the area, but the costs of mining increase in proportion to the depths of digging, hence the incentives for mining are somewhat limited.

Reports on the campus of the University of Denver indicated that some students earn money for college expenses by prospecting in mountain streams in various parts of Colorado. We always enjoyed our trips out to the mountains with the beautiful scenic views, historical reviews and the refreshing mountain air.

London

Following a pleasant overnight flight from Los Angeles via Maine, we crossed the Irish Sea then inland over the colorful British countryside into London. We were met by our guide who would be with us through nine countries and two principalities on our European tour. During our trip from the airport to our hotel, we passed through neighborhoods displaying attractive English homes. Lilacs at the time were in their full glory. Our hotel was adjacent to a park, situated close to a communications tower that had been damaged by a rebellious group from Northern Ireland. During our tours in London, Virginia, Anita and I were much impressed by their bus service and underground rail system. As we viewed the changing of the guard in the vicinity of the royal palace, we were reminded again of traditions of long standing. The solemn atmosphere and architectural grandeur experienced in St. Paul's Cathedral were high lights of our tour in the city. The stately Parliament buildings reflect on the long standing democratic traditions that have prevailed in Great Britain. The ethnic and racial mixture in the city was demonstrated to us as we ordered our meals in various places. The persons who waited on us were natives of former British colonies now residing in London. The British were friendly and very proud of their city. We could identify numerous reasons as to why this is true.

London to Oxford

While we visited in London we were somewhat surprised to learn that waiters in restaurants and clerks in some of the stores spoke very elementary English. Virginia, Anita and I entertained an earlier opinion that we'd have no language difficulty in England in using our basic American vocabulary. However, much of the help in the British Isles apparently comes from earlier British possessions, hence the great variety of linguistic usages. One day while we were tourists enjoying what England had to offer, we opted to go on a tour from London to Oxford. The day was beautiful, the scenery very attractive. In some of the rural areas we were reminded of some of the neat and colorful farms in the U.S. The wooded areas and fields appeared to be very well groomed. Our visit in Oxford was very interesting. The city has characteristics of the Middle Ages as well as the modern and up-to-date. Any visitor would be impressed by the qualities of Oxford University in terms of architecture, libraries, classrooms and laboratories. Oxford offers the traditional, the ancient and modern approaches to learning. As we departed the community later in the day, the three of us commented to the effect that if we were to live in England, the town of Oxford would be our preference.

Rome

Our European tour of 1972 was exciting and stimulating throughout, much of it occurring in what once was the Roman Empire. The magnitude and abiding glory of ancient Rome was revealed more dramatically to us in that city than in any other part of what was a widespread and glorious empire. The glory that was Rome can be seen in artistic statuary and buildings of ancient design that for all practical purposes still serves the public. The Pantheon is an example of the effectiveness of Roman engineering and architectural skill, constructed to serve many gods but now serving as a center of Christian devotion. Within the City of Rome there is an independent nation which serves the Roman Catholic Church as a political and religious unit with a government recognized internationally—the Vatican. Two silent but spectacular reminders of the manner in which Roman officialdom tried to impress the public was in the Coliseum where spectacular events were staged, even to the extent of loss of human and animal life. In the Forum victorious armies marched home following foreign exploits, displaying the spoils of war. But weakness through greed and human selfishness brought the empire down. It was eventually overcome by a sect that was early on bitterly despised and persecuted. In spite of this early treatment, the Christians overcame the weakness of Rome by their eternal strength and dedication.

Pompeii

In June of 1972, Virginia, Anita and I had visited the site of the volcanic destruction that buried the city in 79 AD. The locality has been resurrected to levels of perception that make it seem possible that Pompeii is, in a sense, alive again. The streets, the homes and public buildings are standing as they would have been many years ago except that extensive damage was done to many exteriors.

We did, nevertheless, visit in some homes, possibly residences of the wealthy where artistic forms, including refreshing pools, were still visible. There were displays of human and pet forms dying in excruciating pain from the hot gases and ashes the volcano produced. Out in the main thoroughfares the plumbing was still intact. In a museum which contained artifacts of what once was a great city, there were displays of food common to the place and era, a variety of household tools and utensils, and an assortment of medical equipment typical of practices involved at the time. As we departed Pompeii and viewed Vesuvius in the distance, all was calm and peaceful as life in a measure had been in the city previous to 79 AD.

The Pantheon: Impressive Cathedrals

During our travels we visited many impressive sites, and through the inventory of structures, their interiors, their locations, there are a few that inspired us most in regard to their special outstanding qualities. The Pantheon in Rome is one of these, depicting Roman engineering skills and deep religious fervor. When it was initially erected it was designed to honor all Roman gods of which there were a sizable number. The sturdy appearance of the exterior and the colors and beauty of the interior are overwhelming. When Christianity replaced the early Roman deities, one God was honored along with saints who served him. Centuries following the construction of the Pantheon, new architectural styles were initiated. The construction of stately cathedrals was no less intense than the dedicated efforts centuries earlier by the Romans. The towers reaching skyward, the vast pillared interiors inspired worshippers reverently to respect a God whose might had guided the building of these great monuments of worship. We truly felt the presence of the Almighty as we visited cathedrals in Bourges, France, Cologne, Germany and Uppsala, Sweden. The forces that motivated the building of these marvelous structures truly inspired us to respect the skilled workmen who, with God's help and the dedication of the local congregations, made these notable structures become reality.

Paris

On a beautiful sunny afternoon during our European bus tour, we arrived on a busy thoroughfare in Paris, where along with numerous vehicles of local origin, we passed through the Arch de Triumph on our way to a local hotel. Early impressions of this city were to the effect that Parisians were busily on the move but willing to converse at their convenience. Our hotel was in a theatre district where it was apparent that this is a city of light and degrees of entertainment. In the vicinity of our hotel we learned to enjoy what seemed to be a village situation with shops and homes within the larger city. Early during our stay in this attractive and historical region of France, we ventured to Versailles, a suburb of Paris. The beauty of the gardens, the palaces of the long time royalty, of the nation where within recent times the treaty that ended WWI was signed. Again within the city, we admired the engineering skill of Alexandre Eiffel and his impressive tower. The cathedrals of Paris projected the beauty of artistry in glass and stone. Over the centuries the artisans, the philosophers, the geniuses of science and literature, the musicians and politicians have all left their impressions in this place—in reality a City of Lights.

Vacationing in the Black Hills

In 1983 my daughter, Anita, and I accepted the warm invitation to the Thoreson family for a stay at the Black Hills ranch. Elliot and Berthella met us at the Rapid City airport following our flight from San Diego by way of Salt Lake City. Their welcome, the weather and scenic attractions were comfortably stimulating for both of us. During our stay at the Thoreson's summer home deep within the pine forests of western South Dakota, we had the privilege of visiting Mt. Rushmore, displaying four presidential faces, an especially thrilling sight. Later we viewed Sylvan Lake in all of its beauty. Our tourist train ride through wooden scenery was refreshing. We visited the replicas of a Norwegian stave church near Rapid City which stood close to a typical Norwegian home with a sod roof supporting a colorful meadow. Our tours included visits to places where President Coolidge vacationed in the Black Hills in the 1920s. On one occasion we were guests at a theatre presentation of "Hello Dolly". During the performance, since we were seated next to the stage, we were encouraged as part of the performance to sing along with members of the cast. Anita and I were treated royally during our stay with the Thoresons. We met most of the members of the family with their typical optimism concerning daily affairs. The delicious meals we were served, the beauties of their ranch with the fragrance of wild roses and the stimulating mountain air were profound blessings to us as we recall our very pleasant visit.

Wild Life in the Black Hills

We visited the Black Hills in South Dakota during the summer of 1983 after receiving a warm invitation to spend some time with the Elliot Thoresons of Sioux Falls at their ranch deep in a heavily timbered area. On this occasion "we" refers to my daughter Anita and me, following the death of Virginia, her mother and my wife. Our friendship with the Thoreson family was one of long standing after having met members of the family several years earlier in Denver. One evening shortly after dinner, the suggestion was made that we go out deer viewing. Shadows were lengthening over the landscape at this time of evening when deer would be out foraging. Almost immediately we saw several grazing along the edge of the highway. Later we saw families of four or five until we got the idea that the area must be overrun with deer. Our total viewing brought the number up to 104 by the time darkness had overwhelmed us. When we returned to the Thoreson cottage we could hear wild turkeys calling to each other; judging by the sound effects there must have been a large flock in the area. On another occasion we deliberately sought out a herd of buffalo (bison in some native's parlance). There were numerous animals in the herd, varying from calves to sizable bulls that did not like our car or the people in it. Also coyotes and bear inhabit the area. We did see coyotes but no bear. Seeing any animals in a wilderness setting is a stimulating experience for us all.

Panama Canal, 1985

Early one morning it seemed as though every crew member and every passenger was on deck as we approached the canal. We enjoyed the sunny, balmy weather as we entered the first lock. Our craft was raised to a certain level, then moved through an elevated lake to be lowered at the other end. Digging through mountainous terrain in Panama was extremely demanding which prompted the building of hydraulically operated locks. The lake was formed deep enough so that almost all seagoing traffic could pass through it. A leisurely day was required for transit through the Canal as no one seemed to be in a hurry to arrive at the Pacific Ocean. Typical tropical scenery along the route reminded us that we were near the equator. Several natives had boarded our ship in an attempt to sell colorful garments of various kinds. Much discussion preceded the event of our giving over the Canal to the government of Panama. There have been concerns expressed as to how effectively the Panamanian government can keep the canal going at a high rate of efficiency. Questions arise as to the future of this important international waterway. Will some nation not so friendly to us gain the canal for its own selfish reasons? Will the United States attempt to dig another canal in an area more favorable for the engineering required to build another international waterway in this area? We enjoyed our travel through this famous man made engineering marvel but questions raised regarding its future could be bothersome.

Caracas, Venezuela

During a cruise to the Caribbean, Irene and I opted to go ashore along with other passengers as we docked in the harbor that serves the City of Caracas, a metropolitan area located inland. The people of Caracas were awaiting the arrival of the pope with colorful and appropriate greetings as we entered the city. The city is the capital of Venezuela, displaying attractive and impressive government buildings attesting to the fact that the nation promotes democratic functioning. As we continued our tour in the business district of Caracas, the atmosphere very much in evidence is the effect that this is a busy city. The nation depends upon its petroleum resources in promoting successful business ventures. The earlier Spanish influences are in evidence of architectural manifestations and linguistic usage. The city is modern in so many respects that we felt very much at home as we enjoyed viewing the residential developments and park systems of Caracas. Efforts are being exerted in an attempt to stem the poverty that exists in portions of the community. The suggestions for improvement by governmental offices seemed appropriate for this work. For us, the lasting impressions of the city were in the direction of the citizens acting to accepting good things and basically trying to make them better.

Acapulco

Our cruise ended early one bright January morning in the harbor of Acapulco. We were escorted from our ship to a reception area in one of the local hotels. A bountiful feast had been prepared for us as a kind of welcome to this part of Mexico. Irene and I had reserved a room for a two day stay at one of the local hotels; the facility proved to be an up-to-date apartment which provided us with leisurely comforts. During our stay in Acapulco we toured the city from the busy downtown area to locations where Hollywood movie stars had made their homes. We saw the young male divers leap from rocky ledges into the surging waters below. Their skills were nothing short of sensational. Our tour included the resort where President Kennedy and his first lady enjoyed their honeymoon. The beach resorts, expensive homes and hotels

dotting part of the shoreline pictured an area of considerable wealth. Uncomfortable contrasts were found, however, in places where the so called "common" people
lived, the Mexican laborers who put forth the effort to
build and maintain the more glorious portions of Acapulco. Irene and I enjoyed our accommodations, the food
and the warmth of the weather and reception we received.

World's Fair—1986

Some of the most impressive attractions of our
World's Fair tour were available to us in Seattle. Our stop
there included a tour of the World's Fair grounds of 1962
and the impressive Seattle waterfront. While we visited
the waterfront, we purchased tickets for a boat ride to
Victoria, B.C. The craft had almost all of the accommodations we needed for comfort as we traversed through the
watery and wooded areas between Seattle and Victoria.
The buses that met us at the dock in Victoria transported
us to the Empress Hotel and past government buildings
which house the legislative and executive units of government for British Columbia. As our bus ride continued we
were transported out to the marvelous Bouchart Gardens,
developed in what had originally been a rock quarry. The
flowers, trees, walk-ways, appropriate structures and
tours of these gardens are remarkably impressive. We continued our stay in Seattle for another night after our return
from Victoria. The following day we continued northward through communities displaying attractive homes
and beautifully forested hillsides until we arrived in the
port city of Bellingham. During the course of the evening
we dined at what must have been the most popular buffet

in the area, followed by a visit to the home of a family of friends who soon would depart for the desert.

World's Fair—1986

We continued from Bellingham to the Canadian border through a threat of rain as we journeyed on our way to Vancouver. We engaged hotel rooms shortly after we arrived in the city in an area not far from the fairgrounds. Even though we encountered rain showers we proceeded to the fair and early on found ourselves in a long line of spectators waiting to enter the Alaskan exhibit. From this attraction we moved on to the rest of the fair which involved a stay of several days. The theme of the fair was "Transportation" with exhibits from the space age back to a 1913 steam engine, revealing how progress in travel had become remarkably efficient during the decades of the 20th century. The American and Russian contributions to the fair would enable visitors to project into the 21st century. Our Canadian hosts had done an excellent job preparing for the crowds that came daily to the fairgrounds. All accommodations were exceedingly convenient which made touring at the fair a real pleasure. The fireworks every evening provided a fitting closure for each day's activities. The fair in Vancouver was in some respects a model designed to satisfy visitors of all ages. Our memories of Vancouver and the fair reminds us of the fact that Canadians are friendly and efficient in their work, sensitive companions for the enjoyment of their guests.

World's Fair—Vancouver, BC, 1986

Russ Sommerlot and Vernia had very recently purchased a new car, a Dodge Diplomat. That may have been one of the reasons for planning to do some touring, like making a trip to the World's Fair in Vancouver, B.C. Irene and I were given the opportunity to go with them as we volunteered to share expenses for the opportunity to visit the fair. We began our tour with interest and enthusiasm as we traveled through Los Angeles and beyond into and through Santa Barbara, then to Santa Maria and San Luis Obispo. Between San Luis Obispo and King City we noted the military reminders of World War II as we passed through Camp Roberts, which still had some of the dimensions of a large military post. San Francisco is always an attraction, including the traversing of the Golden Gate Bridge. We stopped for refreshments in Santa Rosa, with a stay overnight in Willets. The next morning we paused in Redway for a coffee break with Steve Symons and his family, giving us a chance to see Steve's updated pharmacy. The following day we toured the state capital in Salem, Oregon, another city with gorgeous floral displays. Portland impressed us as an urban area not much besieged by smog. We stopped in Carmel to visit Ruth and Santa Cruz to visit Dora and her family.

World's Fair—1986

We departed Vancouver in good spirits following our satisfying and most pleasant experiences at the fair. Our itinerary southward from the Canadian border brought us back to Seattle where we reviewed the inspiring sights of Mount Rainier, which we saw from our hotel, then to the capital of Washington at Olympia, and finally to Longview where we spent a restful night before crossing the Columbia River into Oregon. As we continued along the Columbia River we had delightful refreshments near the Multanomah Falls and subsequently impressive views of an engineering marvel, the Bonneville Dam. Following the route along the river we arrived at The Dalles, at which point we turned south with stops at Redmond and Bend. As we toured through this prairie-like area noted for grain production we could see the impressive mountains to the west. Following an overnight stay in Bend we turned west away from Highway 97 for a view of fascinating Crater Lake. From this inspiring part of Oregon we continued to Medford and Ashland for visits with relatives and friends. As we continued from Oregon into California we enjoyed the scenic splendor of Mt. Shasta. Following restful stops in Woodland and Sacramento we continued to the Los Angeles area, and then on to San Diego and home. As recipients of rich memories and deep satisfactions, Russ, Vernia, Irene and I regarded this trip as outstanding in every way.

Denmark

On a beautiful afternoon in June, 1984, we left Los Angeles on a jumbo jet, our destination—Copenhagen, Denmark. The flight was smooth even though we flew through some stormy weather. Anita and I were members of a group that would tour Sweden and Norway beyond our stay in Denmark. The leader of our group was Erik Palmgren who was an excellent instructor of our Swedish classes in San Diego. As always he had all details well in hand so before long we were settled in a great old hotel in downtown Copenhagen. From this vantage point Anita and I could venture out as when we toured what seemed to be a mile long arrangement of stores and shops. On a soap box as we ventured along, we heard a black speaker say unfavorable things about America. We didn't refute him because I doubt that the inattentive group listening was not believing what he said. Our group toured a brewery where a variety of beverages was available, saw the Little Mermaid and the royal palace and courtyard. One evening we had dinner in a great hotel near the Tivoli Gardens. During the course of a good Danish dinner we visited with a group from Japan who almost immediately invited us to visit their homeland. Our tour of the gardens was exciting with all the sights, sounds and color immediately at hand. Anita and I were looking for a good band concert which we didn't find. During our stay in Denmark we shared so many attractions with so much friendliness that basically we didn't miss a thing.

Sweden

Our group went by ferry from Denmark to Sweden where we landed in the community of Malmo. A short drive brought us to Lund where we visited a cathedral displaying actors and musicians performing as the chimes told the hour. In Smoland, where my mother was born, we heard lectures and saw historical displays relative to basic immigration to America. Due to the very limited economy in this part of Sweden, many families left in the 1880s and beyond. Our tour of the Orrefors Glassworks was fascinating as we observed the skill of the blowers and the works of art they created. We saw an ancient castle of Kalmar, crossed the lengthy bridge to the island of Oland. The countryside as we saw it was prospering. The towns and villages were neat and clean, promoting the beauty of June with lavish floral displays. Eventually we arrived in Stockholm, the capital of Sweden. Our group was housed in Old Town which made our stay more exciting. Here we visited Skansen Park with its display of structures from the historical past, later saw the

Warship Vasa which had been raised from its watery grave to its present site, the Carls Milles statuary and the famous town hall. We were guided through the royal castle and grounds where the king and his family live. In Uppsala we visited the cathedral and the campus of its famous university. Our tour bid adieu in Sweden in the industrial city of Goteborg. The contrasts between "Old Sweden" and "New Sweden" have proven to be dramatic. Culturally, socially and scientifically Sweden is one of the most advanced nations in the Western World.

Stockholm

The capital of Sweden. The city is on occasions referred to as the Venice of the North due to the fact that much of Stockholm is built upon numerous islands. The traffic of ocean-going shipping enters the harbor as it leaves the Baltic Sea. Decades ago a warship christened The Vasa was ready to set sail to combat when it sank due to some faulty engineering regarding the imbalance of the craft. The ship was raised in recent times and is now on display in a museum built to honor the craft. Old Town (Gamla Stan) retains its medieval atmosphere architecturally and politically promoting a sense of royal power. The town hall reflects the best in modern day civic construction. This attractive center is the site of the giving of the Nobel prizes each year, except for the peace award which is presented in Oslo, Norway. The royal palace, the Milles sculptural garden and Skansen park are all attractive for people who stroll leisurely and in the process enjoyed the scenic and the artistic. Irene and I are of Swedish descent which enables us to enjoy special pride in this attractive city.

Norway

We boarded a train in downtown Goteborg early one morning for our ride to Oslo, Norway. As in Sweden, so in Norway, the Norwegian farm homes are neat and orderly, the fields efficiently cultivated. Our hotel in Oslo was within walking distance of downtown, past the royal castle. On a tour of the city we saw the king's herd of cattle, a museum housing various kinds of sea craft which had been in the service of the Vikings centuries earlier. Anita enjoyed shopping in establishments displaying typical cool weather garments. All of us were impressed by the artistry incorporated into their town hall. Our tour group traveled by bus from Oslo to Bergen through the sensational Norwegian countryside. We transferred to a sea going craft for a tour of a colorful fiord. The greens and blues blended into majestic formations as we enjoyed the comforts of the boat ride. When we hiked up the trail to our hotel I proposed to Irene and she accepted. On land we traveled to Voss for another colorful overnight stay. The next morning our host helped us observe the 4th of July with flags and music. In Bergen we viewed the structures of the eleventh century merchants, visited the home of composer Edvard Greig, were impressed by their fish and flower markets. From Bergen we flew back to Copenhagen for our return flight to California. Our impressions of the Scandinavian countries we visited, Denmark, Sweden and Norway, were all positive regarding the kindliness of those we met, the great scenic attractions and the beauty and cleanliness within thoroughly modern economics.

Oslo, Norway

Oslo is located inland from the North Sea on a gulf which is suitable for maritime traffic. Much of the history of Norway and Oslo reflects upon the exploits of the early Vikings who explored and plundered large areas of Europe centuries ago. Records indicate that Vikings explored portions of the North American continent as well, especially Greenland. In the Viking Museum of Oslo, the history of the era is dramatically displayed with the long boats revealing skills of nautical design that enabled long distance travel to become a very real possibility. While, Irene, Anita and I would stroll from our hotel to downtown Oslo, we would pass the Royal Gardens and palace. In a larger open area resembling a rural pasture we saw a herd of cattle that was part of an agricultural interest the king possessed. The classical ski jump in Oslo Park revealed the intense interest Norwegians manifest in winter sports. Impressive as well were the Vigeland statuary, revealing in stone the native struggles of typical human beings. The Viking influence, very peaceful in nature currently, very much impressed us as we visited Oslo.

Canada—Colorful and Friendly

On our tour in 1988 we crossed the border into Canada in view of the mighty Niagara Falls. An exciting boat ride enabled us to sample the force and beauty of the water as it moved swiftly down its stream bed. As we followed the shoreline of Lake Ontario we arrived at Toronto, in the center of a thriving metropolitan area. Beyond the city a cruise enabled us to enjoy the island beauty of the St. Lawrence River, then overland to Ottawa, the capital of our neighbor to the north. A tour of the parliament buildings enabled us to sense the power of the great Canadian nation. Our group continued eastward until we arrived at Montreal for a two night's stay. While there we were impressed by the culture and imposing cathedrals of this great city. As guests we enjoyed an Octoberfest that outdid any that I had attended previously or since. As we continued northward our destination was the city of Quebec with its strong French orientation. The English army won a decisive battle on the heights of the city at a time when the English and the French were fighting for positions of territorial acquisition in the New World. In close proximity to Quebec is Ste. Anne De Beaupre, noted for its shrine with its apparent healing powers. Nearby is a diorama revealing the appearance of Jerusalem the day Christ was crucified, an impressive work of brilliant art. We have visited in many parts of Canada on various occasions and find the people and culture to be very much like our own. The fact is that our border with Canada is the longest undefended on the continent. No military protection is located on either side which says much politically and socially regarding our mutual relationship.

Maine and New England

Upon leaving Quebec we enjoyed a bit more of rural Canada before reentering the United States into the state of Maine. Mile after mile we enjoyed the colors of autumn in the wilderness of this great state. From Ogunquit, Maine, we traveled south to Boston for a tour of the area which became especially famous during Revolutionary War days: Bunker Hill, the Old North Church, Faneuil Hall and the Boston Commons have prominent places in the historical records of the American Revolution against the British. Further we sensed the importance of Paul Revere's ride and the work of the Minutemen. Following surges of patriotism in Boston we continued our journey to Plymouth where the "Rock" and replicas of the May-flower are anchored. Even the apparel worn by our host-esses enabled us to understand the intense patriotism and love of religious freedom that motivated the Pilgrims. Fol-lowing our visit to Plymouth we experienced a variety of emotions as we traveled into Rhode Island and a tour of the Breakers, a mansion of note belonging to the Vander-bilt family. The contrast between the life styles of the Pilgrims and the Vanderbilts is inscribed in American history as we note that the freedom of capitalism enabled a few to live in the glowing fortunes of the wealthy. In view of certain historical perspectives, we noted that the Pilgrims and the Vanderbilts both contributed to our cur-rent well being. Our group continued by way of New Ha-ven, Connecticut, where one of our great universities is located. Both President Clinton and Mrs. Clinton were students at Yale University.

Boston

One particularly exciting stop on our "leaf" tour of 1988 was a visit in Boston. Much of the history of this nation, especially in regard to the colonial period and the Revolutionary War, was recorded on the basis of events transpiring in Boston. While we visited the city we felt the intensity of Bunker Hill, Paul Revere's Ride, and the significance of meetings scheduled in public places as how best to deal with the oppressive policies enunciated by the British. Effective planning was required preceed-ing such events as the Boston Tea Party. In more peaceful times such as those we experienced in 1988, our group enjoyed the tours of public structures, churches and places of other political action that stand in respectful dignity even to this day. The relatively large open space referred to as the Commons accommodates livestock on occasions as it did generations ago. Boston has long been famous as a center of higher learning through the presence of schools like Harvard University. Now as a business center of note, Boston serves New England and the nation through insurance and publishing services. The city continues to build its reputation on the basis of its colorful and patriotic history.

Visit in Connecticut

After the "leaf" tour which included much of New England, the Sommerlots, Irene and I left our group for a visit with Irene's and Vernia's relatives, the Brodeens, in Fairfield near New Haven, Connecticut. The date was October, a time when the beautiful trees in the area are displaying their fabulous colors. Both Rev. Gene Brodeen and his wife, Elizabeth, extended us a warm welcome which included a visit at their home plus a delicious dinner. We were impressed by the displays of artifacts at their house, many of which they had purchased during the course of their travels. Mrs. Brodeen excused herself early during our visit enabling her to conduct choir practice at a nearby church where she was the organist. Following our dinner, Gene, the Somerlots, Irene and I experienced a delightful drive through some of the older communities in Connecticut. Along the way I brought up the subject of watch and clock making which helped make the state famous. We stopped at a retirement facility where we had the pleasure of visiting Hannah Munson, Mrs. Brodeen's mother. Upon our return to Fairfield we boarded a New York bound train for a trip to downtown New York City. From Central Station we taxied to our hotel where we rejoined our travel group at the end of another great day of travel.

New York City

Big, loud, in a hurry with blazing billboards and glaring lights. We arrived at night from Fairfield, Connecticut. The Sommerlots, Irene and I detrained at Grand Central Station. A short taxi ride brought us to our hotel for a two night stay. During our tours of the city we traveled by taxi, bus, and water craft. There were so many things to see in the city so crowded with skyscrapers overlooking rough and crowded streets. Two very impressive structures for tourist traffic are Ellis Island and the Statue of Liberty. In Manhattan, the World Trade towers, the Empire State Building, and Radio City Music Hall all attract scores of visitors. The Brooklyn Bridge, the mayor's home and dwellings occupied by movie stars, at least on some occasions, attract attention. Yankee Stadium is very popular with baseball fans, with large numbers attending games during the height of each season. The U.N. Building, Riverside Church and Grant's Tomb are known for reasons historical and religious. The site of an old cemetery in the midst of so much traffic and other plots of ground set aside for historic reasons are reminiscent of the days when Manhattan was a relatively small rural village occupied by thrifty and religious Dutch people. Massive changes made New Amsterdam into New York City where remarkable transitions have occurred over the years.

Two Cultures

We had the privilege of enjoying visits to two distinctive and different cultures as we continued our leaf tour in 1988. The setting of one of the cultures was in Virginia—in the quaint and historic town of Williamsburg. During a return to the 1700s we shared part of colonial times in this community in the shops, on streets, and in legislative halls. Wearing apparel was typical of that era, the materials in places of business were appropriate for tailoring, for kitchen use and for caring for livestock and gardens. The language usage was distinctly English, the legal codes were from British traditions. Power for transportation was provided by well trained horses. Medical and musical supplies were available in terms of limited kinds and qualities. The atmosphere in Williamsburg was friendly with a leisurely kind of lifestyle in evidence. In Pennsylvania we encountered another culture which due to the existence of strict religious regulations was functioning in the 19th century but with evidences of 20th century. The Amish colony we visited was distinctly rural with well kept farm buildings and neatly cultivated fields and meadows in evidence. All power was obtained from well trained horses managed by well disciplined drivers. Farm equipment and buggies for leisurely travel were all pulled by horses. There was no electricity in farm homes or public buildings. Telephone service was severely restricted. Academically, Amish children were limited to eighth grades taught by a teacher who herself was an eighth grade graduate. Visits to these cultures were socially and historically stimulating as we observed how citizens in both areas were adjusting to prevailing conditions.

Philadelphia, Washington and Mount Vernon

In Philadelphia a guide attired in colonial dress enabled us to see the most significant views in our Cradle of

Liberty. The structures where world-changing meetings were held, homes of some of the notables of the times when our nation was being formed and a church where Washington prayed for the success of historical efforts. (Nearly world's farther west on the 4th of July many decades later I visited a replica of a model of Independence Hall at Knott's Berry Farm in the Los Angeles area.) In a room duplicating the meeting place where great decisions were made I heard the voices in recorded form, of those who spoke of "Life, Liberty and the Pursuit of Happiness." I was impressed. When a visit to Washington transcends any low-level politicking and seizes the spirit built into monuments, architectural marvels, resting places for those who died in defense of our nation, it is relatively easy to believe that Washington, D.C. symbolizes what we as a nation believe is right for all of mankind. Tours of Mount Vernon strengthen thoughts and memories of personal greatness in the office of the president of the United States. Any visit to the battlefields of wars fought within our boundaries tend to strengthen the belief that those who served and died there were committed to causes higher than life itself, "these honored dead, fighting for a new birth of freedom."

Ashville, NC, Great Smokies, TN, Nashville: (Leaf Tour)

Irene and I had a pleasant evening in Asheville in tourist surroundings with a visit, as promised, with Clifford Hoffman, a friend of Chick LuPone. The following morning was beautiful as we entered Great Smoky Mountain National Park. Instead of the mists which gave the park its name, the "smoky" now arises from power plants in the area. (Except for much heavy traffic, Great Smoky is scenically like Palomar Park in San Diego County.) We paused at Gatlinburg, Tennessee following the tour of the park. In respect, we paused at the chapel in Gatlinburg which tells the story of Jesus' life. In the vicinity of Nashville we visited Andrew Jackson's home, The Hermitage, where 1000 slaves were employed in a self-supporting enterprise. Near at hand, Nashville is famous for country music, higher education and conservative Protestantism. It is truly an inspiring place.

Memphis, TN, Arkansas, Oklahoma: Leaf Tour

We paused in Memphis where we paid our respects to Elvis at his home, Graceland. It is apparent that thousands of his fans have lavished their feelings and honors on him at that location and elsewhere. If Elvis had had the skills and personality for more respect for his well-being, I would have regarded him more highly. We continued our journey through what appeared to be rice fields and into the scenic wooded areas of Arkansas. Beyond we enjoyed beautiful Lake Eufaula in Oklahoma as well as the Cowboy Museum in Oklahoma City. The ranches in the Amarillo, Texas area, the Spanish and Indian flavors of Old Town, Albuquerque were very attractive. In Arizona we felt concerns regarding the limited attempts involved in preserving the Petrified Forest and the Painted Desert. Irene and I gained considerable insights in our Home Land. The need for conserving our best and wisely using the most of what we have is a source of concern for the present, and especially for decades to come.

Abilene, Kansas

During a cross country tour in 1988, we made a stop in the town of Abilene, Kansas, made famous by a native son, in fact, by the whole Eisenhower family who lived by the railroad tracks in a residential area. Our group visited the family home where hard work and religious fervor had prevailed. The house is only part of an impressive array of historical structures and monuments. Ike and Mamie, along with an infant son, are buried on the grounds in a facility which honors this family in beauty and mournful silence. The Eisenhower library and museum were constructed in a parklike setting where scholars and other visitors pour over documents and personal data encompassing General Eisenhower's military training and service rendered as Allied Commander-in-Chief in Europe during World War II, as well as the eight years of his presidency of the United States, which encompassed years of prosperity in the 1950s. During a campaign tour in Minnesota with a stop in St. Cloud, he crowned the homecoming queen for St. Cloud State University with attended pomp and ceremony. The community shared its dairyland wealth by giving him a tub of butter. As always the Eisenhower smile reflected his confidence and optimism, revealing his strength and his personality.

Land of Lincoln

On tour in 1988 we visited some of the places and locations that were significant in the life of Abraham Lincoln. The reconstructed village in New Salem, Illinois, where he learned significant and honest business practices as well as the skill of reading and thus acquiring a legal background which served him well in years to come.

A stop at Lincoln's home in Springfield revealed interesting historical facts concerning his home and family. One interesting observation was that he was quite tall so it was necessary for him to place a mirror high on the wall for shaving. He was laid to rest in regal splendor in the memorial that bears his name. The monuments which comprise the memorial speak volumes as to Lincoln's humble and unassuming lifestyle. He let others receive the honors and recognition that were often his due. A visit to the site of the Battle of Gettysburg leaves profuse impressions as to the intensity of the fighting, the terrible loss of life and the significance of the fact that this was possibly the battle in which the North overpowered the South, leading to a final victory for the Union. It was at this location that President Lincoln made one of his most profound addresses. In Washington, DC, we viewed Ford's Theater where Lincoln lost his life in one of the foulest deeds committed in American history. As we visited the various places where Lincoln lived, worked and died, we sensed again that in time of greatest crisis, we have had some of our greatest manifestations of leadership, as illustrated by the life of the great emancipator. If his life had extended a few more years some of the agony of the times that followed the Civil War would have been eliminated.

Santa Rosa and Sonoma, California

Two of the most scenic areas in California north of San Francisco are located in the Santa Rosa, and to the east, the Sonoma regions. The streams, the forests, as well as acres and acres of vineyards, are all featured in this part of the state. When my cousin Caroline and her husband, Bob, invited Irene and me as their guests for the enjoyment of their home in Hayward and tours beyond, we enthusiastically accepted. As we journeyed northward through Petaluma and beyond to Santa Rosa, we were impressed by the agricultural development and forested reserves that reflected environmental concerns. In the city of Santa Rosa we were invited to visit the home of Luther Burbank, an internationally known garden plant and tree wizard, who developed high level effectiveness out of the ordinary and the exotic. As we journeyed eastward from Santa Rosa, we were inspired by the beautiful groves of coniferous and hardwood trees in the area. Eventually we became aware of the fact that we were in wine country as numerous vineyards came into view. The Sonoma area is famous for the production of a variety of wines served worldwide. At our stop at one of the wineries we enjoyed a picnic lunch in the shade provided by one of the parks on its premises. Bob and Caroline had provided Irene and me with a new perfect day, including a quiet evening at home following a grand tour and visit.

July 4th, Where?

The weather was becoming warmer, yet warmer, as our troop ship plowed through the relatively calm waters of the Pacific Ocean. There were over 600 of us on board, many of whom preferred to stay on the main deck so as to enjoy the gentle, cooler breezes. We noted the appearance of more flying fish as the days wore on, reminding us of the fact that we were in or near tropical waters. Via radio we received newscasts from time to time updating our knowledge of world affairs. By way of contrast, Virginia and I toured to the top of Mt. Evans on a day that saw readings of 90 degrees in downtown Denver. As we continued upwards of 14,000 feet, the weather became quite winterlike. We encountered a rutted road coated with ice and snow. What appeared to be a snowstorm was covering the mountain landscape with a mantle of white. The plumbing at the rest stop restaurant had frozen so we moved at a snail's pace, enjoying the comforts and scenic beauty at lower elevations. On July 4, 1984, Anita and I toured with a group through an area of snow-dusted peaks in Norway. At breakfast our hostess served us delights with a red, white and blue orientation. During the summers of my teaching assignments in Gunnison, Colorado, we enjoyed a massive, colorful fireworks sponsored by the entire community. At 7000+ elevation, during the 4th of July displays the wearing of heavy jackets was a must. The three of us experienced fire works displays at Superior, Wisconsin, as well, during my summer tenure at the state university at that location. Fourth of July celebrations in Minnesota, Iowa and California have also been memorable with picnics and fireworks. On every occasion we felt that our patriotism was recharged at each event with each serving of potato salad and detonation of each explosive device.

Columbia, Missouri

While visiting with Laurel and Dorothy in their attractive home in Columbia, Missouri, Irene and were shown some of the scenic and historical attractions in the central part of the state. The sight of the biggest oak tree in Missouri was impressive as were the School of Agriculture "providing grounds" where a variety of crops is studied. We saw the palatial home of one of the Walton daughters and the impressive grounds surrounding it. A tour of Jefferson City, and especially the state capitol steeped in history, was encouraging for me as I gained the satisfaction of seeing a noted Benton mural on display. This great work of art depicts the social, economic, and historical dimensions of the state, displayed effectively in an assembly room in the capitol building. Not far from Columbia is the community of Fulton where Winston Churchill gave his "Iron Curtain" speech. In addition to offering his interpretation of world affairs and in honor of his visit, the community was the recipient of a church which had been transplanted from England. The wealth of our visit in Columbia was identified in part by the warm hospitality we received and the grand tours which enabled Irene and me to gain a richer understanding as to what Missouri has to offer.

A Scenic Route

During a period of several years, I worked in the Imperial Valley, California, as a school psychologist, one day a week. My day at selected schools began quite early so I was on the road to my assignments shortly after daybreak. As I drove eastward from San Diego, in the mountains, then down into the Imperial Valley, scenes changed from coastal to desert during a drive of somewhat over 100 miles. On several occasions the eastern sky would display a brilliant shade of red during the early morning hours. During the winter months I would drive through a mountainous wonderland with live oaks and pine trees laden with snow. As I reached an altitude of 4000 feet the early chill of morning and the invigorating fresh air would be most welcome. Mountain lions, bob cats, wild sheep as well as a variety of birds would welcome me through elevated lairs. As I descended to the desert a variety of rock formations would embellish the scenery. A line of demarcation, a water line in some places, would indicate the beach level of a primordial sea. When what seemed to be endless beds of flowers spread out across the desert during the spring seasons following ample rain showers,the colors and fragrances were nearly hypnotic. As colors changed during my afternoon return trips to San Diego, the delightfully fresh air, the shadows, the wild life and the trees all continued to make my Imperial Valley tours a pleasure.

Bed and Breakfast

Anita, my daughter, chose to give Irene and me an unusual anniversary gift—bed and breakfast in a scenic mountainous area near Julian, in East San Diego County. Accommodations were modeled after the best designs of the 1890s. Our bedroom, lounge and bathroom were located in the upper story of a rugged mountain home. We anticipated two nights of comfort in a fresh air setting, anticipations which quickly became reality. Our nights were bathed in moonlight, another unanticipated blessing. Even wilderness sounds asserted themselves when some dogs chased a coyote across the yard beneath our unit. One night a storm passed rapidly through the area, damaging outdoor furniture. Our host and hostess entertained us with snacks, films and good conversation. At breakfast time we received the royal treatment with tender steaks and an abundance of other early morning goodies. Following delicious breakfasts each day our appetites for "later in the day" meals were much modified. During our stay, Irene and I visited a beautiful county park in a heavily wooded area as well as the former mining town of Julian with its quaint buildings and shops. Basically our bed and breakfast experiences were those of pure joy, with all anticipations fulfilled.

XI
ADDITIONAL REVIEWS

ADDITIONAL REVIEWS
Table of Contents

ADDITIONAL REVIEWS

Minneapolis, Minnesota

In September, 1938, I enrolled as a graduate student at the University of Minnesota. During the course of the year '38–'39, I earned my master's degree in the College of Education. Minneapolis was my home. Thanks to the assistance freely given by my friend, Al Madden, I became acquainted with the campus and city quite effectively. One service that I truly appreciated and used regularly was provided by local street car traffic. For 10 cents it was possible to ride to any part of the area. As a student I discovered that excellent entertainment, musically, athletically, and theatrically, was available for very respectable prices. I love trains so every morning as I crossed the bridge from a main traffic thoroughfare, I could see steam powered trains passing beneath me. As I looked from my vantage point on the bridge I could see the Mississippi River and downtown Minneapolis with flour mills near at hand. Shopping in the city proved to be much more convenient than in a small town. The churches and schools from my involvement with them indicated that leadership in the city was highly effective in dealing with community matters. The lakes and parks in Minneapolis have gained national and international reputations for the city. I have departed the city by rail, bus and air on numerous occasions; it always seemed to me upon my return to Minneapolis that I was being beckoned to my second home.

Madison, Wisconsin

Scenically, with its lakes, forested parks and beautiful homes, Madison must be one of the most attractive cities in America. Some urban evaluators have rated it at the top for family living. The business area downtown and the university campus on a hilly part of the city, all reflect a sense of belongingness. Memories of this metropolitan area relate to one of my special assignments at the university in WWII, Virginia and our honeymoon there in 1944. My recollections of Madison are that it is a scenic place with fresh air and clean water. Pollution is apparently at a minimum level in this part of Wisconsin. Charles A. Lindbergh was a student at the University of Wisconsin; at times in the past, political liberals prevailed in Madison. Wisconsin is one of my favorite states and Madison helps foster the indentification. I have great respect for its beauty and its people. Each time I visit Madison a feeling of belongingness prevails as I sense the strength of its many attractions.

Denver, Colorado

While I was completing my work toward a doctorate at the University of Denver, Virginia and I spent a year in the city, enjoying its resident benefits. It's metropolitan qualities with beautiful parks, accommodations for civic affairs, encouragement for the artistic, ample facilities for the academic and political. A well known federal mint is located in Denver. Geographically, in its mile high orientation, commercially and in terms of basic economics, Denver anchors the development of basic agriculture and ranching to the east, to the west the mountains with accounts of fabulous strikes in gold and silver mining location. Much of Colorado's population lives in and north of Denver in places such as Boulder, Fort Collins and Greeley and south in the cities of Colorado Springs and Pueblo. Mountain resorts such as those located in Vail and Aspen attract hordes of tourists who enjoy the snow during the winter season. Near Denver to the west is Golden, noted for its brewery operated by the Coors family. Professional sports have become very popular with local fans, especially in football and baseball. The new airport, some distance from the downtown area, has with its conveniences, improved air travel in Colorado as well as nationwide. The moderate climate, ease of traveling within the city, and opportunities for shopping all form a picture of the local conveniences we enjoyed while we lived in Denver.

Duluth, Minnesota & Superior, Wisconsin

During the course of several pleasant summers in the 1960s, Virginia, Anita and I lived in the Duluth-Superior area while I was a member of the faculty at Wisconsin State University in Superior. The history of this area is very much associated with the discovery of rich deposits of iron ore, especially in Northern Minnesota. Railroads were built for the transportation of ore down to the harbors of Duluth and Superior and for the hauling of supplies and equipment back to the mining communities. The Head-of-the-Lakes region became a busy rail center, providing freight and passenger service to points in Minnesota and Wisconsin. Business and professional services were provided in both communities. Public and parochial schools, colleges and trade schools were developed. Some of the wealth created by the prosperity in this region can be seen by leisurely driving north beyond the business district in Duluth along the famous lake shore drive and viewing the fabulous homes built in this neighborhood. The climate, the attractive lakes beyond Superior, the northwoodsy scenic appeal, the northern lights and ethnic diversity appeal to artists and a variety of tourists for these reasons. We appreciate any opportunity for returning to this wonderful part of America.

Mohave

The Mohave Desert north of Los Angeles must be one of the windiest areas in the United States. In fact the name of the desert, "Mohave", is derived from an Indian name which means "wind." It was in that area that Virginia and I had occasion to visit Molly and Irvin Ortman one chilly weekend. We spent most of our time indoors, visiting and playing yahtzee while the wind kept up a howling song as it buffeted everything in its course. The friendly acceptance of the Ortmans plus Molly's good Southeastern European recipes made us feel welcome. On another occasion during a desert snowstorm while Virginia visited a family of relatives, I was a guest at a session of Irvin's basic psychology class which he taught as a member of the local community college faculty. The whites, greens and browns of the desert on that occasion were intriguing. On yet another Mojave visit with the Ortmans, Virginia and I visited a colorful park in the desert, made of rocks in many shades of red and brown on the hillsides. The Ortmans had come to the desert with their children from their earlier residence in Minnesota; eventually they returned to that state with memories of color, wind and sand.

Fallbrook, San Diego County

One of my assignments in the extension program at San Diego State was to conduct Educational Psychology classes in Fallbrook, near the northern border of our country. The area is especially known for its citrus and avocado groves. The city of Fallbrook is at the eastern edge of Camp Pendleton, a large marine corps base. During my tours into the community I was refreshed by the fragrance of orange blossoms and the lavish floral displays which made the springtime drives to Fallbrook a pleasure. Previous to my class session I would enjoy a coffee break and olollalaberry pie in a quaint restaurant near the school where my class met. All students enrolled appreciated the fact that I would accommodate them by having class sessions in the area where they lived. On one occasion as I was leaving town upon the conclusion of my class reunion, I encountered what seemed to be hundreds of horny toads on the street where I was driving. I deliberately refrained from disturbing them as they enjoyed the cool of a light and refreshing shower.

Vista, California

In the 1958–60s I taught extension classes in Vista, a comfortable drive from San Diego into the North County area. I would stop for gas at Escondido at 30 some cents per gallon. Tree ripened navel oranges were available at warehouse prices in the same location. I would drive on a country road from Escondido to Vista that reminded me of times when North County was truly rural. There was an old school house along the way with its bell tower and bell still intact. The country store where I would shop for fruits and vegetables was as inviting as those places have always traditionally been. When I arrived in Vista I would stop for a coffee break in a restaurant which was part of a large grocery store. As I arrived to teach my course in Child Growth and Development a warm greeting alerted me to the fact that my class was well motivated. The change of pace from the campus was a good source of professional stimulation in a warm and scenic location. The school, a part of the Vista system, was located in a delightfully pleasant neighborhood ideally located for our extension program.

Canning Corn

At the end of our summer session schedule at the University of Denver, 1950, we decided to return to the Midwest for a brief vacation. Upon our arrival in Forest City, Iowa, where Virginia's mother lived, a call had gone out to anyone and everyone to be involved in helping at the local canning factory. The corn was at its peak for processing, so all who could harvest, help in the canning and work in the warehouse were called upon to report to work. Virginia and I were assigned to the warehouse. When the corn had been processed and canned, the boxing and storing in the warehouse began. Sometimes it was midnight or nearly so before our workday ended. The days following offered the same routine: the huskers were out in the fields early to pick the corn, the first loads were brought to the processing plant where the corn was husked and placed in cookers which had been steamed up for the occasion. Color, texture, taste were all regarded as the canned corn was rated, quality-wide. Again Virginia and I did boxing and storing of the freshly prepared corn crop. One morning I was called out early to help load a freight car with boxes of corn for a large grocery

company. The corn was excellent, the workers cooperative and the end result was appetizing.

First Plane Ride

A big stir was created in Northern Iowa one weekend
when an air crew from Texas had flown a military plane
whose maximum mileage limit required that they land in
the Mason City area. The crew apparently continued on
to the Twin City area some other way. Since the plane
was available for public scrutiny, Syrdahl of the Waldorf
science department invited me to go along with him to
see the aircraft. While we were enjoying the viewing of
this relatively ancient aircraft, Syrdahl began chatting
with another friend who was also examining the Army
aircraft. This friend had a plane or two parked at the airport nearby. As the conversation developed, it involved
his planes and me. Shortly I was seated in a Piper Cub
flying over Mason City. On that beautiful summer afternoon in Iowa, the whole landscape, rural and urban,
looked like a beautiful landscaped carpet spread out as
far as the eye could see. At 2000 feet the world was different and very inviting. Of all the flights I have ever experienced, this was one of the most memorable.

Psychology of Cheating

During the summer of 1948 I was professor-in-resi-
dence at the St. Cloud State University Off-Campus Center at Montevideo, Minnesota. One evening Virginia and
I were attracted by a crowd that was attending a fair on
the community grounds not far from the downtown area.
There were various attractions available but one of them
seemed to be especially attractive to me. A crowd had

gathered around a vehicle which was the immediate center of attention. A sales person was explaining and demonstrating the merits of a certain gasoline saving device. His shouting regarding the merits of his device and the manner in which he did the demonstrating aroused my curiosity, even my doubts as to the value of the item he was trying to sell. I asked him what local mechanics thought of his device. His loud and abrasive answer insulted all mechanics in the area. I followed with a request concerning what consumer's research said about the equipment that he was trying to sell. This brought out another verbal blast. About then Virginia escorted me out of the crowd. The best statement I heard about the equipment all evening was from a customer who said the device was worthless. In my way of thinking the person demonstrating employed the psychology of cheating to his advantage.

Trapped

One night following a visit with my parents in Upsala, Virginia and I were driving back to our apartment in St. Cloud. It was a cold, wintry night; both of us were wearing overcoats and heavy overshoes since our car did not have a functional heater. As we were driving through a rural area of fields and meadows I noticed something out in one of the fields that caught my attention. At a distance it looked to me as though a dog out there was fighting an object he could not subdue. I turned our spot light (which was a piece of extra equipment this car displayed) over to the area of activity. As I focused the light on the scene that had caught my attention, I realized that the dog was desperate, caught in a trap. I told Virginia to continue focusing the spotlight on the dog while I would venture out in an attempt to rescue him. As I approached the dog I noticed that one of his legs was caught in a trap. I held out my well-covered right foot in an attempt to see what the animal would do. As I moved closer the dog seemed to know what I was attempting to do. I opened the trap, thus releasing the dog. The animal was so happy it jumped up on my heavy coat and tried to kiss me. I really had gotten my reward. Steel traps of all kinds should be outlawed.

Same Goal, Different Paths

Through to course of the years I have been a worshipper in a variety of Christian churches: Roman Catholic, Lutheran, Methodist, Baptist, Mission Covenant, Mormon, to mention a few. All of the mainline Protestant churches and the Roman Catholic Church all identify the heaven Jesus described to be the final goal of all true Christians. There are varying philosophical and theological paths by which heaven can be gained, based on the writings and lectures of selected religious leaders. There is a conviction widespread among certain Protestant groups that baptism must be formed by complete immersion or the act is not recognized by the church authorities. The Roman Church derives it authority primarily from the papal office in Rome, whereas Protestant churches employ the Bible as their primary authority. The Mormons or Latter Day Saints have gone far afield in developing their theology without apparently being aware of what is written in Revelations 22:19. As a result of some basic differences in theology, recruiting among churches is done in part on the basis of some obvious differences in church practices. The thought that some paths are closer to heaven than others has caused grief and pain within the Christian church. Read Rolvaag's *Their Father's God.* Were that all of our thinking was Christ oriented then the confusion of the choice of pathways would be eliminated.

Boy Scouts

While I was a student at St. Cloud Teachers College, I developed an interest in scouting. During my childhood and adolescent years there were no scout troops available locally that I might have joined. We learned the fundamentals of scouting at St. Cloud and especially during an outing one weekend at Birch Lake. One of the men in our group had forgotten to bring some basic supplies to the event. The fact that it had rained part of the time we were there compelled us to use basics among other skills on how to start and maintain fires. While I taught in Upsala I was assistant scout master for our troop. The boys would come to my classroom following school hours for help in earning merit badges. I enjoyed these opportunities to learn with the boys and in advancing my own efforts as an assistant scoutmaster. On one occasion we decided to prepare baked hole beans. We dug an appropriate hole in a grassy area following the filling of a crock with the appetizing ingredients of the bean recipe we had chosen. Our group placed the crock in the hole we had dug and surrounded it with hot coals. The next day we went to unearth the buried treasure. The crock had broken along with our ambitions for a good dinner. At the end of the school year we encamped near Crosby, Minnesota, in one of the state's iron mining areas. Our facilities were adequately located where a forest of beautiful pine trees had stood. In this location the boys experienced an environmental disaster that had been brought about by greedy lumber barons. If the selective cutting of trees had occurred, the area would still be beautifully forested.

Censorship

In the 1950s sensitivities concerning what people were reading reached a new high in St. Cloud, Minnesota, when it was discovered that a committee of some sort had determined whether or not a certain literature was in the nature of a threat to the basic moral standards of the community. A student at St. Cloud State University had, through some research, discovered that such an organization had been at work in the community for some time, wrote a paper as a class project noting what he had obtained by way of his study. A Minneapolis newspaper reporter read the material prepared by the student at the university and as a result of this discovery, a series of articles on censorship in St. Cloud appeared, revealing the nature of the work done by the local committee. If a member of the censorship group read a paragraph or two from a certain work that he/she did not like, the whole work was censored. The manner in which various works were reviewed was in the nature of a scandal. Sentiment in the community was immediately divided in favor or in opposition to the work the censors had done. Libraries were threatened by the prospect of having books removed, even burned; authors, editorial writers, novelists all felt the sting of censorship. Eventually the feeling in the community arose to the point that the censorship committee was abandoned. How much censorship is still with us anywhere?

XII
IN RETIREMENT

IN RETIREMENT

During my retirement I have:

- Worked in a special teaching program designed to teach non-readers how to read.

- Worked with foreign students at SDSU assisting them in gaining proficiencies in the use of the English language.

- Worked with high school students in San Diego in promoting basic mental health practices.

- Counseled in a medical clinic operated by Dr. Leonard Goldberg—1987–1994. When he retired upon closing the clinic, I resigned from the facility.

- Served as Vice-President of our CSEA unit.

- Served as Chairman of a committee at College Lutheran Church.

- Served as an ombudsman at SDSU.

- Wrote poetry and mental health reviews.

DR. LEONARD GOLDBERG
DIRECTOR, MEDICAL CLINIC

In 1987 Dr. and Mrs. Goldberg interviewed me, and subsequently accepted me for employment as a Clinical Psychologist in his medical facility. I was a professional staff member in his clinic until he closed the center in circa, 1994. During the years that I was a part-time psychologist in the clinic, I learned to know Dr. Goldberg as a person and as a professional. It was a joy to learn to know all the members of his family, his wife and children. As a chiropractor his skills were unexcelled in his field. As a person he was friendly, approachable, cooperative and in every sense, helpful. When he closed the clinic to go into semi-retirement, our friendship, which was established early in our associations, continued. I even had the privilege of counseling his delightful grandchildren.

Verses for the New Year

Age is not finally measured in years but in the depth of
    learning and in gracious deeds,
Through challenges in learning each soul gains power in
    confronting daily needs.

In gracious deeds strength is gained by helping strug-
    gling others,
In life-refreshing love we're strengthened rescuing our
    brothers.

Much learning is gained through dedicated giving and
    forgiving,
To forgive ourselves and those who offended promotes
    sincere and healthful living.

As a new year dawns we reflect upon the memories of
    the passing years,
In joyous thoughts and deep regrets in our laughter and
    our tears.

We are deeply moved by intentions and experiences that
    shape our very beings,
That through the years determine our worldly lot in fail-
    ures and succeedings.

At home and in our communities we gain support
    through patience and warm assistance,
Effectively guided by good will we feel hope in loving
    deep persistence.

Trying assures a measure of success, no attempt assures
    defeat,

Aging years should not be times of depression fear and
cold retreat.

In advanced years discuss our successes with bright and
eager youth,
May our advanced learning help them with much needed,
basic truth.

Love of nature, good health, joy of reading and inspiring travel,
Make every stress and harsh demands quietly unravel.

Then, each new day brings challenges that dispel all
doubts and fears,
Thus, making age a blessing in the passing of the years.

The Night After Christmas

'Twas the night after Christmas
when all through the house,
There was raucous discussing
between husband and spouse.
They had felt that Christmas was
in the giving of things,
Not in giving of themselves to the
new King of Kings.
A costly toy little Rob had received
as a seasonal token,
Had neatly been wrecked,
systematically broken.
Little Amos, just three, received gifts,
computer to sox,
Left him playing most gladly with
each empty box.

Yes, the night after Christmas tells
us more than the eve,
    As to the real spirit of Christmas,
as to what to believe.
    If the love we express in this
season of peace,
    Is to bring untold blessings
that will ever increase.
    We must give of ourselves, to
the Lord in full measure,
    Then each gift of the season will
be a glorious treasure.

Impressions

Grand Canyon, Zion, Bryce May 15th—19th, 1995

From canyon depths to sandy desert scenes,
We saw the works of nature, of men and their machines.
The weather we encountered varied by many degrees,
From the warmth of summer to chilling wintry freeze.
The geological marvels with layered forms and blend,
Yet science does not clearly discern earth's beginning and
    its end.
Geology tells us how marvelous changes have been
    wrought,
But says little about celestial powers who create by word
    and thought.
From churning seas and mighty surging, crushing uplifts,
Come beauty, charm and color in canyons and on cliffs.
In the glory of the depths and sculptured heights of Can-
    yon Bryce,
With each turn of our footsteps, a glorious new surprise.
From Zion's depths it rises shining, bright and lone,

An impressive monument, the glorious Great White
Throne.
And for a delightful change with I-Max on the screen,
In exciting perspective, some sights we'd earlier seen.
Views of the Grand Canyon hold in awe every one and all.
They make our stature and our size seem minimal and
small.
So now as our pleasant journey comes to its appointed
end,
Irene and I wish blessings for our travel mates and
friends.

Coast to Coast
(November 1, 2, 3, 4, 1995)

From the Playas de Tijuana to Mexicali's great canals,
We felt the lure of Mexico in calm and surging spells.
In the foaming surf breaking on Baja's western side,
And the gently rolling waters of Cortez's breaking tide.
The moods of mountain valleys and each sandy, rocky
shore,
Entwined with deep imprints of early Indian lore.
With tigers guarding caves where palatable food was
served,
Appealed to gracious guests all thankful and unnerved.
Fascinating travel brings enlightenment that gently calms
and soothes
Strenghtening and guiding all in many pleasure moods.
In sights and sounds in Tijuana, Ensenada and San Fel-
ipe too
We saw an old Baja Norte with one that's truly new.
The warmth of friendly natives as they greeted with
kindly smiles

Made each journey seem shorter than in accumulated
  miles
With leaders whose knowledge reached beyond most an-
  ticipation
They guided each traveler to new and grander realiza-
  tions.
With wine and brandy or other beverage choices,
Revelers partook with resounding, happy voices.
So now as this remarkable journey comes to its pleasant
  end,
Irene and I extend best wishes to each kindly, traveling
  friend.

In Remembrance, 1996

Memories of another year soon will be
Recorded as historical events by each family.
Of visits with hospitality in royal grace,
Warm receptions extended in each friendly place.
The loving charm of Vanlandingham family members,
Extended warmth that the heart long remembers.
Sharing at Lawrence Welk's in the glory of spring,
Then dinner in a restaurant where all waiters sing.
Cheerful long-distance visits with Vernia, Laurel,
  Evodia, Hugh,
Gave us oral enlightenment, helped see us through.
A year of dental distress, cataract surgery and skin can-
  cer threats,
Survival's the word with no enduring regrets.
A Santa Barbara weekend with history and wine,
A California place with civic appeal and accents divine.
In San Francisco the Rocklitz hosted a reunion of the
  1296th Engineers,

No details overlooked for the comfort of buddies and
   peers.
A delightful day in East County where apple trees thrive,
With Vi and Harry, our hosts, in a glorious drive.
We review '96 with memories of joy and of pain,
Yet we have much to be thankful for in all that we gain.
In blessings we share with all who peruse this review,
Warmest greetings for 1997 to each one of you.

Memories—1997

As days shorten and candles brightly glow,
We reflect on recent memories and those of long ago.

Of the Nativity, family dinners and anticipated gifts,
Skiing, Christmas lights and snow in heavy drifts.

Entering the New Year with optimistic solutions,
And the warmth of kindly greetings and cheerful resol-
   tions.

More recently in California, fruit trees and fields of brilliant flowers,
Glistening breakers, towering mountains revealing nature's powers.

Our guests at Welk's resorts enjoyed sights and sun,
Sharing each repast intensified our fun.

Then visual surgery for Irene and nasal for my plight,
Brought degrees of healing comfort for breathing and for
   sight.

A tour of Northern Arizona, Flagstaff and the Canyon Grand,
By bus and by rail we enjoyed this scenic land.

As the memories of the past and present intertwine,
We see each day as a blessing, a glorious gift of time.

We are blessed by warmest greetings from relatives and friends,
So our memories grow richer as another old year ends.

Journey in October 1997

On a cool and cloudy morning before the break of day,
A group of happy travelers went merrily on their way.

Through grooves of avocados, past fields now fallow and the desert's quiet life,
We arrived about at noontime in warm and sunny Blythe.

Then Wickenburg in Arizona with museums most appealing,
Containing sculptures, paintings and facts of history, most revealing,

We viewed Indian dwellings where history was shaped in stone and cleft,
With mystery surrounding every scene as to why the natives left.

In Sedona where nature's handiwork appears in redstone monuments,
Here an upbeat mood prevails that brings no great laments.

311

In the Flagstaff area with piney woods, cinder cones and
   mountain peaks,
There a mood of solemness gave respite that the weary
   traveler seeks.

From Williams to the South Canyon rim with all its grandeur revealing,
On beaten rails, through ranching lands with entertainment appealing.

We saw the grandest Canyon with its color, its hues
   daily changing,
While way below in gorges deep the mighty Colorado's
   raging.

But in Laughlin a change of moods to gambling and to
   guessing,
As coins were absorbed and reluctantly dispensed in devices most possessing.

Now all the memories, the happiness seem like a fading
   song,
Combine to make this trip a grand sojourn for all who
   were along.

So now as our most pleasant journey comes to its pre-
   dicted end,
Irene and I wish the best to you, each travel-mate and
   friend.

Copper Canyon

From the streets of Tijuana to the shores of Cabo Sur,
We enjoyed the sights and sounds of a great & pleasant
    tour.
In Los Mochis in the early morning darkness and gentle
    falling rain,
We boarded a fast smooth-riding Pacific railroad train
At Bahuichino we went from comfy train to a very
    crowded bus,
Unaware of the excitement that was in store for us.
On miles of hills, curves and through rough road therapy,
We arrived a La Mision and were welcomed graciously.
The wood burning stoves, the brief moments of electri-
    cal power,
Made us feel the primitive life with each short passing
    hour.
The Tarahumara Indians, their children and their wares
Seemed far removed from our lives with their burdens
    and their cares.
The beauty of the canyons, the mountains and each ver-
    dant forest glen,
Made us feel the delightful urge to see them all again
At Pasada Barrancas each hour was true delight,
The crisp air, the hospitality and each new depth and
    height.
The marvels of this ancient land and the glories of each
    view,
Were great for soul and body and gave us strength anew
El Feurte with its mansion house and colorful parade,
The Viva Mexico observance made us glad that we had
    stayed.
The ancient face of La Paz and the modern city too,
Revealed the pride of Mexico to generations old and new

Lovers' Beach and Todas Santos with all their native
  graces,
Made us thankful for these lovely great and scenic places.
And can we forget the Indians' great athletic skills,
Their homes in caves, their meager coops carved out of
  cliffs and hills.
The feasts we had in fiestas and Italian cuisine,
The friendly chats, the walks and treats as in a pleasant
  dream.
Then so we from our memories send as this great jour-
  ney ends,
Best wishes from Irene & me to all our traveling friends.

Our Memories, Our Hopes
(2–01–99)

In this season days and events of this century will be past,
Events will become memories in sunshine lightly are cast.
May the years to come in the new era bring hopes to
  renew,
Anticipations of showers of blessings that will truly
  accrue.
When we reflect upon the history of the greatest genera-
  tion then recall,
How we survived in wars and depressions and recovered
  from them all.
The pains of wanting and the weight of fighting to gain
  each victory,
With peace and recovery our greatest and significant vale-
  dictory.
In satisfaction reflecting upon the security of future generations,
Making certain that their anticipations will be satisfying
  realizations.

314

With all our generation accomplished in a positive way,
In saving lives, shortening distances and giving wings to
all we say.
Do we appreciate all the social and scientific gain?
Or with distressed condemnation see mainly stress and
strain?
Truly great accomplishments survive in an air of great
acceptance and cooperation,
In a truly patient mood of trust and conservation.
When memories inspire and most effectively guide,
Hopes then are realized and great blessings will abide.
Irene and I send warmest greetings for the
Christmas season and happiness for years to come.

Alive at 85
(09–26–1999)

Four score and five, alert, healthy, ambitious, alive,
Living fully each day, thus I happily survive.
There are pains, frustrations, general physical slowing,
Some exercise in bicycling, gardening and neat yard
mowing.
Tradition weighs heavily as occasionally I drive,
Maximum highway speed for me is still 65.
Most drivers are speeding as they go rapidly by,
If I pass someone going 60, he's older than I.
When I refer to the hard times of the Great Depression,
Anita says such thoughts encourage unnecessary re-
gression.
One pill a day is the extent of my prescription,
Try to eat sensibly in following each nutritional de-
scription,
My memory needs sharpening, at times I pause and stall,

But I depend upon a wealth of experiences for accurate
   recall.
Many relatives and friends have departed this life,
Among them my parents and loving first wife.
The supports given me by those who remain,
Are a blessing to me as they share laughter and pain.
I have often been strengthened on the local scene,
And almost world-wide in what I have done and have
   seen.
Academic awards and professional recognitions,
Identified degrees of success and strengthened ambitions.
Will I reach 90, 100 in the millennium to come?
Reach my goals as akin to earlier victories won?
Much encouragement comes from family and friends,
Thus strength in faith is renewed as each pleasant day
   ends.

NORTH AMERICAN
FISHING CLUB

Members'
Cookbook

Edited by
Steve Pennaz
Ron Larsen
Colleen Ferguson

Published by the North American Fishing Club
Minnetonka, Minnesota 55343

We would like to thank the following people for their help:

NAFC Charter Members who submitted the great variety of fish recipes for this year's Members' Cookbook, and for supporting the lifetime sport of fishing by joining the North American Fishing Club. This book is dedicated to our members' further enjoyment of fishing in an environment that is both safe and satisfying.

NAFC Staff Members: Publisher Mark LaBarbera, Managing Editors Steve Pennaz and Ron Larsen, Editorial Assistants Colleen Ferguson and Cara House, Art Director Dean Peters, Vice President of Product Marketing Mike Vail, Marketing Manager Cal Franklin and Project Coordinator Laura Resnik.

A special thanks to Boating Safety Specialist Tim Smalley of the Minnesota Department of Natural Resources for all his help and information on water safety.

Cover photo courtesy of Lund Boats; photos on page 23 courtesy of Minnesota Department of Natural Resources Boating Safety Section. All illustrations created by David Rottinghaus.

Address reprint requests and orders for additional books to:
NAFC Cookbook Editor
P.O. Box 3403
Minnetonka, MN 55343

ISBN 0-914697-40-4
Copyright 1991, North American Fishing Club

The North American Fishing Club offers a line of fraternal products for members. For information, write: NAFC, P.O. Box 3408, Minnetonka, MN 55343.

Contents

Good Meal, Safety Are No Accident

With a light, but steady breeze coming out of the southeast, NAFC Charter Member Rod Mysliwiec and his brother Robin expected nothing more than a pleasant day of walleye fishing. But about mid-afternoon, Rod spied a boat moving toward their anchored craft. At first, he thought it was another angler moving in to share the good walleye action they were enjoying, but as the boat moved closer and closer, its operator failed to throttle down. The hair on Rod's neck began to rise. He tapped Robin on the shoulder to get his attention, and pointed toward the oncoming boat.

"Watch it Robin, I think this boat is going to hit us!" said Rod.

There wasn't time to lift the anchor or even start the motor before the boat smashed into, and then, over them. Luckily, Rod and Robin were able to jump clear of the collision and weren't injured in the accident. Their boat, however, wasn't so lucky. Water began rushing in the huge gash opened along the bow and the boat immediately began to sink. Two nearby anglers rushed to help, and after pulling Rod and Robin from the cold water, were able to tow the damaged craft to shore before it sank.

Rod and Robin found out later that the man who almost killed them was legally drunk. Several thousand dollars in repair bills later, he was also broke.

Early in the planning stages for this NAFC Members' Cookbook, we held a roundtable discussion at Club headquarters to select a theme. A number of great ideas were presented, ones that I'm sure will appear in the coming years. But one seemed to stand out in the minds of many attending the meeting—fishing and boating safety.

To be honest with you, I was against the idea in the beginning. I thought our members would find the topic too dry, and besides, is a cookbook really the place to cover boating safety? Then, I talked to Tim Smalley, the boating safety specialist with the Department of Natural Resources in Minnesota, the state that regularly ranks highest in boat ownership per capita. Tim related a couple recent examples of fishermen who lost their lives in boating accidents—accidents that could have been prevented with a little common sense. He also armed me with several meaningful statistics from the National Safe Boating Council, Inc. Things you can keep in mind while plying the water for your next fishing trophy.

•The three most common causes of boating fatalities are capsizing (37 percent), falls overboard (24 percent) and collision with another boat or object (14 percent).

•Nationwide there were 896 boating fatalities and 3,635 injuries reported for 1989—the most recent statistics available.

•Boating accidents cause more than $25 million in property damage each year.

•Of the 8,020 boats involved in accidents in 1989, more than half (4,078) were open motorboats, and 5,834 were less than 26 feet in length.

•In more than 80 percent of all boating fatalities, the victim was not wearing a personal flotation device.

•About 75 percent of 1989 accidents occurred when the water was calm or choppy. Only 10 percent occurred when the water was characterized as rough or very rough.

•More than half of all boating accidents occurred on Saturday or Sunday.

Smalley also reported that almost 50 percent of boating fatalities over the past six years have been alcohol-related. And 76 percent of those arrested for piloting a boat while intoxicated had previous arrests for alcohol-related auto driving violations.

Boaters, like drivers, need to moderate consumption and drink responsibly. The right time to celebrate fishing success is in safe surroundings. What good is this great fish cookbook NAFC members have helped us compile if you don't get home to enjoy the fish you save for the family table? Please keep these points in mind whenever you're on the water. We'd like you to have the opportunity to try the great recipes your fellow NAFC members have submitted and enjoy the years of fishing and boating fun still ahead of you.

Steve Pennaz
Executive Director
North American Fishing Club

COOKBOOK ABBREVIATIONS

tsp. = teaspoon
T. = tablespoon
pt. = pint
oz. = ounce
lb. = pound
pkg. = package

MEASUREMENT CONVERSIONS

1 pinch = less than $1/8$ tsp.
1 tbsp. = 3 tsp.
2 tbsp. = 1 oz.
4 tbsp. = $1/4$ cup
5 tbsp. + 1 tsp. = $1/3$ cup
8 tbsp. = $1/2$ cup
10 tbsp. + 2 tsp. = $2/3$ cup
12 tbsp. = $3/4$ cup
16 tbsp. = 1 cup

1 cup = 8 oz.
1 pint = 16 oz.
1 quart = 32 oz.
1 gallon = 128 oz.

1 cup = $1/2$ pint
2 cups = 1 pint
4 cups = 1 quart
2 pints = 1 quart
4 pints = $1/2$ gallon
8 pints = 1 gallon
4 quarts = 1 gallon
8 gallons = 1 bushel

Section 1

BOATING SAFETY

An Often Neglected Topic

Laws You Should Know

Lowhead Dams: Dangerous Drowning Machines

Basic Rescue Techniques

Uniform State Waterway Marking System
Regulatory Markers

Boat Exclusion
Area

Danger

Controlled
Area

Information

Buoys used
to display
regulatory
markers

Aids to Navigation

Mooring
Buoy

Red-Striped
White Buoy
Do not pass
between buoy and
nearest shore

Black-Topped
White Buoy
Pass to north or
east of buoy

Red-Topped
White Buoy
Pass to south or
west of buoy

Solid black or green and solid red buoys
(Pass between)

Port
Side ------ Looking Upstream ------ Starboard
Side

These examples of regulatory and navigation markers are reproduced here to help fishermen traverse various waterways safely. While the navigation aids shown are primarily for deeper-draft commercial vessels, fishermen should be aware of what these markers mean. To learn more about these systems, take a boating safety course near you or call the United States Coast Guard.

An Often
Neglected Topic

If there is one topic fishermen don't talk about much, it's
boating safety. That changes, however, if a group member
has a close call or a fishing buddy actually drowns. Then,
boating safety becomes the priority topic for awhile as each
group member recounts his or her near-tragedies. Such stories
can almost be worn as medals of valor; testaments of conquest
over almighty Mother Nature.

If you stop to think about your many years on the water, it's a
safe bet that you have at least two or three "war stories" of
your own to tell; times that you pushed your luck a little too far,
but came away unscratched. Maybe it was fishing during a
lightning storm. How about the times you fished when the
waves were a bit too high for your boat? Do you take enough
life jackets with you on every trip? Tragedy can strike at any
moment, as many boating accident victims can attest, but there
are numerous things you can do to reduce the odds that you

will be involved. Most are common sense, others are carefully described in the following chapters.

Boating should be fun and exciting, so the best time to talk about safety is before an accident happens. It is our goal to arm you with the tools you need to enjoy fishing and boating without accidents on today's waterways—and enjoy the great recipes that follow. Let's get started.

Types Of Boating Accidents

The following chart (which is based on 100 deaths in the water over a period of one year for a state that has over 600,000 boats registered) breaks down water-related accidents with their corresponding percentages of deaths.

Accident Category	Percent of Deaths
Boating	44
Swimming, Wading or Diving	39
Falls Into the Water (Non-boating)	10
Falls Through the Ice	6
Scuba Diving	1
Total	100

In understanding why boating accidents occur, it is necessary to look at the types of accidents and how they happen. Various state and federal agencies annually compile boating accident statistics. Most divide them into two groups: fatalities (where a death occurs) and non-fatal accidents (where only an injury or property damage occurs).

Generally, most boating fatalities occur in small, open boats powered by outboard motors (less than 40 horsepower) or in non-powered canoes. The following are the three most common types of fatalities:

1. Capsizing (tipping over)—These accidents are commonly associated with three unsafe boating practices.

•Overloading or improperly distributing the weight of passengers and gear in the watercraft, making it unstable and hard to handle.

•Sudden and sharp high speed turns.

•Boating in bad weather or ignoring the obvious signs of an approaching storm.

2. Falling overboard—Many fishermen and other boaters drown every year when they unexpectedly fall, or are thrown

Passing: Port to Port

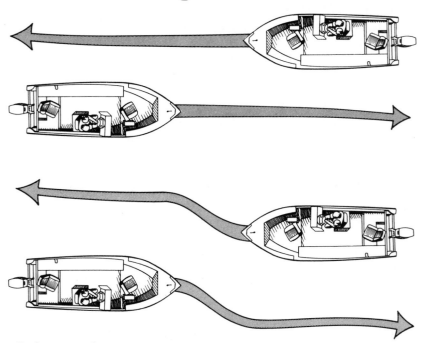

Each watercraft must pass on the port side of the other when meeting port to port, or head to head.

overboard. They might be standing up to start an outboard motor, or trying to net a fish. In any case, they lose their balance and end up falling into the water.

3. Swamping—This occurs when a boat takes in water over the sides or stern. Most swamping accidents occur when the operator disregards hazardous water conditions. A small, open boat, especially one that is improperly loaded or handled, can take in large amounts of water in a short time.

Most non-fatal boating accidents involve higher-powered craft (over 40 horsepower). Non-fatal accidents result in personal injuries and property damage. The following are the two most common types of non-fatal accidents:

1. Collisions—Boating collisions usually involve two boats, or a boat and a fixed object. Collisions occur between boats when operators do not pay attention to where they are going, or if the "rules of the road" were not being followed. Collisions with fixed objects often happen when the operator is unfamiliar with an area, ignores navigation markers or simply does not keep a sharp forward lookout.

2. Fires or Explosions—These accidents often occur when the proper safety equipment, such as ventilation systems and fire extinguishers, have not been installed or properly used. They also happen when proper fueling procedures are not followed, or the fuel system is not properly maintained.

Here are other points to note about boating accidents:

•In most cases, lifesaving devices are on board the craft but are not in use at the time of the accident.

•The use of alcohol is involved in about half of all boating accidents.

•Cold water (less than 70 degrees Fahrenheit or 21 degrees Celsius) is a major factor in many fatal accidents.

•Most boating accidents occur during the day and in clear weather.

•The majority of boat operators involved in accidents have considerable experience in using their craft but have never taken a formal boating safety course.

You Are The Key To Water Safety

Your safety depends on you, your equipment and other people who, like yourself, enjoy spending leisure time on, in or near the water.

Let's look at your responsibilities:

As boat operators, you are the "captain of the ship." You are expected to know federal, state and local regulations that apply to your watercraft and the waters in which you are operating.

It is your obligation to have the safety equipment required by law, to keep it in good condition and always on board, and to know how to properly use these devices.

You must have a complete knowledge of your boat, its handling characteristics and the boating rules of the road.

You are also responsible for your passengers, their safety and their actions. If any of your passengers are acting in a manner that jeopardizes their safety or the safety of all on board, take corrective measures.

The water user has a final responsibility which frequently is overlooked. This is an obligation to recognize that others who don't fish may also enjoy being on the water. There are great numbers of persons who enjoy sailing, skiing, canoeing or skin

Crossing

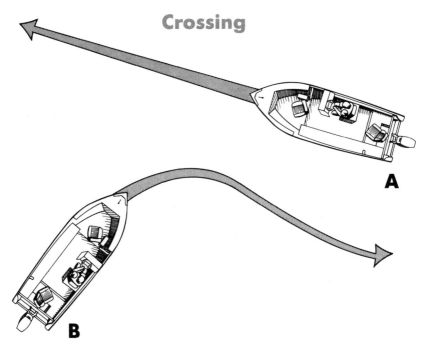

A

B

When two boats approach each other at a right angle, the boat on the starboard (right) side has the right-of-way. The privileged boat (A) must hold course and speed while the burdened boat (B) must keep clear and pass behind the boat with the right-of-way.

diving. Everyone has the right to pursue their interests and a right to use public waters, so long as they do not interfere with another person's right to enjoy his favorite activity.

Boat Handling

Before heading out to open water, learn how your boat maneuvers. Unlike an automobile, a boat turns at the rear (stern), not at the front (bow). You turn a motorboat by pushing the stern in the opposite direction of the turn. Outboards and stern drive units are much like a car—they respond almost instantly because the propeller and rudder turn as a unit.

As you turn, your bow makes a small circle while the stern swings out widely. Keep this "stern swing" in mind when in tight quarters.

How fast can a watercraft stop? Does it take a longer or shorter distance than a car traveling at the same speed? It depends on the craft and numerous other factors.

Every operator should know his boat's stopping distance at various speeds after the throttle has been closed. Boats do not have brakes like automobiles! The only way to slow a boat quickly is to shift it into reverse. However, this should be done *only* at *slow* speeds or it can damage the motor and possibly sink the craft.

A feeling for a craft's behavior can be developed by doing several turns at various speeds. A smart skipper never makes tight, sudden, high-speed turns. You could flip the craft or throw your passengers overboard. Many capsizing accidents are caused by sharp turns at high speeds.

To prevent damage to the motor, care must be taken to keep the lower unit from hitting the lake bottom or any other object. Remember, most larger engines are outfitted with a power trim and tilt unit that prohibits the motor from kicking up if an object is hit thereby increasing the likelihood you will damage or destroy the engine.

Rules Of The Road

There are traffic rules afloat, as well as on our highways. Common sense tells us we should know what to do when passing, meeting and crossing the path of another craft. These rules are simple and provide uniform patterns of passing and direction that otherwise would not exist.

1. Non-motorized craft have the right-of-way over motorized craft in all situations, except when the non-motorized craft is overtaking or passing.

2. When two boats approach each other head on, each must alter their course to the right to avoid a collision.

3. If two boats approach each other at a right angle, the one on the right (starboard) has the right-of-way.

4. Small boats should not insist on the right-of-way when approaching large commercial vessels, which are limited in maneuverability.

5. When passing another boat going the same direction, maintain sufficient distance to avoid collision or endangering the other craft with your wake. If you are being passed, do not alter your course or speed.

Take a moment every so often to review these rules of the road so they remain fresh in your mind. The explanations and illustrations apply to boats on inland waters. Rules on different waterways are generally similar. However, you should study the

Overtaking

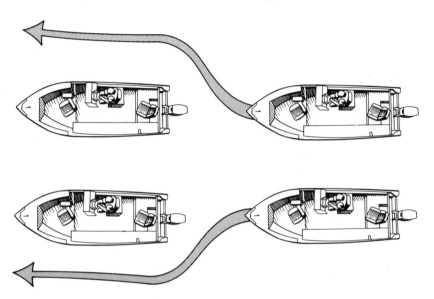

In an overtaking situation, the boat being overtaken has the right-of-way but it must hold to its course and speed. To overtake and pass, signal well in advance by one short whistle blast for passing to starboard, two short blasts for passing to port. A boat should not pass until it receives a similar signal in answer from the boat being overtaken.

rules applying to the lakes and rivers in your area.

Mindful Boating Procedures

The following provisions, though not *rules of the road*, will aid in developing orderly and safe boating patterns:

1. Operate your watercraft at a slow, no-wake speed when you are close to swimming areas, docks, rafts, moored watercraft and fishing boats, or when signs or buoys direct you to do so.

2. Do not enter prohibited areas which are lawfully marked by buoys or signs.

3. Keep to the right in narrow channels and operate at slow speeds.

4. At night, running lights indicate which boat has the right-of-way. The green light is on the starboard (right) and a red light on the port (left) side of the craft. If the red and white lights are the only ones visible, then that boat is privileged and has the right-of-way, and the other boat should give way.

5. Though *you* may have the right-of-way, always use common sense. Just because you're in the right, don't assume the other boat will yield.

The Weather—Its Importance

Weather is a major concern of fishermen and other boaters. Weather can change suddenly and some of the worst storms seem to strike when least expected. There are a number of good sources of weather information. Before you set out, check local television and radio stations, read the forecast in the newspaper or call the nearest National Weather Service office, especially if the weather looks threatening.

A portable radio tuned to a local station is also a valuable source of weather information. Most stations broadcast routine weather forecasts and in addition, notify listeners of serious, unexpected storms. If you're listening to an AM station and start having problems with static, there may be a thunderstorm in the vicinity.

Above all, be alert to weather you can see. There are no hard and fast rules regarding weather, but there are signs that do indicate changes:

•A rising barometer indicates fair weather and a rise in wind velocity; a falling barometer indicates stormy or rainy weather.

•Watch for wind shifts.

•Watch for distant lightning in addition to the rough water that comes with most storms. Remember, your boat will be the tallest point in the immediate area and could be hit. Sailboats with metal or wooden masts are even more vulnerable to lightning strikes.

What To Do If You're Caught In A Storm

If an unusually severe storm hits and you are unable to reach shore, the following are some emergency procedures to remember:

1. Put on your personal flotation device if you haven't done so already.

2. Head for shore if possible.

3. Head into the waves at an angle.

4. Reduce your speed, but keep just enough power to maintain headway.

5. Seat your passengers in the bottom of the boat, have them put on their PFDs and stay as close to the centerline as possible.

6. Keep bilges free from water.

7. If motor fails, trail a sea anchor on a line from the bow to keep the boat headed into the waves. A bucket or a shirt with neck and sleeves knotted together will do the job in an emergency.

8. Drop an anchor and ride out the storm if all else fails.

If Your Boat Does Start To Sink:

•Find out where the leak is coming from and attempt to plug it with anything that's handy. If you can't plug it, start to pump or bail out water.

•If you have an inboard or stern-drive engine, let the engine help bail the boat by disconnecting the water intake hose from the inlet valve and holding it below the water level in the boat. Don't forget to close the inlet valve.

•Signal for help by blowing your horn, waving a flag or any other way to attract attention.

•Stay with your boat if it stays afloat, even if it capsizes!

Alcohol's Impact On Boating

It's been estimated that the over-use of alcohol is involved in approximately half of all boating accidents. This includes not only the collisions, but anglers who drown after falling out of their boats on peaceful afternoons.

The responsible consumption of alcohol and boating have often been associated with one another. However, over-use and abuse of alcohol have the same undesirable effects on the boater as they do for the driver on the highway. Here is a summary:

1. Balance—Most people who die in boating accidents fall out of a craft which may or may not have capsized in the process. Balance is one of the first things affected by alcohol. You may not notice this decrease, but your body will, and a small boat is not the most stable platform to debate this point.

2. Coordination—As the alcohol level in your body increases, your ability to coordinate diminishes. An intoxicated boater will have extreme difficulty in trying to swim or reach a lifesaving device, regardless of his or her swimming abilities while sober.

3. Vision—Vision is also affected by alcohol. For example, glare recovery time is reduced. Add the "tunnel vision" effect induced by boat vibrations, and you further handicap the boat operator.

4. Judgment and Risk Taking—The average person is more likely to lose his or her ability to reason after too many drinks, possibly causing them to take unnecessary chances.

5. Reaction Time—Physical reflexes can be slowed by over-consumption of alcohol. This can create a dangerous delay if the operator has to react quickly.

With a little common sense, boating is one of the safest pastimes in our way of life. It's up to you, however, to apply that common sense to your consumption of alcohol when you engage in these activities.

Laws You Should Know

There are many federal, state and local laws that apply to boating. It's to all boaters' advantage to read through the regulations every year or so to keep up on law changes and avoid potential trouble with the law.

We will not cover all federal, state and local laws here because they can vary from location to location. What we will cover are some of the federal laws that apply directly to personal safety. Most of these items are common sense, but in the course of a fishing trip may be forgotten.

For a complete set of rules contact the nearest Coast Guard station and your local law enforcement office.

Law Enforcement

A vessel underway, when hailed by a Coast Guard vessel, is required to maneuver in such a manner that permits a boarding officer to come aboard.

Other federal, state and local law enforcement officials may board and examine your vessel at any time, whether it is numbered or not.

It's important to note that the Coast Guard may impose a civil penalty up to $5,000 for failure to comply with the unified Inland Rules of the Road (Inland Navigation Rules Act of 1980).

Boating While Intoxicated

Operating a vessel while intoxicated became a specific federal offense effective in 1988. This law set standards for determining when an individual is intoxicated. A Blood Alcohol level of .10 percent or higher (.08 percent in Utah) is considered intoxicated for operators of recreational vessels being used only for pleasure. Violators are subject to civil penalty not to exceed $1,000 or criminal penalty not to exceed $5,000, one year imprisonment or both.

Negligence

Negligent or grossly negligent operation of a vessel which endangers lives and property is prohibited by law. The Coast Guard may impose a civil penalty for negligent operation. *Grossly negligent operation* is a criminal offense and an operator may be fined up to $5,000, imprisoned for one year or both. Some examples of actions that may constitute negligent or grossly negligent operation are:

- Operating a boat in a swimming area.
- Operating a boat while under the influence of alcohol or drugs.
- Excessive speed in the vicinity of other boats or in dangerous waters.
- Hazardous water skiing practices.
- Bowriding, also riding on seatback, gunwale or transom.

Termination Of Use

A Coast Guard boarding officer who observes a boat being operated in an *unsafe condition*, specifically defined by law or regulation, and who determines that an *especially hazardous condition* exists, may direct the operator to take immediate steps to correct the condition, including returning to port. This law may be applied when:

- Insufficient number of Coast Guard approved personal

Alcohol Concentration Chart

| Drinks* | \| Body Weight In Pounds | | | | | | | | BOAT OPERATION |
	100	120	140	160	180	200	220	240	
1	.04	.03	.03	.02	.02	.02	.02	.02	BE CAREFUL
2	.08	.06	.05	.05	.04	.04	.03	.03	
3	.11	.09	.08	.07	.06	.06	.05	.05	OPERATION IMPAIRED
4	.15	.12	.11	.09	.08	.08	.07	.06	
5	.19	.16	.13	.12	.11	.09	.09	.08	
6	.23	.19	.16	.14	.13	.11	.10	.09	
7	.26	.22	.19	.16	.15	.13	.12	.11	DO NOT OPERATE
8	.30	.25	.21	.19	.17	.15	.14	.13	
9	.34	.28	.24	.21	.19	.17	.15	.14	
10	.38	.31	.27	.23	.21	.19	.17	.16	

*Subtract .015% for each hour of drinking.
(1 glass wine = 1 bottle of beer = 1 highball)

By the chart above, you can see that only two drinks impair the functioning of people under 160 pounds! Remember, alcohol isn't the sport. Fishing is the sport. Enjoy it safely.

flotation devices (PFDs) on board.
•Insufficient fire extinguishers on board.
•Craft is loaded beyond manufacturer's recommended safe loading capacity.
•Improper navigation light display.
•Fuel leakage.
•Fuel in bilges.
•Improper ventilation.
•Improper backfire flame control.
•Operating in regulated boating areas during predetermined adverse conditions (applies in 13th Coast Guard district only).
•Voyage deemed manifestly unsafe.

An operator who refuses to correct the condition can be cited for failure to comply with the directions of a Coast Guard boarding officer, as well as for the specific violations which were the basis for the termination order. Violators may be fined not more than $1,000 or imprisoned not more than one year or both, depending on the situation.

Personal Flotation Devices (PFDs)

PFDs must be Coast Guard approved, in serviceable condition and of appropriate size for the intended user. Wearable PFDs must be readily accessible, meaning you must be able to put them on in a reasonable amount of time in an emergency (such as vessel sinking or on fire). They should not be stowed in plastic bags, in locked or closed compartments or have other gear stowed on top of them. Throwable devices must be immediately available for use. Though not required, a PFD should be worn when the vessel is underway. A PFD can save your life, but only if you wear it.

Boats less than 16 feet in length (including canoes and kayaks of any length) must be equipped with one Type I, II, III, IV or V PFD (see diagram) for each person aboard.

Boats 16 feet and longer must be equipped with one Type I, II, III, or V for each person aboard, plus one Type IV.

Federal law does not require PFDs on racing shells, rowing skulls and racing kayaks; state laws vary.

Types Of PFDs

A Type I PFD, or Off-Shore Life Jacket provides the most buoyancy. It is effective for all waters, especially open, rough or remote waters where rescue may be delayed. It is designed to turn most unconscious wearers in the water to a face-up position. The Type I comes in two sizes. The adult size provides at least 22 pounds of buoyancy, the child size, at least 11 pounds.

A Type II PFD, or Near-Shore Buoyant Vest is intended for calm, inland waters or where there is a good chance of quick rescue. This type will turn some unconscious wearers to a face-up position in the water. The turning action is not as pronounced as a Type I PFD and it will not turn as many persons under the same conditions. An adult-size device provides at least 15 ½ pounds of buoyancy; a medium child size provides 11 pounds. Infant and small child sizes each provide at least 7 pounds of buoyancy.

A Type III PFD, or Flotation Aid is good for calm, inland water, or where there is good chance of quick rescue. It is designed so wearers can place themselves in a face-up

Off-Shore Life Jacket

Near-Shore Buoyant Vest

Flotation Aid

Throwable Devices

There are a number of different types of PFDs approved by the United States Coast Guard. They include the Type I Offshore Jacket, Type II Near-shore Buoyant Vest, Type III Flotation Aid, and Type IV Throwable Device.

position in the water. The wearer may have to tilt his head back to avoid turning face-down in the water. The Type III has the same minimum buoyancy as a Type II PFD. It comes in many styles, colors and sizes and is generally the most comfortable type for continuous wear. Float coats, fishing vests and vests designed with features suitable for various sports activities are examples of this type of PFD.

A Type IV PFD, or Throwable Device is intended for calm, inland waters with heavy boat traffic; where help is always present. It is designed to be thrown to a person in the water and grasped and held by the user until rescued. It is not designed to be worn. Type IV devices include buoyant cushions, ring buoys and horseshoe buoys.

A Type V PFD, or Special Use Device is intended for specific activities and may be carried instead of another PFD only if used according to the approval conditions on the label. Some Type V devices provide significant hypothermia protection. Varieties include deck suits, work vests, board sailing vests and hybrid PFDs.

A Type V Hybrid Inflatable PFD is the least bulky of all PFD types. It contains a small amount of inherent buoyancy, and an inflatable chamber. Its performance is equal to a Type I, II or III PFD (as noted on PFD label) when inflated. Hybrid PFDs must be worn when underway to be acceptable.

Visual Distress Signals

All vessels, used on coastal waters, the Great Lakes, territorial seas and those waters connected directly to them, up to a point where a body of water is less than two miles wide, must be equipped with visual distress signals. Vessels owned in the United States operating on the high seas must be equipped with visual distress signals. The following vessels are not required to carry day signals but must carry night signals when operating from sunset to sunrise:

•Recreational boats less than 16 feet in length.
•Boats participating in organized events such as races, regattas or marine parades.
•Manually propelled boats.

Pyrotechnic visual distress signals must be Coast Guard approved, in serviceable condition and readily accessible. They are marked with a date showing the service life, which must not be expired. Launchers manufactured before January 1, 1981, intended for use with approved signals, are not required to be Coast Guard approved. If pyrotechnic devices are selected, a minimum of three are required. That is three signals for day use and three signals for night. Some pyrotechnic signals meet both day and night use requirements. Pyrotechnic devices should be stored in a cool, dry location. A watertight container painted red or orange and prominently marked "distress signals" is recommended.

United States Coast Guard (USCG) approved pyrotechnic visual distress signals and associated devices include:

•Pyrotechnic red flares, hand-held or aerial.
•Pyrotechnic orange smoke, hand-held or floating.
•Launchers for aerial red meteors or parachute flares.

Non-pyrotechnic visual distress signals must be in serviceable condition, readily accessible and certified by the manufacturer as complying with USCG requirements, they include:

•Orange distress flag.
•Electric distress light.
The distress flag is a day signal only. It must be at least 3x3 feet with a black square and ball on an orange background. It is most distinctive when attached and waved on a paddle or boathook or flown from a mast.

The electric distress light is accepted for night use only and must automatically flash the international SOS distress signal. This is an unmistakable distress signal. A standard flashlight is not acceptable as a visual distress signal.

Under Inland Navigation Rules, a high intensity white light flashing at regular intervals from 50-70 times per minute is considered a distress signal. Strobe lights used in inland waters shall only be used as a distress signal.

Regulations prohibit display of visual distress signals on the water under any circumstances except when assistance is required to prevent immediate or potential danger to persons on board a vessel.

All distress signals have distinct advantages and disadvantages, no single device is ideal under all conditions or suitable for all purposes. Pyrotechnics are excellent distress signals, universally recognized. However, there is potential for injury and property damage if not properly handled. These devices produce a very hot flame and the residue can cause burns and ignite flammable material. Pistol launched and hand-held parachute flares and meteors have many characteristics of a firearm and must be handled with caution.

Fire Extinguishers

Approved extinguishers are classified by a letter and number symbol. The letter indicates the type of fire the unit is designed to extinguish (Type B is designed to extinguish flammable liquids such as gasoline, oil and grease fires). The number indicates the relative size of the extinguisher (minimum extinguishing agent weight).

Approved extinguishers are hand-portable, either B-I or B-II classification and have the following characteristics:

Classes	Foam (gals)	CO_2 (lbs)	Dry Chemical (lbs)	Halon (lbs)
B-I	1.25	4	2	2.5
B-II	2.5	15	10	10

Fire extinguishers are required if any one or more of the following conditions exist:
- Inboard engines.
- Closed compartments under thwarts and seats where portable fuel tanks may be stored.
- Double bottoms not sealed to the hull or which are not completely filled with flotation materials.
- Closed living spaces.
- Closed stowage compartments in which combustible or flammable materials are stored.
- Permanently installed fuel tanks. Fuel tanks secured so they cannot be moved in case of fire or other emergency are considered "permanently" installed.

There are no gallon capacity limits to determine if a fuel tank is portable. If the weight of a fuel tank is such that persons on board cannot move it, the Coast Guard considers it permanently installed.

Dry chemical fire extinguishers without gauges or indicating devices must be inspected every six months. If the gross weight of a carbon dioxide extinguisher is reduced by more than 10 percent of the net weight, the extinguisher is not acceptable and must be recharged.

Check extinguishers regularly to ensure gauges are free and nozzles are clear.

Minimum number of hand portable fire extinguishers required:

Vessel Length	No Fixed System	With Approved Fixed System
Less than 26'	1 B-I	0
26' to 40'	2 B-I or 1 B-II	1 B-I
40' to 65'	3 B-I or 1 B-II and 1 B-I	2 B-I or 1 B-II

Coast Guard Approved extinguishers are identified by the following marking on the label: Marine Type USCG Approved, Size ..., Type ..., 162.208 ...

Navigation Rules

The Navigation Rules establish actions to be taken by vessels

Lights

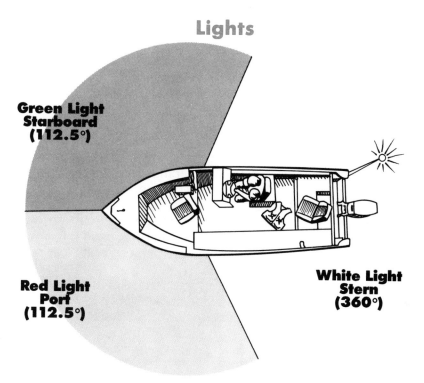

**Green Light
Starboard
(112.5°)**

**Red Light
Port
(112.5°)**

**White Light
Stern
(360°)**

All boats must display lights after sunset. This illustration shows a common light placement on motorboats.

to avoid collision. The vessel operator is responsible for knowing and following applicable navigation rules. There are different whistle signals and actions used by recreational vessels in crossing, meeting and overtaking situations.

Navigation Lights

Recreational vessels are required to display navigation lights between sunset and sunrise and other periods of reduced visibility (fog, rain and haze). The U.S. Coast Guard Navigation Rules, International-Inland encompasses lighting requirements for every description of watercraft.

Reporting Boating Accidents

All boating accidents must be reported by the operator or owner of the vessel to the proper marine law enforcement authority for the state in which the accident occurred.

Immediate notification is required for fatal accidents. If a person dies or disappears as a result of a recreational boating accident the nearest state boating authority must be notified without delay, providing the following information:
- Date, time and exact location of the accident.
- Name of each person who died or disappeared.
- Number and name of the vessel.
- Names and addresses of the owner and operator.

A formal report of a fatality must be filed within 48 hours. If, as a result of a boating or related equipment accident, a person sustains injuries that require more than first aid, a formal report must be filed.

Accidents involving more than $200 damage must be reported within 10 days. A formal report must be made if property damage exceeds $200; or there is a complete loss of a vessel.

If you need further information regarding accident reporting, please call the Boating Safety Hotline, 800-368-5647.

Lowhead Dams:
Dangerous Drowning Machines

ollowing a late September storm some years ago, a tragic chain of events connected with a lowhead dam on the rain-swollen Susquehanna River at Binghamton, New York. By the time the episode had ended 24 hours later, three persons were dead and four others had been injured. It should have taught river users and rescue personnel valuable lessons about dam safety. But it would be another five years and a number of fatalities later before thinking would change about the most dangerous of drowning machines: lowhead dams.

The tragedy at Binghamton started in early evening when two persons, who were rafting on the Susquehanna, were swept over the Rockbottom Dam and were trapped in the recirculating current below the dam. First, three fishermen in a boat attempted to rescue the pair, but their craft was caught up in the turbulent water. It capsized, and all three were thrown into the roiling water. One drowned, but the other two fishermen and the two rafters were rescued. However, the tragedy didn't end there.

The following day the local fire chief and two firemen in an outboard-powered boat attempted to recover the body of the drowned fisherman. As they attempted to reach the base of the dam, their craft was caught up in the recirculating current and the boat overturned. Attempts to rescue the firemen from shore failed and a second rescue boat carrying two sheriff's deputies, also trained in water rescue, met the same fate in the turbulent water. Fortunately, two of the firemen and the two deputies were rescued.

People began asking, "Why did this tragedy occur?"

Drowning Machines

Dams come in many sizes and shapes, ranging from huge, lock-and-dam structures on large rivers to small, lowhead dams on rivers and streams. Although there obviously are hazardous situations involving the larger dams, their size and design do not present the same kind of threat that the seemingly harmless lowhead dams do.

These dams are basically simple barriers and are usually no more than 10 feet high. They have no gates or devices to control water flow. Usually, water flows constantly over them. Most were built to provide water power for milling or to power generators or to control lake levels. In fact, they can be pleasant places in the summer when water levels are low.

During the spring or during other periods of high runoff, it can be a different story. Large volumes of water pouring over these dams create a churning backwash or recirculating current. This hydraulic, as it is often called, can pull any object, including a person, to the face of the dam where it is pushed to the bottom, released to the surface and then sucked back to the face of the dam to start the cycle all over again. This can continue indefinitely, and it can be impossible for a person to break out of the cycle by himself.

Adding to the life-threatening nature of the situation are these factors:

•Both faces of the dam usually consist of a vertical concrete abutment. Even if a victim struggles to the edge of the structure, chances are poor that he or she will have enough strength to climb the wall.

•Branches and other debris trapped in the hydraulic create an additional hazard to the victim.

•Temperature of the water at times of high runoff is usually low, decreasing survival time.

•Finally, air bubbles mixing in the water decrease its buoyancy by one-third. The victim has a hard time staying afloat, even with a personal flotation device (life preserver).

The combination of these factors makes these lowhead dams the nearly perfect drowning machine.

A Nationwide Concern

Problems with these dams are not confined to New York state. Fatal accidents like this have occurred in virtually every state. Several thousand of these dams are sprinkled across the country. Most were built in the 1800s and early 1900s; many have been abandoned or are not being used for their original purpose.

One such dam located on the Crow River in central Minnesota claimed the lives of three persons. As tragic as these deaths were, others have died in similar accidents elsewhere in the country in recent years. Even though warning signs and patrolling authorities attempt to keep people from these dangerous situations, fishermen, canoeists and adventurers continue to press their luck at the base of these "drowning machines."

Rescue Techniques: The Latest Advances

Only a few fortunate rescuers have survived a trip through the current below a lowhead dam. Dennis Lutz, a Miamisburg, Ohio fireman, described his experience attempting to rescue a teenager:

"You can't believe how powerful the current is. As my buddy and I approached the dam, the boat seemed to rise and move rapidly forward. It's like being caught by a monster. It just won't let go."

The rescue boat filled with water and capsized as the strong current sucked it into the dam. Lutz was dragged down into the hydraulic, battered along the bottom, caught in a submerged tree, wrenched free and pushed to the surface, only to have the cycle repeated. Lutz was finally rescued, but his companion and the teenager drowned.

In response to this 1980 tragedy, the Ohio Department of Natural Resources' Division of Watercraft, with the assistance of firemen and the Red Cross, developed techniques that can help anyone faced with a fast-water rescue problem.

These techniques have been put into practice across the U.S. in recent years.

"In any rescue operation, we first reassure the victims," says James French of the Ohio DNR. "Next we try to rescue from shore. As a last resort, we attempt direct rescue from a boat. But we never take the boat into the hydraulic of a dam. The risk is simply too high."

Lowhead dam rescues are either shore- or boat-based. Shore-based rescues are used on dams up to 300 feet wide which have accesses at both ends. If rescue by throw-line is not possible, a line with a rescue buoy in the center is placed across the river. This can be done with a line gun, or by using a boat downstream from the dam. Rescuers on both sides of the river then work the line up to the victim and pull him to shore.

Dams where access to both ends is not possible or dams that are wider than 300 feet generally require a boat-based rescue, using two boats which are connected by a safety line. One boat attempts to get close enough to cast a flotation device on a line to the victim. The second boat stands by downstream to assist in the rescue and keep the first craft from being pulled into the dam.

Specialized watercraft and a coupling which allows an ordinary fire hose to be inflated with compressed air and pushed out to a victim also have been used successfully.

The basic rule is that rescue techniques must be realistic and simple. Dams *are* dangerous so it's important that NAFC members and other river users give them the respect they deserve. No fish is worth risking your life.

Basic Rescue Techniques

An accident can happen whenever you are fishing despite all the precautions you may have taken. If an accident does occur, follow these simple steps:

1. Assist yourself and others who are in trouble, if at all possible. A number of tips are outlined in this chapter.

2. Never risk your life or the lives of others to save equipment.

3. Summon help, if necessary.

4. Report all boating accidents to the county sheriff as soon as possible. (This is required by law if there is substantial property damage, injury or a death.)

Survival

In a boating accident you may be forced into the water or thrown overboard. Stay with the boat if it is still afloat and not in danger, and attempt to reboard if at all possible. If this isn't possible, hang on to the boat and use it as a support. Most newer craft have built-in flotation and can support the weight of the occupants even after capsizing or swamping. A boat, even if it's overturned and partially submerged, can be spotted by rescuers more easily than someone floating in the water.

If your boat does sink or drift away, you have several other options. Here are some suggestions, with emphasis placed on the problems associated with cold water (generally less than 70 degrees Fahrenheit or 21 degrees Celsius) commonly associated with boating fatalities in Northern states.

1. Put your PFD on, and make sure it's securely fastened.

2. Items left floating after an accident (boat cushions, gas cans, minnow buckets, coolers and oars) can be used as improvised flotation devices.

3. Ordinary clothing will preserve body heat in cold water and help you float. Avoid undressing unless your clothing severely hampers movement. A shirt or coat can be used as a flotation aid by simply buttoning it up at the collar and forcing air into the torso by blowing in the space between the top buttons and collar. Hip boots and waders will also hold air and assist in floating.

4. Survival floating or treading water may be necessary until help arrives if you have no other means of support. In cold water, treading water is preferred over survival floating, since there is less heat loss when the head remains out of the water.

5. Swimming for shore should be considered only as a last resort if no other means of survival are at hand. It has been shown that in water of 50 degrees Fahrenheit, a good swimmer has only about a 50 percent chance of making it to shore that is one mile away! Weigh your odds before starting out. Swimming may be advisable in warmer water if shore is close.

Hypothermia And Its Impact On Survival

Hypothermia is a factor in many boating fatalities each year. Hypothermia simply means that the body is losing heat faster than it is producing it, causing a decrease in the body's inner temperature. The greatest danger to those persons using boats is from immersion in cold water (less than 70 degrees Fahrenheit). Here are a few suggestions to increase your survival time in cold water in addition to those mentioned previously.

Hypothermia Chart

Water Temp. (F.)	Exhaustion Or Unconsciousness	Expected Time Of Survival
32.5	Under 15 Min.	Under 15-45 Min.
32.5-40.0	15-30 Min.	30-90
40-50	30-60 Min.	1-3 Hr.
50-60	1-2 Hr.	1-6 Hr.
60-70	2-7 Hr.	2-40 Hr.
70-80	3-12 Hr.	3-Indef.
Over 80	Indef.	Indef.

This chart shows times of exhaustion or unconsciousness and expected time of survival when immersed in varying water temperatures. These times are approximate only. They may vary from person to person.

1. Reboard your craft, even if it's filled with water or capsized. The more of your body you can get out of the water, the better off you are, since water takes heat from the body many times faster than air at the same temperature.

2. Don't take off your clothing unless it's absolutely necessary, since it helps trap body heat like a diver's wet suit.

3. Remain still. Swimming, treading water or survival floating all use up valuable energy and increase the rate of heat loss.

4. Wear your PFD. A PFD increases survival time in cold water in two ways: It decreases the movement necessary to remain in cold water, and retains heat.

Basic Rescues

Many drownings occur each year within a few feet of safety. Even a nonswimmer can save a life if he or she knows how to use these basic rescue techniques.

1. If the victim is within arm's reach, lie flat on the dock and extend your arm to the victim. Grasp the victim's hand or wrist and pull to safety. Do not overreach or you may be pulled into the water.

2. If the victim is beyond reach, use a shirt, towel, branch, oar, pole rope or other object. Allow the victim to grab one end and pull him or her back to safety.

3. If the victim is too far away for a reaching-type rescue, throw them a paddle, spare tire, gas can, insulated jug or anything else that floats. Be careful not to *hit* him or her.

4. If a row boat is handy, row to the victim and extend an oar or paddle. Do not allow them to board unless the boat is stable. Row slowly back to safety while the victim hangs on to the back of the boat. If the victim is too weak or too scared to hang on, hold them until more help arrives.

5. If a motorboat is used, *stop the engine a few feet away and glide* to the victim from the downwind or leeward side. Moving the shift lever to neutral *may not* stop the propeller. Pull the victim into the craft.

6. Even though you may be considered a good swimmer, if you're not trained in lifesaving techniques, you should not attempt a rescue involving direct contact with a person in trouble. The result could be both of you drowning. Instead, swim close enough to extend a towel, shirt or any object that floats so the person may cling to it until rescued.

First Aid

Most fishermen run into situations where knowledge of first aid comes in handy. This brief guide will help in those situations, but does not take the place of a complete course in first aid or cardiopulmonary resuscitation (CPR). Such courses are offered by the American Red Cross. Also, make sure you outfit your boat with a good first aid kit.

Artificial Respiration

The most effective way to restore normal breathing is to use mouth-to-mouth (or mouth-to-nose) resuscitation. Follow these steps:

1. Begin immediately.

2. Place the victim on his or her back if at all possible. However, if the victim can't be moved, but the airway is clear, mouth-to-mouth breathing can be given with the victim in any position, even in the water.

3. Clear the airway of any foreign matter or obstruction.

4. Tilt the head backward to open the air passage.

5. Pinch the nostrils to prevent air leakage.

6. Place your mouth over the victim's mouth so that you form an airtight seal.

7. The first breath should determine whether or not there is a clear air passage. You should be able to see the victim's chest rise and fall.

8. Listen for the rush of air from the victim as you remove your mouth. If you do not hear air coming, recheck the head and jaw position and clear the victim's mouth.

9. The breathing rate should be 12 times a minute for adults, and 20 times a minute for small children.

Wounds And Bleeding

Bleeding from wounds, whether serious or not, can usually be controlled by applying direct pressure. Press the wound with a clean cloth or your bare hand. For serious bleeding a large cloth should be applied and bandaged into place. If it becomes soaked with blood, more layers of cloth should be added without removing the original dressing.

If an arm or leg is bleeding severely, but is not broken, it should be raised slightly while applying direct pressure to stop the bleeding. Removing a fish hook which has penetrated the skin is not difficult. If the hook doesn't penetrate deeply enough for the barb to catch, simply remove the hook by backing it out. If the barb is embedded and a physician is unavailable, push the hook through until the barb protrudes and snip off with wire cutter. Cleanse the wound and cover it with a bandage. See a physician as soon as possible.

Burns

A burn is a serious and painful injury and should be treated carefully. First aid objectives are to relieve pain, prevent infection and treat for shock.

Burns are classified into three degrees. First degree burns redden the skin, second degree burns blister the skin and third degree burns char the burn area.

Burns that are not serious should be placed immediately in cold (not ice) water. Do not apply water if the skin is broken or charred. Ointments, sprays or antiseptics should *not* be applied to any severe burn. Apply a dry, sterile dressing to the burn area and have the victim drink liquids if conscious. Leave all additional treatment to a physician.

Sunburn can be just as severe and painful as other burns. The only completely effective method of prevention is coverage by clothing. A sun cream that filters out the harmful rays should be used freely and often on exposed skin.

Broken Bones, Dislocations And Spinal Injuries

Chances are that the most serious injury a fisherman will have to deal with is a barbed hook stuck in the finger, but that long-awaited trip into the wilderness to a little-known lake where the fish are "this big" can sometimes result in accidents. Help may be some distance away, so it pays to be prepared to deal with emergencies that might arise.

Broken bones or fractures are of two general types, closed and open. A closed fracture does not break the skin. An open fracture has a connecting wound. First aid for the two types is similar, though the wound and bleeding must also receive attention in open fractures. Swelling, change of shape, pain or change in color are indicators of common fractures. If a fracture is suspected, a splint that immobilizes the broken bone and the joints above and below it should be used. Padding between the limb and the splint should be used to protect the limb.

A dislocation is the slipping of the end of a bone from a joint. Don't try to put a dislocated bone back into place. Immobilize and protect the dislocation in its most comfortable position until the victim can reach medical care.

Injuries to the neck, head and back may result from water accidents. If the victim is conscious, see if he or she can move their feet, legs, arms and hands. If there is any loss of movement, or feeling, or if there is pain in the back or neck, a spinal injury should be suspected.

Never move the victim of a spinal injury any more than necessary. Don't allow his head to turn forward or sideways, or his back to bend. If he is in the water and not in danger, *do not remove him!* Water acts as an excellent support until proper help can be obtained. If transportation is absolutely necessary, use a firm, full-length support, such as a door or picnic bench. If mouth-to-mouth breathing is necessary, tip the

Levels Of Hypothermia

Core Temp. F	Symptoms
99.6	"Normal" rectal temperature
98.6	"Normal" oral temperature
96.8	Elevated metabolic rate
95.0	Maximum shivering
93.2	Victim still conscious and responsive
91.4	Severe hypothermia below this temperature
89.6	Consciousness clouded; pupils dilated; shivering stops
86.0	Progressive loss of consciousness; muscle rigidity increases; pulse and blood pressure difficult to obtain; breathing decreases
82.4	Ventricular fibrillation possible if heart irritated (by jostling victim or performing CPR)
80.6	Voluntary motion ceases; pupils nonreactive to light.
78.8	Victim seldom conscious
77.0	Ventricular fibrillation may develop spontaneously
68.0	Heart standstill
64.4	Lowest accidental hypothermia victim to recover
48.2	Lowest artificially cooled hypothermia patient to recover

This chart shows levels of body temperature and the symptoms that will arise when hypothermia sets in. These are generalizations; symptoms may vary from victim to victim.

head back only as far as needed to open the airway.

If the victim is unconscious you should suspect a head injury. Some symptoms of a head injury are bleeding from the head, ears or nose, unequal pupil size; and either a slow and strong or fast and weak pulse rate. Make the victim comfortable and seek medical attention immediately.

Hypothermia

The effects and symptoms of hypothermia can vary with the temperature and length of exposure. One of the first indicators is uncontrollable shivering which may give way to muscle spasms and loss of the use of arms and legs. During the time these symptoms are occurring, the victim may be confused and deny that there is a problem. As the victim's body temperature continues to fall, pulse and breathing decrease and his or her heartbeat becomes uneven. If no action is taken by a rescuer at this point, their body temperature will continue to drop and the victim will die from heart and respiratory failure.

If you rescue someone who has been in cold water here are the important points to remember:

1. Get the victim out of the water and into a protected area.

2. Replace wet clothing with dry and wrap victim in a sleeping bag or blankets to keep warm.

3. Transport the victim to a hospital as soon as possible.

4. Handle hypothermia victims gently, do not allow them to walk unless absolutely necessary.

5. If semi-conscious or worse, try to keep the victim awake. If there is difficulty in breathing insure an open air passage. If breathing stops, use mouth-to-mouth resuscitation or, if you are properly trained, cardiopulmonary resuscitation (CPR) if no pulse is detected.

6. If you encounter a victim who has been immersed in cold water (less than 70 degrees Fahrenheit) for a long period of time and is not breathing, begin mouth-to-mouth resuscitation and CPR immediately, even if it appears hopeless. In some cases, victims of cold-water accidents have been successfully resuscitated without brain damage after periods of almost one hour underwater.

Section 2

RECIPES

Bass	Halibut	Sole
Bluefish	Mahi Mahi	Striper
Bluegill	Muskie	Sturgeon
Carp	Northern	Swordfish
Catfish	Panfish	Trout
Cod	Perch	Tuna
Crappie	Pickerel	Walleye
Flounder	Redfish	Yellowtail
Grouper	Salmon	Chef's Choice
Haddock	Snapper	

Stuffed Bass

Serves: 4-6
Prep Time: 20 minutes

1 3-lb. bass	¹/₄ cup parsley, minced
¹/₂ cup butter	¹/₂ cup dry bread crumbs
¹/₂ cup onion, finely chopped	1 T. lemon juice
	1 tsp. salt
¹/₂ cup fresh mushrooms, chopped	¹/₂ tsp. pepper

Wash fish in cold water and pat dry with paper towel. Place butter in 2-qt. microwave-safe casserole dish. Cook on high for 45 seconds until melted. Stir in remaining ingredients and pack lightly into fish. Close with toothpicks. Place fish in 12x18-inch baking dish. Cover head and tail with aluminum foil, then cover dish with plastic wrap. Ventilate by puncturing in two places. Cook on high power 16-18 minutes or until fish flakes easily. Let stand 5 minutes before serving.

Jan Rutledge
Killeen, Texas

Bermuda Bass

Serves: 2
Prep Time: 1 hour

1 lb. striper fillets, skinned butter	juice of 1 lemon
	1 cup white wine
1 Bermuda onion, thickly sliced	6 bay leaves
	8 oz. sour cream

Butter bottom of 1¹/₂-qt. casserole dish and place onion at bottom. Lay fish on onion and pour lemon juice and white wine over fish. Top with bay leaves and sour cream. Bake in 350-degree oven for 30 minutes. Remove fish and whisk juices together. Pour over fish.

Walter Womack
Las Vegas, Nevada

Baked Stuffed Bass

Serves: 6
Prep Time: 1 hour

1 3-lb. bass	pinch of garlic powder
1 onion, chopped	pinch of oregano
1 green pepper, chopped	lemon juice
stuffing mix	salt and pepper to taste
margarine	

Saute onion and green pepper in margarine until tender, then add to stuffing mix with oregano and garlic salt. Add enough water to stuffing mix until mixture reaches desired consistency. Sprinkle salt and pepper inside bass, then fill with stuffing mix. Close fish and secure. Place fish in baking dish lined with aluminum foil and brush with butter. Sprinkle with seasoning salt. Bake at 350 degrees for approximately 12 minutes per pound. Baste with margarine and lemon juice.

Raymond Smith
Morgantown, West Virginia

Bass With A Touch Of Class

Serves: 2
Prep Time: 20 minutes

1 bass fillet	1 small can crab meat,
salt and pepper	drained
seasoned salt	1 medium onion, chopped
	butter

Lay bass in microwave-safe dish. Sprinkle with seasoned salt and pepper, chopped onion and butter. Cover with waxed paper and cook on high for 10 minutes. Remove and place crab meat over top of fish. Sprinkle with a little more seasoned salt and a touch more butter. Cover with waxed paper and cook 3 more minutes. Serve.

Tom Polkey
Escanaba, Michigan

Bass Cakes

Serves: 4
Prep Time: 30 minutes

4 medium bass halves	**2 T. butter**
3 cups potatoes, diced	**$^1/_4$ tsp. pepper**
1 egg	**$^1/_4$ cup vegetable oil**
1 T. salt	

Chop bass into small pieces. Boil diced potatoes until soft. Drain and beat with hand mixer. Add egg, salt, butter and pepper. Add bass pieces. Do not mix. Drop by tablespoon onto hot skillet and turn when browned. Serve immediately.

Marvin Bailey
Sebring, Florida

Bass Melt

Serves: 2-4
Prep Time: 30 minutes

$1^1/_2$ cups bass, cooked	**$^1/_8$ tsp. pepper**
$^1/_4$ cup cucumber, finely chopped	**$^1/_2$ tsp. onion powder**
1 T. radish, chopped	**4 large tomatoes, thinly sliced**
1 T. mayonnaise	**4-8 bread slices, toasted**
1 T. sour cream	**4 American cheese slices**
$^1/_2$ tsp. salt	

Set oven to broil. In small bowl, mix fish, cucumber, radish, mayonnaise, sour cream, salt, pepper and onion powder. Place mixture on tomato slices on each piece of bread. Spread fish mixture over tomatoes and spread to edges. Top each piece with 1 cheese slice. Place on baking sheet and broil 2-3 inches away from heat until cheese melts, or about 2 minutes. Top each sandwich with another piece of toast, if desired.

Doug Frick
North Richland Hills, Texas

Smothered Bass Steaks

Serves: 4
Prep Time: 30-45 minutes

2 1-lb. bass steaks	1¹/₂ cups milk
¹/₂ tsp. salt	2 onions, sliced
¹/₄ tsp. pepper	1 T. lard
¹/₄ cup flour	2 bacon slices, chopped

Combine salt and pepper with flour and sprinkle over fish. Place in baking dish and add milk. Bake at 425 degrees for 10 minutes. Brown onions in lard. Place bacon pieces and onions on fish and bake another 10-15 minutes or until fish flakes with fork.

Brad Woodward
Oxford, Pennsylvania

White Bass Delight

Serves: 4
Prep Time: 30 minutes

8 white bass fillets	1 4-oz. can mushroom
2 T. oil, butter or	pieces
margarine	¹/₂ tsp. garlic powder
1 cup onion, chopped	¹/₂ tsp. black pepper
³/₄ cup green or red bell	1 tsp. paprika
pepper, chopped	lemon juice

Remove lateral line from fresh fillets. Cut fillets in half, then cut each piece in three equal parts. In large frying pan, heat oil. Add onion, bell pepper, mushrooms and fish. Mix garlic powder, pepper and paprika. After frying 2 minutes, sprinkle mixture over fish pieces and stir gently so as not to break up fish. Cover pan for 4 minutes. Stir gently again and flip fish. Cover and cook 3 minutes. Check fish for flakiness. When cooked, sprinkle with lemon juice and serve.

Peter Barnes
Marietta, New York

Bass Fillets

Serves: 2
Prep Time: 30 minutes

4 bass fillets	cooking oil or butter
1 cup pancake mix	paprika
salt and pepper	parsley
2 eggs, beaten	lemon slices

In pie dish, combine pancake mix and salt and pepper. Coat fillets with beaten eggs and coat with pancake mix. In large frying pan, heat butter or oil on medium heat. Drop coated fillets into pan and cook each side until golden brown. Sprinkle lightly with paprika and garnish with parsley and lemon slices. Serve.

Carlos Whitney
Greenville, New Hampshire

Arizona Bass

Serves: 4
Prep Time: 1 hour, 30 minutes

1 lb. bass fillets	$^1/_4$ tsp. pepper
1 large carrot, sliced	1 cup fresh mushrooms
$^1/_2$ cup onion, chopped	1 green pepper, chopped
4 potatoes, sliced into	4 oranges, quartered
$^1/_4$-inch pieces	$^1/_4$ cup butter
$^1/_2$ tsp. salt	

Butter Dutch oven and put in half of carrots, onions and potatoes. Then, layer bass fillets over vegetables. Lay rest of vegetables over fish and sprinkle with salt and pepper. Add mushrooms, green pepper and oranges for the final layer. Pour 2 cups water into oven and lay pats of butter over the combination. Bake at 350 degrees, turning once after 30 minutes. Bake another 30 minutes.

Lynn Adkins
Phoenix, Arizona

Baked Stuffed Freshwater Bass

Serves: 6
Prep Time: 30 minutes

1 **3- to 5-lb. freshwater bass**
  juice of 1 lemon
2 **T. butter**
6 **shallots, chopped**
1 **leek, use white part**
1 **T. parsley, chopped**
4 **tsp. capers, chopped**
2 **cups bread crumbs**
1 **tsp. salt**
$^1/_2$ **tsp. pepper**
1 **tsp. paprika**
  pinch of nutmeg
2 **cups sherry**
$^1/_2$ **cup melted butter**
3-4 **bread slices**

Clean fish and pat dry with paper towel. Rub fish all over with lemon juice. Melt butter in saucepan and add shallots, leek part, parsley and capers, then cover. Cook over low heat for 3 minutes. Add bread crumbs, salt, pepper, paprika, nutmeg and just enough sherry to moisten stuffing. Slice fish and insert stuffing. Secure with toothpicks. Place fish in greased baking dish. Combine melted butter and remainder of sherry. Wrap bread slices around fish and secure with toothpicks. Pour some butter and sherry mixture on bread. Bake at 350 degrees uncovered for 1 hour and 30 minutes for 4 lbs. of fish; 15 minutes less for 3 lbs. Baste occasionally with remainder of butter and sherry mixture. Remove bread slices 30 minutes before finished baking time.

Harold Delanty
Neola, Iowa

Missouri-Style Crispy Bass

Serves: 6
Prep Time: 15 minutes

3 lbs. bass fillets	**1 tsp. pepper**
1 cup cornmeal	**1 cup milk**
1/2 cup oat flour	**4 T. melted margarine**
1/2 tsp. baking powder	**salt and pepper to taste**
1 tsp. garlic powder	
1 tsp. dill weed	
1/2 tsp. basil	
1/2 tsp. oregano	

Combine dry ingredients. Dip fish into milk, then coat with cornmeal mixture. Place fish in broiler-safe dish. Brush or sprinkle melted margarine onto fillets. Broil fish uncovered on middle rack for 10 minutes or until golden brown. Season to taste and enjoy.

Barry Poulton
Columbia, Missouri

Mike's Texas Fried Bass

Serves: 4
Prep Time: 20 minutes

2 lbs. bass fillets
Italian salad dressing
2 cups cornmeal
salt and pepper to taste
cooking oil

Marinate fillets for 1 hour in salad dressing in refrigerator. Place cornmeal and salt and pepper in bag. Put fillets in bag and shake. Fry in hot oil until golden brown, about 3 minutes. Serve with French fried potatoes, catsup and hot sauce for a Texas-style treat.

George Anderson
Orange, Texas

Zesty Bass

Serves: 4
Prep Time: 6 hours

2 2 ¹/₂-lb. bass fillets
1 small jar Italian dressing
   lemon pepper
   salt and pepper
1¹/₂ cups Italian bread
   crumbs

Marinate fish overnight in refrigerator in salad dressing. Shake lemon salt and salt and pepper over fish, then roll in bread crumbs. Lay fillets in 8x14-inch baking pan. Cook at 400 degrees for 15 minutes. Turn and cook another 15 minutes.

William Pelath
Austin, Texas

Flaky Baked Bass

Serves: 4
Prep Time: 1 hour

3 lbs. bass fillets, boneless
³/₄ tsp. melted butter
¹/₃ cup lemon juice
   parsley
   garlic
   salt and pepper to taste

Spread bass fillets in single layer in large glass baking pan. Slice each side of fillet to allow penetration of seasoning. Pour melted margarine over fillets. Pour lemon juice into bottom of pan (not over fillets). Sprinkle parsley over fish and season with garlic and salt and pepper. Cover pan with aluminum foil and bake at 350 degrees for 1 hour or until done.

Michael Cline
Shawnee, Oklahoma

Baked Bass

Serves: 4
Prep Time: 30 minutes

1 large bass, skinned	$^1/_2$ cup bread crumbs
1 garlic clove, minced	$^1/_2$ cup melted butter
1 T. parsley flakes	salt and pepper to taste

Rub fish with garlic. Place fish in buttered baking dish. Add remaining ingredients. Bake 30 minutes at 350 degrees.

Leonard Svetich
Boise, Idaho

Mike's Zesty Bass

Serves: 4
Prep Time: 30 minutes

2 lbs. bass fillets	4 T. lemon juice
Italian salad dressing	$^1/_2$ cup melted butter

Marinate fillets in salad dressing for 1 hour in refrigerator. Add lemon juice and melted butter. Place in baking dish. Cover with aluminum foil and bake at 350 degrees for 15 minutes.

George Anderson
Orange, Texas

Breaded Italian Bass

Serves: 3
Prep Time: 30 minutes

6 bass fillets	1 egg
1 cup cooking oil	1 cup Italian bread
$^1/_2$ cup milk	crumbs

Heat cooking oil over medium heat. In separate bowl, mix milk and eggs. Dip fish in egg and milk mixture, then roll in bread crumbs. Fry 2-3 minutes or until golden brown.

Mike Swayngim
Ocala, Florida

Grilled Bass

Serves: 4
Prep Time: 10 minutes

8 large bass fillets	**1 lemon**
salt and pepper to taste	**¹/₂ cup melted butter**
garlic powder to taste	

On grill, place bass with salt, pepper and garlic powder in aluminum pan. Cook about 10-15 minutes. Drain water and pour lemon juice and butter over fish. Cook 5 more minutes.

Stephen Hieronymus
Washington, Illinois

White Bass With Mustard

Serves: varies
Prep Time: 10 minutes

white bass fillets	**cornmeal**
salt	**cooking oil**
prepared mustard	

Cut fillets in half if they are large. Season with salt and apply mustard liberally to each piece. Roll in cornmeal and drop into hot oil for approximately 5 minutes. Cook until flaky. Serve.

Gerald Jackson
Shoreview, Minnesota

Cajun Fried Bass

Serves: 4
Prep Time: 30 minutes

2 lbs. bass fillets	**1 cup flour**
1 T. mustard	**1 cup cornmeal**
3 T. creole seasoning	

Cut fish into 3-inch pieces. Place in bowl and add mustard and seasoning. Mix well. Combine flour and cornmeal in bowl. Lightly coat fish. Deep-fry fish until floating. Serve hot.

Orange Grilled Bass

Serves: 4
Prep Time: 1 hour, 30 minutes

4 bass fillets	**¹/₄ tsp. dried mustard**
4 orange slices	**4 T. green onion, chopped**
4 T. butter	
4 T. orange juice	
¹/₂ tsp. salt	

Place fillets on sheet of heavy-duty aluminum foil and top with orange slice and a little onion. Melt butter in small saucepan with orange juice, salt, mustard and green onion. Mix well and spoon mixture over each fillet. Seal foil tightly and grill over hot coals, about 8 inches from heat. Cook for 20 minutes, checking fish for flakiness. Serve immediately.

Pete Reiter
Grey Eagle, Minnesota

Bar-B-Q Baked Bass

Serves: 4
Prep Time: 1 hour

4 large bass fillets	**barbecue sauce**
2 white onion slices	**3 pats of butter**
2 lemon slices	
salt and pepper	
white cooking wine	

Heat grill. Place fillets on large piece of aluminum foil. Separate onion rings and cover fillets. Place half the lemon slices on fillets. Salt and pepper to taste. Fold aluminum foil into "pan," adding just enough cooking wine to cover bottom. Place a dab of barbecue sauce on each fillet, then top with pats of butter. Close foil completely, leaving small steam vent, and grill.

Wayne Godwin
Jackson, Missouri

Bluefish Salade

Serves: 8-10
Prep Time: 15 minutes

bluefish, cooked and
chilled
2 T. lemon juice
2 T. lime juice
1 T. balsamic vinegar
³/₄ tsp. salt
1 tsp. Dijon mustard
ground black pepper
2 tsp. tarragon
2 T. dill
6 T. olive oil

4 plum tomatoes,
quartered
¹/₂ red onion, sliced
¹/₃ lb. green beans, cooked
6 new potatoes, cooked

Mix everything together, except vegetables, fish and potatoes, in bowl. Break fish into large pieces. Combine all remaining ingredients. Toss, keeping in mind that the more you toss salad, the smaller the fish pieces will be. Serve chilled.

Vito Ancona
Lisbon Falls, Maine

Broiled Bluefish

Serves: 2
Prep Time: 30 minutes

1 lb. bluefish fillets
¹/₂ cup lemon juice
2 T. Worcestershire sauce

2 tsp. Old Bay seasoning
2 tsp. butter

Skin and wash fillets, then soak in lemon juice and Worcestershire sauce for 1 hour. Sprinkle with Old Bay seasoning and place 1 tsp. butter on each fillet. Broil 15-20 minutes or until fish flakes with fork.

Ben Slider
Wagontown, Pennsylvania

Baked Bluefish

Serves: 4
Prep Time: 30 minutes

1 tsp. seafood seasoning
parsley sprigs

2 **bluefish fillets**
2 **T. butter**
1 **pt. oysters**
1 **T. lemon juice**
hot sauce

Put butter in large, shallow baking dish and add fillets. Drain oysters, keeping broth, and place evenly on fillets. Pour 1 cup oyster broth over fillets and oysters (add water if necessary to make 1 cup). Sprinkle with lemon juice, hot sauce and seafood seasoning. Dot with butter. Cover with aluminum foil and bake for 15-20 minutes at 350 degrees. Garnish with parsley sprigs and serve.

Michael L. McGinley
Bucksport, Maine

Bluefish Batter

Serves 2-4
Prep Time: 30 minutes

$^1/_2$ **lb. bluefish fillets**
$^3/_4$ **cup flour**
$^1/_4$ **cup cornstarch**
$^1/_2$ **T. baking powder**
$^1/_2$ **T. baking soda**
$^3/_4$ **cup water**
1 **egg**

Mix dry ingredients. Stir in water and egg. Beat until smooth and frothy. Thoroughly coat fillets in mixture and deep-fry until golden brown.

Brad Woodward
Oxford, Pennsylvania

Rick's Bluefish Dish

Serves: 4-6
Prep Time: 2 hours

**4-6 bluefish fillets,
1-1¹/₂-inches thick
Italian salad dressing
lemon juice
garlic salt
Mrs. Dash seasoning
pepper**

In baking dish or pan, pour thin layer of salad dressing to cover bottom. Sprinkle lemon juice and seasonings on one side of fillets and place in dish. Cover remaining sides of fillets with lemon juice and seasonings and cover with dressing. Place dish in refrigerator and marinate 2-4 hours. Bake in middle rack of oven at 350 degrees for 30 minutes. When fish flakes easily with fork, remove from oven. Serve with hush puppies.

Rick Peery
Salem, Virginia

Bluefish A La Microwave

Serves: 1
Prep Time: 10 minutes

**1 bluefish fillet
3 garlic cloves
3 parsley sprigs
1 T. butter or margarine**

Wash fillet and put in microwavable, covered dish. Cut approximately 3 slits into fillet. Mince garlic and parsley, then combine and stuff into slits. Cut butter into 2 pats and place on top of fish. Cook (covered) on high for 3 minutes. Voila!

Gene Natale
Brooklyn, New York

Fried Bluefish

Serves: 4
Prep Time: 30 minutes

2 bluefish fillets
1 cup milk
1 cup flour
salt and pepper to taste
2 eggs
milk or water
1 cup seasoned bread
crumbs

Dip fillets in milk, then roll in flour with salt and pepper. Dip coated fillets into beaten eggs (may add milk or water to thin), then roll in seasoned bread crumbs. Fry in oil until fish flakes with fork, about 15 minutes on moderate heat. Serve.

Michael L. McGinley
Bucksport, Maine

Marinated Bluefish

Serves: 4
Prep Time: 1 hour

2 lbs. bluefish fillets
1/4 cup Italian dressing
1/4 cup Catalina dressing
1 tsp. ground cayenne
pepper

1/2 tsp. basil
1/2 tsp. oregano

Mix above ingredients and pour over fillets in shallow, non-metal bowl. Marinate in refrigerator for 2 hours. Place fillets and marinade in non-stick skillet over low heat. Simmer 2-3 minutes, then turn. Continue simmering for 2-3 minutes or until fish flakes. Serve with lemon wedges. Remaining marinade may be used as sauce for fish.

Richard Strecker
Hertford, North Carolina

Bluegill Fish Cakes

Serves: 4
Prep Time: 1 hour

2 **cups bluegill, flaked**
³/₄ **cup crushed oyster crackers**
1 **egg, beaten**
³/₄ **cup milk**
2 **T. onion, minced**
¹/₂ **T. salt**
¹/₂ **T. pepper**

2 **T. melted butter**
3 **T. lemon juice**

Preheat oven to 350 degrees. Mix bluegill, cracker crumbs, egg, milk, onion, salt, pepper, butter and lemon juice together. Toss with fork, then press into 8 cakes. Lay on greased pan and bake 55 minutes. If desired, serve with the following sauce: ¹/₄ cup melted butter, ¹/₄ cup lemon juice, ¹/₈ tsp. salt.

Phillip Wright
Warren, Ohio

Bluegill Niblets

Serves: 6
Prep Time: 30 minutes

1 **lb. bluegill fillets, cut into bite-size pieces**
1 **bottle beer**
¹/₂ **cup catsup**
1 **tsp. horseradish sauce**

dash of Tabasco sauce
pinch of garlic powder

Cut fillets into thin, bite-size pieces. Pour beer into saucepan and bring to a boil. Add fish by the handful. Continue to boil 3-5 minutes, then sift with slotted spoon. Serve with sauce made with the remaining ingredients.

Robert Casper
Deltona, Florida

Baked Carp Fillets

Serves: 2
Prep Time: 45 minutes

2 carp fillets
1 cup stuffing mix
flour
$^1/_2$ cup beer

Mix above ingredients except fillets. Cut a slit in fillets and stuff mixture in fish. Place fillets in baking pan and bake in moderate oven for approximately 45 minutes or until fish flakes with fork. (Be sure to use fillets from a carp weighing 10 lbs. or more in order to avoid a lot of bones.)

W. R. Hedrick
Reno, Oklahoma

Cajun Catfish

Serves: 4-6
Prep Time: 15 minutes

4-6 catfish fillets
vegetable oil
2 cups yellow mustard
3 eggs, beaten
1 T. Tabasco sauce
1 cup ground cornmeal
1 cup yellow cornmeal
1 cup flour

1 cup Italian bread
crumbs
2 tsp. salt
1 tsp. garlic powder
1 tsp. paprika
lemon wedges

Rinse fish and pat dry. In 12-inch skillet, heat 1 inch of oil to 350 degrees. In medium bowl, combine mustard, eggs and Tabasco sauce. Pour mixture into 13x9-inch baking pan. In another bowl, combine remaining ingredients (except lemon wedges), then pour into another 13x9-inch baking dish. Dredge fish in mustard mixture, coating well. Shake off excess mixture. Place fish, one at a time, in hot oil. Fry until golden brown and crispy, about 6 minutes per side. Drain on paper towels and serve with lemon wedges.

A.C. Donohue
Lexington, Kentucky

Broiled Catfish

Serves: 4
Prep Time: 10 minutes

2 lbs. catfish fillets
1 tsp. salt
1 tsp. pepper

1 lemon
butter

Salt and pepper fillets. Squeeze lemon over fillets and broil in oven for 5 minutes or until fish flakes with fork. Spread butter on fillets and serve.

Jason Safcik
Peoria, Arizona

Chinese Catfish

Serves: 4-6
Prep Time: 10 minutes

4-6 catfish fillets	**soy sauce**
1 bell pepper	**cayenne pepper**
3 medium onions	
2 celery stalks	
2 carrots	
1¹/₂ sticks margarine	
cajun creole spices	

Thinly slice bell pepper and onions. Slice celery and carrots at a 45-degree angle. Melt half of margarine in wok or pan over low flame. Season catfish fillets to taste with creole seasoning and spread in single layer in pan or wok. Sear both sides of fillets, then remove and coat with soy sauce. Set aside. Melt remaining margarine and add vegetables. Add pepper and soy sauce to taste, cooking until vegetables are crisp-tender. Stir constantly. Return fillets to wok and gently stir, then cover and reduce heat. Cook until fish is white and flaky. Serve over steamed rice.

William Pope
Alexander, Arkansas

Pecan Catfish

Serves: 4
Prep Time: 20 minutes

4 catfish fillets	**3 T. Dijon mustard**
2 T. milk	**1 cup ground pecans**

In small bowl, combine milk and mustard. Dip fillets into mixture, then roll in ground pecans. Lightly shake off excess. Place on greased baking sheet. Bake in oven at 500 degrees for 10 minutes or until fish is flaky.

Gary Kibbe
Drayton Plains, Michigan

Steamed Spanish Catfish

Serves: 4-6
Prep Time: 1 hour

2 lbs. catfish fillets	**$^1/_4$ tsp. ground oregano**
$^1/_4$ cup flour (seasoned with salt and pepper)	**$^1/_4$ tsp. ground saffron**
	$^1/_2$ cup instant rice
$^1/_4$ cup olive oil	**9 oz. artichokes, frozen**
2 carrots, peeled and sliced	**6 small shelled clams, washed**
$^1/_2$ cup onion, chopped	**8 oz. shrimp**
1 garlic clove, minced	
2 T. pimiento, chopped	

Coat catfish fillets with flour and brown in hot oil. In steaming bowl, combine remaining ingredients, except artichokes, clams and shrimp. Place catfish fillets on top of ingredients in steaming dish and steam for 45 minutes. Add artichokes, clams and shrimp. Cover and steam for an additional 15 minutes. Serve.

Robert Perry
Clifton, Colorado

Catfish Burgers

Serves: 3
Prep Time: 15 minutes

1 lb. raw catfish, boned	**salt and pepper to taste**
1 egg, beaten	**1 garlic clove, minced**
$^1/_2$ cup bread crumbs	**3 drops of Tabasco sauce**
1 onion, finely chopped parsley, chopped	

Put fish through meat grinder or food processor. Mix ground fish with remaining ingredients. Form into patties and put on plate. Cover with waxed paper and let stand 30 minutes. Grill and serve without bun.

Vince Pugiliese
Pittsburgh, Pennsylvania

Catfish Parmesan

Serves: 4
Prep Time: 10 minutes

4 6-oz. catfish fillets
$^1/_2$ cup dry bread crumbs
$^1/_2$ cup Parmesan cheese, grated
2 T. parsley, chopped
$^1/_2$ tsp. paprika
$^1/_4$ tsp. oregano
$^1/_4$ tsp. basil

$^1/_4$ tsp. ground pepper
$^1/_3$ cup milk
2 T. vegetable oil

Preheat oven to 450 degrees. Lightly grease 13x9-inch baking pan. On waxed paper, combine bread crumbs, cheese and seasonings. In shallow bowl, dip fillets in milk and coat with bread crumb mixture on both sides. Arrange fish in prepared baking dish. Drizzle oil on top of fish. Bake 8-10 minutes or until fish flakes easily with fork.

Ira Craig
Roy, Utah

Salsa-Baked Catfish

Serves: 4
Prep Time: 30 minutes

1$^1/_2$ lbs. catfish fillets
2 T. butter
$^1/_2$ cup plain yogurt
1 cup of your favorite salsa

2 cups mozzarella cheese, grated
salt and pepper to taste

Butter bottom of large baking dish. Place fish in single layer in dish. Season with salt and pepper. Spread yogurt evenly over fish. Top with cheese and salsa. Cover and bake 15-20 minutes. Serve with additional warm salsa.

M. B. "Con" Smoll
Encitas, California

Catfish Stew

Serves: 6
Prep Time: 90 minutes

12 **medium catfish fillets**	8 **bacon strips, uncooked**
margarine	**salt and pepper**
2 **celery stalks, cut**	1½ **cups water**
lengthwise	
2 **carrots, cut lengthwise**	
4 **onions, sliced**	
6 **potatoes, sliced**	

Grease cast iron Dutch oven with margarine. Place celery and carrots in bottom. Put in a few onion slices and layer fish fillets, potatoes, onions and bacon strips over carrots and celery. Season to taste. Pour in water and cover. Bake in preheated oven at 375 degrees for 1 hour or cook over a campfire while you fish!

Ned Caudill
Winnabow, North Carolina

Catfish Chowder

Serves: 6
Prep Time: 40 minutes

1 **lb. catfish fillets**	**pepper to taste**
½ **cup onion, chopped**	2 **cups milk**
2 **T. butter**	1 **8-oz. can cream-style**
2 **cups potatoes, diced**	**yellow corn**
1 **cup boiling water**	
¾ **tsp. salt**	

Skin fillets and cut into 1-inch pieces. Fry onion in butter until tender. Add potatoes, water, salt, pepper and fish. Cover and simmer for 15 minutes or until potatoes are cooked. Add milk and corn. Stir again and simmer until hot.

Richard Paschke
Janesville, Wisconsin

Fried Catfish Supreme

Serves: 2
Prep Time: 10 minutes

2 12-inch catfish fillets
   milk
1¹/₂ cups yellow cornmeal
1 tsp. salt
1 tsp. pepper

1 T. cayenne pepper
¹/₂ lb. bacon

Wash and dry fillets. Place in bowl of milk, with enough milk to cover fillets. Mix cornmeal and seasonings together in pie plate. Coat fillets with cornmeal mixture and lay out on paper towels in refrigerator for 1 hour. Meanwhile, cook bacon and retain grease. Fry catfish in bacon grease for approximately 3 minutes on each side or until golden brown. Drain on paper towels and serve. Eat bacon as an accompaniment to the fish.

Ed Lowe
Santa Clara, Utah

Steamed Catfish

Serves: 3
Prep Time: 45 minutes

3 lbs. whole catfish,
   dressed
5 ginger root slices
³/₄ cup sesame oil

¹/₂ cup green onions,
   chopped
¹/₄ cup soy sauce

Using steamer, boil water with ginger slices. Meanwhile, prepare fish and put into steamer. Cover and steam 20 minutes. When fish flakes with fork, it is done. When cooked, remove from steamer and place on platter. Cook sesame oil to the point of smoking and slowly pour over catfish. Sprinkle with onions and soy sauce. Serve immediately.

J. D. Gagliardo
Oxnard, California

Blackened Catfish

Serves: 6
Prep Time: 30 minutes

3 lbs. catfish
1½ sticks butter
2 tsp. lemon pepper
2 tsp. thyme
2 tsp. basil
1 tsp. garlic powder
1 tsp. onion powder
1 tsp. salt
¼ tsp. cayenne pepper
3 lemons, cut in wedges
3 T. Worcestershire sauce

In saucepan, melt butter over low heat. Add lemon pepper, thyme, basil, garlic powder, onion powder, salt and cayenne pepper. Remove from heat and let cool slightly. Dip each fillet in butter mixture, coating thoroughly. Place fish in shallow dish and pour remainder of butter mixture over fillets. Cover dish with plastic wrap and refrigerate for 1 hour. Preheat cast iron skillet or griddle over hot coals for 10 minutes. Melt remaining butter in saucepan and add Worcestershire sauce, then set aside. Grill fillets 2-3 minutes per side. Serve with butter sauce and lemon wedges.

Earl Ball
Phoenix, Arizona

Pan-Fried Catfish

Serves: depends on size of fish
Prep Time: 30 minutes

catfish
1 cup flour
1 cup cornmeal
1 cup cooking oil
1 T. lemon juice

Skin catfish. Mix flour and cornmeal together. Roll catfish in mixture. Place catfish in hot cooking oil. Cook until meat falls apart with fork. Apply lemon juice before serving. This is delicious when cooked over campfire in cast iron skillet.

Patricia McKinney
Carthage, Missouri

Cod Melt

Serves: 2
Prep Time: 30 minutes

1½ **lbs. cod**	**spaghetti sauce**
cooking oil	**mozzarella cheese slices**
3 **eggs**	
2 **T. milk**	
Italian bread crumbs	

Fill half of fry pan with oil and bring to a high temperature. Roll fillets in eggs beaten with milk, then roll in bread crumbs. Coat well. Fry on both sides until fish is golden brown. Place fried fish in casserole dish and pour enough spaghetti sauce over to cover fish. Lay strips of cheese over sauce. Place in preheated oven at 350 degrees for 5 minutes or until cheese melts.

Richard Beaupre
Westfield, Massachusetts

Savory Microwaved Cod

Serves: 4
Prep Time: 10 minutes

4 **cod fillets**	¼ **cup soy sauce**
1 **tomato, sliced**	¼ **cup sherry or rice wine**
1 **small onion, sliced**	
1 **green pepper, sliced**	
salt, pepper and garlic	
powder to taste	
¼ **cup rice wine vinegar**	

Place fish in microwave-safe 8x8-inch baking dish with tomato, onion and green pepper. Season with salt, pepper and garlic. Pour vinegar, soy sauce and wine over mixture. Cover and microwave 5-10 minutes, or until fish flakes easily with fork.

George Blanchard
Seattle, Washington

Shrimp and Fish Casserole

Serves: 4
Prep Time: 15 minutes

1 lb. cod
1 medium onion, thinly
   sliced
1 T. butter
2 garlic cloves, minced
3 T. water
   salt and pepper

lemon juice
1 cup sour cream
1 T. Dijon mustard
1 cup baby shrimp, cooked

Wipe fish with damp cloth and cut into cubes. Saute onion in
butter until soft. Add garlic and fish. Sprinkle water, salt and
pepper over fish. Simmer for 10-20 minutes, or until fish is flaky.
Sprinkle with lemon juice. In small bowl, mix sour cream with
mustard, then heat slightly. Add baby shrimp to sour cream
mixture and serve with fish. Garnish with dill or parsley.

Greg Boling
St. Joseph, Missouri

Cod Potato Loaf

Serves: 6
Prep Time: 1 hour

2 cups cod, boiled and
   minced
1½ qt. mashed potatoes
2 eggs

salt and pepper to taste
1½ cups bread crumbs
½ tsp. onion and parsley,
   finely chopped

Line 1½-qt. baking dish with mashed potatoes, covering bottom.
Fill dish with boiled cod. Combine eggs, salt and pepper,
bread crumbs, onion and parsley. Then, mix with minced
codfish in dish. Spread thick layer of mashed potatoes over fish
and bake at 350 degrees for 1 hour in moderate oven. Serve
hot.

Joe Tolen
Philadelphia, Pennsylvania

Broiled Crappie

Serves: 4
Prep Time: 30 minutes

**4 crappie slabs, scored
   crosswise
   lemon juice
   melted butter
   Worcestershire sauce
   salt and pepper
   garlic powder
   paprika**

Score crappies crosswise on both sides. Place on broiler pan.
Sprinkle lemon juice on top-side of fish. Brush with butter, then
sprinkle both sides with Worcestershire sauce, salt, pepper,
garlic and paprika. Place pan in oven and broil until fish flakes.
Serve with lemon wedges or tartar sauce.

Abner Straughan, Jr.
Prattville, Alabama

Crappie Tidbits

Serves: 4
Prep Time: 5 minutes

**6 crappie fillets
   water
   salt
   barbecue sauce (any
   kind)**

Place fillets in boiling water. Add salt and boil for 3 minutes.
Drain well. Place in freezer for 1 minute. Remove fillets from
freezer and serve in small bowls, after dipping in your favorite
barbecue sauce.

Jim Stefanic
Youngstown, Ohio

Cornbread Crappie

Serves: 4-6
Prep Time: 30 minutes

10 crappie fillets	**1 cup milk**
¹/₂ cup cornmeal	**2 eggs**
¹/₂ cup flour	
salt and pepper	
¹/₂ cup cracker crumbs	
2 T. lemon pepper	
peanut oil	

Mix all ingredients together except fish, oil, milk and eggs. Mix milk and eggs together in separate bowl. Heat 1 inch of oil in skillet. Dip fillets in egg and milk mixture, then roll in breading. Fry until golden brown. Remove and drain on paper towels.

Gary Ashley
Marion, Indiana

Crappie Chips

Serves: 2
Prep Time: 20 minutes

1 lb. crappie fillets	**1¹/₂ cups milk**
cooking oil	**1 egg**
1¹/₂ cups Italian bread crumbs	
1 tsp. salt	
1 tsp. lemon pepper	
1 tsp. Old Bay seasoning	

Skin and wash fillets. Heat 1 inch of oil in skillet. In separate bowl, mix bread crumbs and seasonings. In another bowl, mix milk and egg, then soak fillets. Roll in bread crumb mixture, then cook in oil 2-3 minutes or until golden brown.

Ben Slider
Wagontown, Pennsylvania

Flounder With Cheese Sauce

Serves: 4
Prep Time: 25 minutes

4 flounder fillets
2 cups clam juice
3 T. butter
¹/₂ cup green onions,
chopped
2 T. flour

3 T. sour cream
2 T. dry white wine
salt and pepper to taste
¹/₄ cup mozzarella cheese,
grated

Place clam juice in large frying pan and bring to a boil. Add fillets and poach for 3 minutes. Remove and drain on paper towels. Butter baking dish and arrange fillets in a single layer. In frying pan, saute onions until lightly browned. Stir in flour and a little clam juice, until thickened. Add sour cream, wine and salt and pepper. Coat fillets with sauce and top with grated cheese. Broil until fish is cooked thoroughly and cheese melts (about 4-5 minutes).

N. C. Hanks
Crowley, Louisiana

Grilled Flounder With Crab

Serves: 2-4
Prep Time: 45 minutes

2-4 flounder fillets
¹/₂ lb. diced shrimp
(optional)

1¹/₂ lbs. crab
lemon juice
melted butter

If using shrimp, cook and remove shells. Drain. Mix crab and diced shrimp together. Lay flounder fillet out and add crab mixture, then roll and insert toothpicks to hold. Combine lemon juice and melted butter in separate bowl. Place fillets on hot grill to brown. Reduce to medium heat and baste with lemon and butter mixture. Turn fish every 5 minutes, until fish flakes (about 30 minutes).

Bill Vegle
Chester, Virginia

Sweet & Sour Flounder

Serves: 4
Prep Time: 30 minutes

4 flounder fillets	**2 T. catsup**
³/₄ cup flour	**¹/₂ tsp. chili powder**
1 tsp. baking powder	
1 tsp. salt	
water	
1 tsp. salad oil	
1 16-oz. can sweet and	
sour sauce	

Combine flour, baking powder, salt and ³/₄ cup water in bowl. Heat 1 inch of salad oil in skillet to 370 degrees. Coat fish with flour mixture. Fry in oil until golden brown, turning once. Drain well on paper towels, then place on platter and keep warm. In small saucepan, heat sweet and sour sauce, catsup and chili powder over medium heat until hot, stirring occasionally. Spoon over fish and serve.

James Campbell
Evington, Virginia

Tarragon Flounder

Serves: 3
Prep Time: 30 minutes

2 lbs. flounder	**¹/₄ tsp. salt**
1 cup tarragon vinegar	**¹/₈ tsp. pepper**
¹/₂ cup yellow cornmeal	**¹/₄ cup butter**
¹/₂ cup flour, sifted	

Arrange flounder in shallow baking dish. Pour on vinegar and marinate 10 minutes. Meanwhile, combine cornmeal, flour, salt and pepper. Coat fillets with mixture evenly on both sides. In hot skillet, melt butter and saute fish until golden brown on each side. Serve with cucumber slices.

Paul Tofil
East Hartford, Connecticut

Fabulous Cheese Flounder

Serves: 4
Prep Time: 15 minutes

4 **flounder fillets**
lemon juice
3 **T. melted butter**
3 **T. mayonnaise**
3 **T. Parmesan cheese,**
grated

1 **T. onion, chopped**
dash of Worcestershire
sauce

Place fillets in shallow baking dish. Sprinkle with lemon juice and bake at 350 degrees for about 10 minutes. Remove from oven and pour off juice from fish. Turn oven to broil. Mix butter, mayonnaise, cheese, onion and Worcestershire sauce in bowl. Spread over fish and place under broiler. Broil until golden and bubbly (1-2 minutes).

Ben Carr
Gloucester, Virginia

Fish Packages

Serves: 4
Prep Time: 30 minutes

4 **flounder fillets**
1 **cup fresh mushrooms,**
sliced
1 **cup carrots, thinly sliced**
1 **cup zucchini, sliced**
butter

salt and pepper to taste
4 **10-inch rounds of**
aluminum foil

Lightly saute vegetables in butter, then season with salt and pepper. Grease shiny side of foil rounds and place one-fourth of vegetable mixture on each piece. Place fish on top of vegetables. Close package, sealing out as much air as possible, but not tearing foil. Bake at 450 degrees for 10 minutes.

Daniel Silvestro
Bronx, New York

Grilled Grouper With Pineapple Salsa

Serves: 4
Prep Time: 30 minutes

4 grouper fillets
¹/₂ fresh pineapple, cubed
1 jalapeno pepper
1 small red onion, minced
2 tomatoes, peeled and
    diced
    salt and pepper to taste
2 T. tomato paste

Salt and butter grouper fillets, then cook over hot grill until white and flaky. Meanwhile, mix above ingredients together and spoon over fish when cooked.

Daniel Silvestro
Bronx, New York

Grouper In Green Sauce

Serves: 4-6
Prep Time: 30 minutes

1¹/₂ lbs. grouper meat
1 cup vegetable oil
¹/₂ onion, chopped
1 cup fresh parsley
1 tsp. salt
2 T. vinegar
¹/₂ cup white wine
1 tsp. garlic, minced

Mix together all ingredients, except fish and oil. Place fish in frying pan and cover with sauce. When sauce boils, cover pan and simmer for 15 minutes. Remove and serve with wild rice.

Oswaldo Tapanes
Miami, Florida

Baked Haddock

Serves: 2
Prep Time: 45 minutes

1 lb. haddock
1 pkg. white cream sauce
lemon juice
¹/₄ cup buttered bread
crumbs
dash of paprika

Prepare white sauce as indicated by directions on package. Lay fish in buttered, shallow pan. Sprinkle with lemon juice. Pour white sauce over fish, then sprinkle with bread crumbs and paprika. Bake at 350 degrees for 35 minutes.

William Macera, Sr.
Horc, Massachusetts

Baked Fillet Of Haddock

Serves: 6
Prep Time: 20 minutes

1-3 lbs. haddock fillet
3 T. butter
¹/₂ tsp. salt

Place haddock in buttered pan and dot with butter. Sprinkle salt over fish. Bake at 350 degrees for 20 minutes. Place under broiler burner for 2-3 minutes to brown.

Donald Martin
North Port, Florida

Alaskan Halibut Royale

Serves: 4-6
Prep Time: 12 minutes

2 lbs. halibut steaks
1 cup dry white wine
2 tsp. salt
$^{1}/_{2}$ cup mayonnaise
$^{1}/_{2}$ cup sour cream
$^{1}/_{3}$ cup green onion, chopped

$^{1}/_{4}$ cup bread crumbs
paprika

Combine wine and salt. Pour over halibut. Marinate in refrigerator for 1 hour. Drain and dip both sides of steaks in bread crumbs. Place in shallow, glass baking dish. Combine mayonnaise, sour cream and green onion, then spread over halibut steaks. Sprinkle with paprika. Bake at 450 degrees for 12 minutes or until fish flakes with fork.

Capt. Bruce Warner
Homer, Alaska

Cherry-Grilled Halibut

Serves: 2
Prep Time: 30 minutes

2 lbs. halibut fillets
1 tsp. ground black pepper
$^{1}/_{2}$ tsp. salt
$^{1}/_{2}$ T. garlic powder
$^{1}/_{2}$ T. ground red pepper

$^{1}/_{2}$ cup butter (soft)
$^{1}/_{2}$ cup cherry wood chips

Leave skin on one side of fillet. Cover fish with spices (meat-side only). Spread butter over spices. Let stand for 20 minutes. Light gas grill and spread chips on evenly. Set on lowest setting. Coat grill with oil. Cook fillets for 10 minutes, skin-side down, keeping lid closed on grill. Remove and enjoy.

Ronald Shipe
Taft, California

Crunchy Baked Halibut

Serves: 6
Prep Time: 90 minutes

2 lbs. halibut
¹/₂ cup French salad
dressing
2 T. lemon juice
¹/₄ tsp. salt
1 can French fried onions

¹/₄ cup Parmesan cheese,
grated

Cut fish into serving-size pieces. Place in shallow, baking pan. In separate bowl, combine salad dressing, lemon juice and salt. Pour sauce over fish and let stand for 30 minutes, turning once. Crush and add onions. Add cheese and mix thoroughly. Sprinkle over fish. Bake at 350 degrees for 30 minutes.

Dawn Shockley
Crystal, Minnesota

Saucy Cheese Halibut

Serves: 4-6
Prep Time: 15 minutes

4-6 halibut steaks
¹/₂ cup mayonnaise
¹/₂ cup sour cream
2 tsp. flour
1 T. shallots, chopped
1¹/₂ tsp. lemon juice

¹/₂ cup cheddar cheese,
grated

Rinse and dry fish. Place in 9x13-inch greased baking dish. Combine mayonnaise, sour cream and flour until smooth. Add shallots and lemon juice. Spoon over fish, covering evenly. Bake at 425 degrees for 12-15 minutes or until fish is flaky. Sprinkle with cheese and cook another 2-3 minutes or until cheese melts. Serve immediately.

F.L. Calkins
Butte, Montana

Halibut Hawaiian

Serves: 4-6
Prep Time: 10 minutes

2 lbs. halibut, poached
1 8-oz. can pineapple
   chunks
2 T. brown sugar
4 tsp. cornstarch
1/4 cup white vinegar
1 T. soy sauce
1/2 red pepper, cubed

1/2 green pepper, cubed
1/4 cup green onion,
   chopped

Cover halibut chunks with boiling, salted water for 10 minutes or until white. Drain pineapple and save syrup. Add enough water to syrup to equal 1 cup. Combine brown sugar, cornstarch, vinegar and soy sauce in separate bowl. Cook until mixture thickens, then add pineapple, peppers and green onion. Cook until peppers are semi-tender. Serve over poached halibut.

Capt. Bruce Warner
Homer, Alaska

Parmesan Dill Grill Fish

Serves: 4
Prep Time: 20 minutes

   halibut fillets
1/2 cup mayonnaise
2 T. margarine
1 T. dill
   Parmesan cheese

Mix mayonnaise, margarine and dill together thoroughly. Brush mixture on both sides of fish fillets. Sprinkle Parmesan cheese on both sides of fillets and bake at 350 degrees for 5 minutes. Then, broil for 5 minutes.

Steve Willner
Englewood, Colorado

Mahi Mahi With Mushrooms

Serves: 4-6
Prep Time: 45 minutes

 2 lbs. mahi mahi
 $\frac{1}{2}$ cup butter
 3 onion slices (thin)
 2 cups mushrooms
 3 green pepper rings
 1 cup water
 2 cups white wine
   salt and pepper
 1 T. lemon juice
 $\frac{1}{4}$ cup flour
 $\frac{1}{2}$ cup cream
   cayenne pepper
   pinch of chives
 1 egg, hard boiled
 5 olives, sliced

Butter large baking pan with $\frac{1}{4}$ cup butter. Spread onions, mushrooms and pepper rings over bottom of pan. Place fish over vegetables. Pour water and white wine over fish. Salt lightly and drizzle with lemon juice. Cover with foil and poach in preheated oven at 375 degrees for 15-25 minutes. Remove fish and keep warm. Melt remaining butter ($\frac{1}{4}$ cup) in another saucepan and blend in flour, stirring until it bubbles. Reduce broth from baking pan by half, strain and stir into roux. Cook until thickened. Blend in cream and cayenne pepper and heat thoroughly. Salt and pepper to taste. Add strained mushrooms and onion. Pour sauce over fillets and garnish with chives, sliced egg and black olives.

Arthur Jarvis
El Cajon, California

Ceviche

Serves: 8
Prep Time: 12 hours

1 lb. mahi mahi fillets,
   diced
1 cup fresh lemon or lime
   juice
1 small onion, diced
   serrano peppers, diced
¹/₄ cup olive oil

³/₄ tsp. dried oregano
¹/₈ tsp. pepper
2 medium tomatoes,
   chopped

In non-metallic bowl, cover fish with lemon and lime juice.
Cover bowl and place in refrigerator overnight (stir
occasionally). Add all other ingredients and gently mix. Chill
and serve with English water biscuits or crackers.

Ray Tiller
Miami, Florida

Mahi Mahi On The Grill

Serves: 4
Prep Time: 30 minutes

2 lbs. mahi mahi
¹/₈ tsp. salt
¹/₈ tsp. pepper
¹/₂ cup lemon juice
¹/₂ stick butter
¹/₂ onion, sliced or chopped

Cut blood line out of fillets. Put fillets in foil that is twice the size
of fillet. Fold foil so both ends of foil meet in middle of fillet.
Fold ends up to keep in all juices. Pour lemon juice over fish.
Sprinkle salt and pepper over fish, then place sliced onions on
top. Fold up foil so it can easily be opened to check flakiness.
Grill fillets at 450 degrees for 15 minutes. if not done, grill for 8
more minutes.

Mark Poedtke
Coral Springs, Florida

Muskie Fillets In Cream

Serves: 4
Prep Time: 20 minutes

4 **muskie fillets**	3 **cups light cream**
4 **T. butter**	**paprika**
1½ **cups onion, chopped**	
¼ **tsp. salt**	
2 **cups dry white wine**	

Melt 3 T. butter in heavy skillet and saute onions. Dust fillets lightly on both sides with salt. Place in skillet and pour wine over fillets. Simmer 3-4 minutes, then slowly add cream. Cover and cook over low heat for 10 minutes. Dot fillets with remaining butter and sprinkle with paprika.

Edmund DeMaria
Levittown, Pennsylvania

Baked Muskie With Dill Sauce

Serves: 4
Prep Time: 45 minutes

4 **muskie fillets**	1 **T. lemon juice**
1 **can cream of celery soup, condensed**	⅓ **cup melted butter**
½ **cup milk**	
2 **T. fresh dill, minced**	
½ **tsp. parsley, chopped**	

Combine soup and milk, stirring over low heat until hot. Add dill and parsley. Place fillets in oiled baking pan. Brush with lemon and butter mixture. Cover with aluminum foil and place in preheated oven at 375 degrees. Bake 30 minutes, basting with lemon and butter mixture twice. Remove fish and spoon prepared dill sauce over fish. Serve.

Peter Widrlechner
Mt. Prospect, Illinois

Baked Northern

Serves: 4
Prep Time: 45 minutes

6-8 lbs. fresh northern
¹/₂ cup butter
3 cups bread crumbs
¹/₂ cup celery, chopped
¹/₂ cup onion, chopped

¹/₂ cup fresh tomato,
chopped
1 tsp. curry powder
1 cup hot water

Clean fish and slit lengthwise. In saucepan, melt butter and add bread crumbs, celery, onion, tomato, curry powder and hot water. (Dressing should be just wet enough to stick together.) Stuff fish and tie with string. Score fish in three places and stuff slits with butter. Bake at 400 degrees for 45 minutes or until fish flakes easily.

Arthur Runston
Sauk Rapids, Minnesota

Tomato Baked Northern Pike

Serves: 6
Prep Time: 2 hours

10 lbs. northern pike
2 onions, sliced
salt
lemon pepper
butter

1 lb. bacon (lean)
2 cans stewed tomatoes
2 tomatoes, sliced

In large broiler pan, place cleaned fillets. Cover with layer of sliced onion. Salt and pepper to taste, then brush with melted butter. Cover onion with layers of bacon strips. Combine stewed tomatoes and sliced tomatoes. Cover everything with tomatoes, then seal pan with aluminum foil. Bake at 275 degrees for 90 minutes or until fish flakes and bacon is cooked.

Eugene Madsen
Lake City, South Dakota

Jackson's Northern Chowder

Serves: 4
Prep Time: 40 minutes

2 cups northern fillets, cut in 1-inch pieces	1 cup potatoes, finely diced
1 bay leaf	1 cup celery, finely diced
1 qt. water	$^{1}/_{4}$ tsp. salt
2 T. instant chicken bouillon	$^{1}/_{4}$ tsp. pepper and oregano
$^{1}/_{2}$ cup onion, chopped	2 cups medium white sauce
1 cup carrots, finely diced	

In large pan, put fish, bay leaf, water and bouillon. Bring to a boil, then simmer slowly for 20 minutes. Add vegetables and spices, simmering until tender. Make medium white sauce in separate pan and thin with hot soup stock, then slowly stir all of white sauce into soup. Garnish with chopped parsley. (If soup is too thick, add some whole or evaporated milk.)

Gerald Jackson
Shoreview, Minnesota

Pickled Northern

Serves: 2
Prep Time: 2 days plus 1 hour

1 northern fillet	2 cups white vinegar
salted water	$^{3}/_{4}$ cup sugar
white vinegar	1 T. pickling spice
1 cup water	1 cup Muscatel wine

Cut northern in bite-size pieces, bones and all (except large "Y" bones). They will dissolve. Soak fish for 24 hours in water salty enough to float an egg. Then, wash fish in cold water and cover with white vinegar. Soak for another 24 hours, then drain. Mix 1 cup water, 2 cups vinegar, sugar and pickling spice for syrup and boil for 5 minutes. Cool syrup and add wine. Pour mixture over fish and put in covered container and refrigerate 3-4 days. Tastes just like herring.

Milbert Schaffer
Pierre, South Dakota

Panfish Pizza

Serves: 4
Prep Time: 1 hour

1 lb. panfish fillets	**2 tomatoes, thinly sliced**
2 9-inch pizza crusts, frozen	**8 oz. mozzarella cheese, grated**
pizza sauce	
1 cup green stuffed olives, sliced	
¹/₄ cup capers	
1 small onion, thinly sliced	

Thaw crusts and spread with pizza sauce. Place remaining ingredients evenly over fish, then top with grated cheese. Be sure fish is broken up. Bake at 375 degrees for 15 minutes or until crust is brown and crispy.

Walter Womack
Las Vegas, Nevada

Microwave Fillets

Serves: 2
Prep Time: 3-5 minutes

8-10 panfish fillets
1 tsp. Lawry's seasoning salt
2 T. butter
2 T. real lemon juice

Place fillets in microwave cooking container. Be careful not to put one on top of another. (They won't cook if stacked.) Sprinkle seasoning salt, butter and lemon juice evenly over all the fillets and cook on full power in covered container until fillets are white and flaky.

Garry Roeker
Sherburn, Minnesota

Chipped Perch

Serves: 4
Prep Time: 15 minutes

2 lbs. perch fillets
1 cup Caesar salad
dressing
1 cup potato chips, finely
crushed
$^1/_2$ cup cheddar cheese,
grated

Dip fillets in Caesar salad dressing, then lay in lightly greased baking dish. Cover with crushed potato chips and cheddar cheese. Bake at 375 degrees for approximately 12-15 minutes.

Shawn Sanner
Keyport, Washington

Quick Fillets

Serves: 2
Prep Time: 40 minutes

perch fillets
$^1/_2$ stick butter
lemon juice
lime juice
tartar sauce
cocktail sauce

Place large fry pan on stove, heat to medium range and melt butter in pan. Turn heat to medium-low range. Coat fillets with lemon and lime juice. Place enough fillets in pan to fill it. Cover pan and slow cook for approximately 15 minutes or until fillets become white and fluffy. Remove fillets from pan and place on plate. Coat fillets with your favorite tartar and cocktail sauce.

Richard Rooney
Laramie, Wyoming

Stack's Perch

Serves: 2
Prep Time: 40 minutes

4 perch fillets
Townhouse crackers
1 egg, beaten

1 T. milk
peanut oil

Crush crackers to near-dust. Dip fillets in beaten egg and milk, then dip in cracker crumbs. Fry in peanut oil, turning when one side is golden.

Francis Stack
Lorain, Ohio

Yellow Perch Jambalaya

Serves: 3
Prep Time: 1 hour

1 lb. perch fillets
¹/₂ cup bacon, chopped
1 cup onion, chopped
¹/₂ cup green peppers,
  chopped
1 garlic clove, chopped
1 chicken bouillon cube
1 can tomato sauce
¹/₄ cup parsley, chopped
1 T. salt

1 cup boiling water
1 cup rice, uncooked
1 can whole tomatoes

Cut fillets into 1-inch pieces. Cook bacon until crisp. Add onion, green pepper and garlic to same pan, cooking until tender. Dissolve bouillon cube in boiling water. Combine all ingredients and pour into well-greased 2-qt. casserole dish. Cover and bake at 350 degrees for 50 minutes, or until rice is tender and fish flakes easily.

William Thennes
Bark River, Michigan

Baked Pickerel In Mushroom Cheese Sauce

Serves: 4
Prep Time: 25 minutes

1½ **lbs. pickerel fillets**
1 **10 ½-oz. can cream of mushroom soup**
¼ **cup cheddar cheese, grated**
½ **cup mushrooms, sliced**
¼ **cup dry sherry**
1 **T. parsley, chopped**

Place fish in shallow, buttered baking dish. In separate bowl, mix soup, cheese, mushrooms, sherry and parsley. Spread over fish. Bake in preheated oven at 375 degrees for 25 minutes. Serve with rice and garnish with parsley.

Gred Shadler
Toledo, Ohio

Baked Redfish

Serves: 4
Prep Time: 30 minutes

4 redfish fillets
lemon pepper seasoning
salt
butter
1 medium onion, sliced
1 lemon, sliced

On barbecue grill, place fillets on sheet of aluminum foil.
Sprinkle with lemon pepper and salt. Lay pats of butter, onion
slices and lemon slices on fish after 1 minute or when fillets are
warm enough to melt butter. Wrap fillets in foil and bake on
uncovered grill for 20-30 minutes.

Richard Mechler
San Antonio, Texas

Skillet-Fried Redfish

Serves: 4
Prep Time: 1 hour

2 lbs. redfish
1 qt. buttermilk
1 box cornflake crumbs
1 tsp. salt
¹/₂ tsp. cayenne or red
pepper
2 cups sunflower or
safflower oil

Trim bloodline from fillets. Soak fillets in buttermilk for 2 hours
in refrigerator. Mix cornflake crumbs, salt and cayenne pepper.
Remove fillets from buttermilk and dip into crumbs, coating
thoroughly. Place in hot oil and cook for a few minutes on each
side, or until golden brown.

Jeffrey Wise
Abilene, Texas

Blackened North Carolina Redfish

Serves: 4
Prep Time: 25 minutes

4 lbs. redfish fillets	**¹/₂ stick butter (unsalted)**
1 lb. hickory chips, soaked in water	**4-6 T. cajun spices**
	juice of 1 lemon

Heat gas grill. Place large, cast iron skillet or griddle on gas grill. Add soaked hickory chips on top of lava rocks in grill. Turn grill to highest heat for 20-30 minutes with lid closed. Meanwhile, melt butter and coat fillets. Sprinkle cajun spices on both sides of fillets. Carefully place fillets in preheated skillet. Pour lemon juice over each fillet and close lid. Cook 1-2 minutes. Turn fillets and pour remaining lemon juice over them. Cook another 2 minutes. Fillets will form a slightly blackened crust on outside while remaining moist on inside.

Richard Strecker
Hertford, North Carolina

Barbecued Redfish

Serves: 2 persons per fish
Prep Time: 1 hour, 30 minutes

4-20 lbs. large fish
Italian dressing
creole seasoning to taste

Fillet fish, leaving skin and scales. Cut out ribcage. Marinate fish in Italian dressing or red cooking wine for 1 hour. Light charcoal and let burn to get low heat. Season fish to taste and put on grill. (Caution: Scales will stick to grill until after they are "burnt.") Use egg spatula to gently pry off. Fish is cooked when meat flakes off of skin with fork, or cooked longer until drier, if desired. Serve with small dish of shrimp stew, it really enhances the meal.

Paul Pontiff
Baldwin, Louisiana

Salmon Quiche

Serves: 6
Prep Time: 1 hour

2 **cups salmon, fresh or canned**
1 **9-inch sweet pie shell, cooked**
6 **eggs, beaten**
3 **green onions, chopped**
2 **T. butter or margarine**

1 **cup cream**
1/2 **tsp. wine mustard**
2 **T. lemon juice**
salt and pepper to taste
2 **cups Monterey Jack cheese, shredded**

Brush bottom of pie shell with 2 tsp. beaten eggs. Cook at 350 degrees for 1-2 minutes or until glazed. Saute onions in butter until soft. Add salmon and stir until coated with butter. Pour salmon and onions into pie shell, covering bottom. In bowl, combine eggs, cream, mustard, lemon juice, salt and pepper and 1 cup cheese. Stir well and pour over salmon mixture in pie shell. Sprinkle with 1 cup cheese. Bake at 350 degrees for 30-45 minutes until quiche passes clean-knife test when knife is inserted in the middle of it. Serve hot or cold.

Bruce Morse
Santa Cruz, California

Jiffy Salmon Casserole

Serves: 4-6
Prep Time: 45 minutes

1 **cup canned or cooked salmon, flaked**
1 **10-oz. can cream of mushroom or chicken soup**

1/4 **cup milk**
1 1/2 **cups peas, cooked**
potato chips

Grease 1-qt. casserole dish. Combine all ingredients and top with potato chips. Bake at 350 degrees for 35 minutes.

John Curran
Flora Vista, New Mexico

Hot And Spicy Smoked Salmon

Serves: 10-14
Prep Time: 1-2 days

10 **lbs. salmon fillets (with skin on)**	3 **cups kosher salt**
2 **garlic cloves, minced**	3 **gals. water**
2 **T. onion powder**	1 **cup sugar**
4 **T. black pepper**	
2 **tsp. Tabasco sauce**	
4 **T. Worcestershire sauce**	

In 2 cups water, bring garlic, onion powder, black pepper and Tabasco and Worcestershire sauces to a boil. Simmer 5 minutes. Combine salt with water, mixing until salt is completely dissolved. Add spices to salt water. (This must be in plastic or steel container—not aluminum.) Add sugar. Slice fillets into 2-inch strips, then completely submerge in brine for 18 hours. Remove from brine and place on racks of smoker. Pat meat with paper towels and let air-dry for 1 hour before smoking. Place in smoker. Cook 16-18 hours.

Michael Tersney
Alpena, Michigan

Simi Salmon Pate'

Serves: 12-15
Prep Time: 20 minutes

1 **6-oz. can smoked salmon**	2-3 **dashes of Tabasco sauce**
2 **8-oz. pkgs. cream cheese**	**crushed nuts of your**
$^1/_8$ **tsp. garlic powder**	**choice**
$^1/_2$ **tsp. onion powder**	

Flake salmon well. Mix cream cheese, garlic powder, onion powder and Tabasco sauce. Form into a half ball and roll in crushed nuts. Chill for 2 hours before serving.

Doug Frick
North Richland Hills, Texas

Microwaved Salmon A La King

Serves: 4
Prep Time: 30 minutes

15 oz. salmon
1 medium onion, chopped
¹/₄ cup green pepper, chopped
¹/₄ cup butter or margarine
¹/₄ cup flour
¹/₂ tsp. instant chicken bouillon cubes, crushed

1 cup light cream
¹/₂ cup water
1 4-oz. can mushroom pieces
2 T. pimiento, chopped

Break salmon into bite-size pieces and set aside. In large casserole dish, combine onion, green pepper and butter. Cook (covered) on full power for 2 minutes, or until vegetables are crisp-tender. Stir flour and bouillon into mixture. Add cream and water. Cook (uncovered) another 5 minutes or until thick, stirring every minute. Fold in salmon, mushrooms and pimiento. Cook on full power for 1-2 minutes, stirring once. Serve over English muffin halves.

Mary Flowers
Austin, Colorado

Fisherman's S.O.S. (Salmon On Shingle)

Serves: 1-3
Prep Time: 5-12 minutes

1 15 ¹/₂-oz. can salmon, pink or red
1¹/₂ cups V8 Juice
garlic, fresh or powder

salt and pepper
1-3 bread slices, toasted
1-3 cheese slices

Pour and heat V8 Juice in frying pan. Add salmon. Put in spices and heat. Put mixture on toast and place cheese slice on top. Serve when cheese melts.

Stephen Krajcirovic
Allentown, Pennsylvania

Barbecued Salmon Steaks

Serves: 4
Prep Time: 6 hours

4 salmon steaks, cut 1-inch thick	**¹/₄ tsp. salt**
¹/₄ cup orange juice	**dash of pepper**
¹/₄ cup cooking oil	
¹/₄ cup dry white wine	
3 T. snipped parsley	
2 garlic cloves, minced	

Place salmon in shallow dish. In separate mixing bowl, combine orange juice, oil, wine, parsley, garlic, salt and pepper. Pour over salmon, coating well. Cover and marinate 6 hours (or overnight), turning at least once. Drain salmon, saving marinade. Pat salmon dry with paper towel. Grill steaks on uncovered grill over medium-hot coals for 7 minutes. Turn and grill another 7 minutes or until fish is cooked and flaky. Brush occasionally with marinade.

Frank Coombs
South Burlington, Vermont

Salmon Pasta

Serves: 4-6
Prep Time: 30 minutes

1 lb. salmon	**¹/₂ stick butter**
1 cup celery	**1 cup broccoli, chopped**
1 cup carrots, shredded	**1 lb. thin spaghetti**
1 cup sliced mushrooms	
1 large onion, chopped	

In large pan, combine above ingredients except spaghetti. Cook on medium heat until vegetables are tender. Serve over cooked spaghetti.

Frank Wolfe
Northtown, Pennsylvania

Oriental Salmon Salad

Serves: 4
Prep Time: 20 minutes

1^{1}/$_{2}$ **cups salmon, cooked and flaked**
1^{1}/$_{2}$ **cups boiling water**
1^{1}/$_{2}$ **cups instant rice**
1 **small onion, chopped**
^{1}/$_{3}$ **cup sour cream**
2 **T. cold water**
1 **T. soy sauce**
^{1}/$_{2}$ **tsp. garlic powder**
^{1}/$_{2}$ **tsp. salt**
^{1}/$_{8}$ **tsp. pepper**

^{1}/$_{2}$ **tsp. ground ginger**
2 **T. parsley, chopped**
1 **pkg. oriental vegetables, cooked**
^{1}/$_{2}$ **red pepper, chopped**

Pour boiling water over rice and onion in 2-qt. bowl. Cover and let stand 5 minutes. In separate bowl, mix sour cream with cold water, soy sauce, spices and parsley. After rice is cooked, pour sour cream dressing into rice. Add remaining ingredients and toss lightly. Serve on crisp bed of lettuce.

Mrs. D. Sailer
Mauston, Wisconsin

Smoked Salmon Dip

Serves: 8-10
Prep Time: 30 minutes

2-3 **lbs. smoked salmon, moist**
1 **16-oz. pkg. cream cheese**

6-8 **green onions**
2 **T. lemon juice**
1 **tsp. Tabasco (optional)**

Remove all bones from salmon. Combine all ingredients and mix by hand (like meat loaf). Serve cold with celery, carrots, crackers or any vegetable you like. Add Tabasco if you like tangy food.

Jerry Lee Peterson
Colorado Springs, Colorado

Gravlax

Serves: 4
Prep Time: 30 minutes

- **1 lb. salmon fillets, boned
  with skin on**
- **1 cup white sugar**
- **²/₃ cup salt**
- **2 T. dry dill weed**

Cut fillets into an even number of hand-sized pieces. Mix sugar, salt and dill together and rub firmly onto meat-side of fillets. Place fish in deep glass or ceramic bowl, stacking them meat-to-meat and skin-to-skin. Place a plate that just fits on top of fish, and then a heavy weight, such as full cans, clean rocks etc., on the plate. Refrigerate 48 hours. Drain fish and wipe clean. Slice thinly on the diagonal. This Norwegian delicacy is served with cream cheese, sliced onion, rye bread, bagels and crackers.

Lloyd Wester
Guilcene, Washington

Hot Cheeks

Serves: 2
Prep Time: 15 minutes

- **¹/₂ lb. salmon cheeks**
- **1 cup white vinegar**
- **1 tsp. salt**
- **1 tsp. ground black pepper**
- **¹/₂ cup water**

Skin and bone cheeks. Mix ingredients together in bowl and add fish cheeks. Stir occasionally and let stand for 15 minutes. Serve with vegetables.

Ronald Shipe
Tart, California

Salmon Steaks With Mushroom Stuffing

Serves: 6
Prep Time: 45 minutes

6 salmon steaks	**¹/₈ tsp. pepper**
¹/₂ tsp. salt	**1 cup light cream**
¹/₄ cup butter	
¹/₄ cup onion, finely chopped	
3 cups soft bread crumbs	
2 cups sliced mushrooms	
2 T. lemon juice	
¹/₄ tsp. salt	

Sprinkle salmon with salt. Melt butter and saute onions in butter until tender. Combine with crumbs, mushrooms, parsley, lemon juice, salt and pepper. Place salmon in buttered baking dish. Place stuffing on salmon. Cover with rest of salmon. Pour cream over top. Bake at 350 degrees, basting occasionally for 30-40 minutes or until salmon flakes.

Anthony Proctor, Jr.
Eaton Rapids, Michigan

Peppered Salmon Steaks

Serves: 2
Prep Time: 15 minutes

2 1-lb. salmon steaks	**¹/₄ cup brown sugar**
1 stick butter	**³/₄ cup peppercorns,**
2 garlic cloves	**crushed**
3 T. lemon juice	

Melt butter. Add garlic cloves, lemon juice and brown sugar. Mix well. Dip salmon steaks in sauce and roll in crushed peppercorns. Grill 5 minutes on each side and serve.

Dean Donarico
Lilburn, Georgia

Salmon Shore Lunch

Serves: 2-4
Prep Time: 1 hour

2-4 **large salmon fillets**	**salt and pepper to taste**
2 **sticks butter**	**paprika**
1 **can stewed tomatoes**	
2 **medium onions,**	
quartered	
1 **can large peeled**	
potatoes	

Tear off sheet of aluminum foil longer than fillet. Bend sides to form "tray" and line with pats of butter. Place fillets on butter. Top fillets with pats of butter. Drain tomatoes and add to foil along with onion, potato, salt and pepper. Seal tight with another piece of aluminum foil. Grill on open grill for 15 minutes, then turn and cook for another 15 minutes. Sprinkle with paprika before serving.

Dale Bee, Jr.
Taylor, Michigan

Salmon Loaf

Serves: 4
Prep Time: 40 minutes

2 **cups salmon**	1 **tsp. salt**
1 **cup bread crumbs**	**pinch of pepper**
1 **T. onion, chopped**	**water**
2 **eggs**	
1 **T. parsley**	

Mix all ingredients, except water, and shape into loaf. Add ½ cup water. Bake at 350 degrees for 35 minutes. If desired, pour a cream sauce of your choice over loaf when served.

Paul Hennion
Wyckoff, New Jersey

Spiced Salmon & Scalloped Potatoes

Serves: 4
Prep Time: 25 minutes

16 oz. salmon, cooked	cajun spicing
4 medium potatoes, pared and thinly sliced	¹/₂ tsp. cilantro
	¹/₂ tsp. lemon pepper
2 medium onions, peeled and thinly sliced	4 eggs
	2 cups milk
3 T. dill weed	2 T. butter
1 tsp. salt	¹/₂ cup bread crumbs
¹/₄ tsp. pepper	parsley, chopped

Break salmon into fairly large chunks and set aside. Cook potatoes in boiling, salted water for 10 minutes. Drain. Butter shallow casserole dish. Lay half of potatoes and half of onions in dish. Sprinkle with dill, salt, pepper, cajun spices, cilantro and lemon pepper. Add salmon. Layer with remaining potatoes and onions. In separate bowl, whisk eggs and milk, then pour over casserole evenly. Melt butter and mix with crumbs, then sprinkle over the top. Bake uncovered at 350 degrees for 30 minutes or until potatoes are tender. Garnish with parsley.

Victoria Starkey
Albany, Oregon

Onion Broiled Salmon

Serves: 4
Prep Time: 25 minutes

2 salmon fillets	garlic salt
lemon pepper	1 onion

Cut fillets in half and lay on broiling pan and sprinkle garlic salt over them to taste. Shake a generous portion of lemon pepper over entire fillets. Slice onions into rings and cut in half. Lay plenty of onion slices over fillets. Broil for 15-20 minutes until fish flakes easily.

David Rose
Traverse City, Minnesota

Hot Salmon Surprise

Serves: 6
Prep Time: 25 minutes

2 lbs. salmon fillets
1 large onion, diced
1 green bell pepper, diced
2 garlic cloves, minced
¹/₄ cup butter
¹/₂ tsp. hot curry
¹/₄ tsp. marjoram
¹/₈ tsp. chili powder
¹/₄ tsp. oregano
¹/₄ cup soy sauce

2 cups rice
2 cups water

In large skillet, cook onion, bell pepper, garlic and half of butter for 10 minutes over medium heat. Remove. Coat fillets with butter and place in skillet, adding remaining ingredients. Mix well and cover, simmering for 45 minutes or until salmon is cooked.

Don Wilson
West Milton, Ohio

Salmon In Sour Cream

Serves: 3
Prep Time: 20 minutes

3 lbs. salmon
1 T. onion juice
juice of 1 lemon

salt and pepper
1 cup sour cream

Grease bottom of baking dish. Place salmon in baking dish and pour with combined onion juice, lemon juice and salt and pepper. Spread sour cream over fish and bake 45 minutes in moderate oven. Do not overcook.

Edward Jaye
Garfield Heights, Ohio

Crispy Salmon Steaks

Serves: 6
Prep Time: 30 minutes

6 large salmon steaks	**6 lemon wedges**
¹/₂ cup melted butter or	**6 parsley sprigs**
margarine	
2 tsp. salt	
¹/₈ tsp. paprika	
1 cup crushed saltines	
1 cup crushed potato chips	

Combine butter, salt and paprika. Dip steaks into mixture, then roll into combined crushed saltines and potato chips. Arrange steaks on lightly-greased broiler rack in broiler pan. Broil 6 inches from heat for 5 minutes. Turn and broil another 5 minutes or until fish flakes easily with fork. Serve with lemon wedges and parsley sprigs.

Paul Tofil
East Hartford, Connecticut

Salmon Bake

Serves: 10
Prep Time: 30 minutes

1 large whole salmon
2 lbs. carrots, chopped
2 lbs. onions, sliced
2 celery bunches, chopped
5 lbs. potatoes, chopped
salt and pepper
¹/₂ lb. butter

Place all ingredients on large sheet of aluminum foil. Dot with butter and seal well. Cook over hot coals for 1 hour or until vegetables are tender.

Stephen Hieronymus
Washington, Illinois

Salmon Delight

Serves: 4-6
Prep Time: 1 hour

3-4 lbs. salmon fillet
1 pkg. onion soup mix, dry
1 medium onion
5-6 small potatoes

Preheat oven to 350 degrees. Place salmon fillet on heavy aluminum foil sheet that's large enough to fold into tent shape. Peel potatoes and cut into 1-inch cubes. Place potatoes around fillet. Peel onion and cut into rings. Toss onion rings over fillet. Sprinkle soup mix over fillet, potatoes and onion. Fold foil edges into tent shape to keep in moisture. Place on middle rack of oven and bake 1 hour.

Phil Deardorff
Lawrenceburg, Indiana

Breezy Salmon Bake

Serves: 6
Prep Time: 30 minutes

2 lbs. salmon steaks, fresh
or frozen
2 T. onion, grated
1¼ tsp. dill weed
1 T. butter or margarine
1 tsp. salt
dash of pepper
¾ cup light cream

Place steaks on well-greased 12x18-inch bake-and-serve platter. Combine remaining ingredients. Brush steaks with sauce. Broil (about 4 inches from heat source) 10-15 minutes or until steaks flake easily when tested with fork.

Rob Kimball
Huachuca City, Arizona

Salmon Loaf Supreme

Serves: 4
Prep Time: 1 hour, 30 minutes

2 cups salmon, flaked	**1 tsp. lemon juice**
1/2 cup salad dressing	**1 cup fine bread crumbs**
1 cup cream of celery soup, condensed	
1 egg, beaten	
1 tsp. salt	
1/2 cup onion, chopped	
1/4 cup green pepper, chopped	

Combine salad dressing, soup, egg, salt, onion, green pepper and lemon juice. Mix well. Add salmon and bread crumbs. Bake in greased 8x2½-inch loaf pan for 1 hour at 350 degrees. Garnish with lemon wedges and cucumber twists, if desired.

Elizabeth Butchkavitz
Scranton, Pennsylvania

Broiled Salmon Steaks

Serves: 6
Prep Time: 30 minutes

2 lbs. salmon steaks
1 bottle lite Italian salad dressing
salt and pepper

Place steaks in oblong cake pan and pour salad dressing over fish. Cover and refrigerate for at least 1 hour. Remove from refrigerator and place fish on broiler pan. Broil 5-8 minutes per side, basting with marinade. Salt and pepper to taste. Fish is cooked when it flakes with fork.

Paul Krizmencic
Denver, Pennsylvania

Stuffed Salmon Rolls

Serves: 4
Prep Time: 1 hour

- **4 small salmon fillets**
- **1 pkg. broccoli au gratin rice mix**
- **butter**
- **1 can cream of mushroom soup**

Prepare rice. Let cool. Meanwhile, roll salmon fillets around your hand and hold together with toothpicks. Stuff center with rice mixture. Place in baking dish, topping each with a pat of butter. Bake 15 minutes at 350 degrees or until fish is done. Remove toothpicks before serving. While fish is cooking, prepare cream of mushroom soup, using half the amount of water or milk as stated on can. Pour soup over fish and serve.

Robert Beeman
Arvada, Colorado

Volcanic Spread

Serves: 10
Prep Time: 15 minutes

- **1 pt. salmon**
- **1 8-oz. pkg. cream cheese**
- **2-4 T. hot taco sauce**
- **3 drops of liquid smoke mayonnaise (optional) salt and pepper**
- **1 cup cheese, shredded**

Mix fish, cream cheese, taco sauce and liquid smoke to desired consistency, adding mayonnaise to soften. Salt and pepper to taste. Form large ball and roll in shredded cheese. Serve as an hors d'oeuvre with crackers.

Jack Hensley
Lincoln, Nebraska

Sure-Fire Smoked Salmon

Serves: 10
Prep Time: 11 hours

10 lbs. salmon
1 cup rock salt
1 cup regular salt
2 cups brown sugar
1-1½ qts. water

Combine salts and sugar in large bowl. Add water and mix well to make brine. Prepare salmon, cutting slices 4 inches wide. Add to brine. Seal so it's completely airtight. Soak for 5 hours. Pour fish into colander and let air-dry for 1 hour. Place on smoking racks, sprinkling with brown sugar. Smoke fish for 5 hours (longer for thick fish pieces).

Mark Bunney
Everett, Washington

Salmon Party Ball

Serves: 15
Prep Time: 30 minutes

1 can salmon or fresh
   salmon
8 oz. soft cream cheese
1 T. onion, finely chopped
1 T. lemon juice
¼ tsp. liquid smoke
¼ tsp. salt
⅓ cup chopped nuts
¼ cup snipped parsley

Mix all ingredients, except nuts and parsley. Shape into ball. Cover and refrigerate at least 8 hours but no longer than 4 days. Mix nuts and parsley together and coat ball with mixture.

Max Lovegren
Clatskanje, Oregon

Fiesta Salmon

Serves: 2
Prep Time: 1 hour

8 oz. salmon
¹/₂ can cheddar cheese soup
3 T. chili peppers, chopped
2 tsp. onion, chopped
3 T. milk
³/₄ cup tortilla chips,
coarsely chopped

Steam salmon for 15 minutes or until flaky. Meanwhile, combine soup, peppers, onion and milk in saucepan. Heat until bubbly, stirring well. Stir in salmon and ¹/₂ cup tortilla chips. Pour mixture into two 8-oz. individual casserole dishes. Bake uncovered at 375 degrees for 30 minutes. Serve with steamed broccoli.

Mark Bunney
Everett, Washington

Salmon Patties

Serves: 4
Prep Time: 30 minutes

4 lbs. salmon
2 onions, chopped
2 eggs
³/₄ cup flavored bread
crumbs
2 T. mayonnaise
salt and pepper to taste

Boil salmon until it falls off bones. Let cook until flaky. Mix all ingredients together and form into patties. Place ¹/₂ cup bread crumbs in separate dish and coat patties on both sides. Fry in hot oil with a touch of butter until golden brown.

Anne Kosek
Plains, Pennsylvania

Baked Salmon On BBQ Grill

Serves: 4
Prep Time: 1 hour

> **5 lbs. coho salmon**
> **salt**
> **pepper**
> **1 medium onion, sliced**
> **butter**
> **1 lemon**

Light charcoal grill. Season inside of salmon with salt and pepper. Place onion slices and butter on inside and outside of fish. Wrap in aluminum foil and fold seams so juices will not leak. Place on grill about 12 inches from coals and cover. Turn fish after 25 minutes, then cook another 20 minutes. Before eating fish, discard skin. Serve with lemon.

Roger Schmitt
Winter, Wisconsin

Salmon Avocado Spread

Serves: makes 2 cups
Prep Time: 15 minutes

> **8 oz. salmon, canned or**
> **fresh**
> **1 ripe avocado**
> **1 T. olive oil**
> **1 garlic clove, minced**
> **1¹/₂ tsp. onion, grated**
> **¹/₂ tsp. salt**
> **4 drops of Tabasco sauce**

Remove skin and bones from salmon and flake. (If using fresh salmon, cook it first.) Peel avocado, remove seed and smash. Combine all ingredients and toss lightly. Serve on crackers.

Virginia Walker
Waterloo, Oregon

Morse's Salmon Patties

Serves: 6
Prep Time: 15 minutes

2 cups canned salmon, cooked
³/₄ cup canned salmon juice or broth
1 egg
¹/₂ lb. saltine crackers, crushed
cooking oil

Process or roll crackers until fine and set aside. In bowl, mix salmon, broth, egg and half of cracker crumbs until salmon is broken into small, uniform pieces. Shape 10-12 patties and coat with rest of cracker crumbs. Fry quickly in hot oil in skillet until brown on both sides. Serve plain, with lemon or your favorite sauce.

Bruce Morse
Santa Cruz, California

Tangy Chinook

Serves: 12
Prep Time: 45 minutes

12 lbs. chinook
1 onion, sliced
1 lemon, sliced
1 orange, sliced
seasoning salt

salt and pepper
1¹/₂ sticks butter

Make tinfoil bed and lay chinook or salmon (with head on) in it. Stuff with onion, 4 lemon slices, 4 orange slices and 1 stick butter. Season fish with seasoned salt and salt and pepper. Put rest of lemon, orange and butter on top of fish. Cover with tinfoil. Cook for 45 minutes.

Michael Lesperance
Menominee, Michigan

Marinated Salmon Steaks

Serves: 4
Prep Time: overnight plus 30 minutes

4 **salmon steaks, 1-inch
thick**
¹/₄ **cup cooking oil**
¹/₄ **dry white wine**
1 **tsp. lime peel, finely
shredded**

2 **T. lime juice**
1 **T. capers, drained**
2 **garlic cloves, minced**
¹/₄ **tsp. pepper**

Place salmon in shallow dish. For marinade, combine remaining
ingredients and pour over salmon. Turn to coat. Cover and chill
for 6 hours or overnight, turning occasionally. Drain salmon and
reserve marinade. Pat salmon dry. Grill on uncovered grill
directly over medium-hot coals for 2 minutes. Turn and grill
while brushing occasionally with reserved marinade for 6-8
minutes or until salmon flakes.

Bill Guertner
Eatonville, Washington

Smoked Salmon

Serves: 10
Prep Time: 24 hours

5-10 **lbs. salmon chunks**
²/₃ **cup brown sugar**
¹/₄ **cup salt**
1¹/₂ **cups soy sauce**
1¹/₂ **cups water**

¹/₂ **tsp. onion powder**
1 **tsp. garlic**
¹/₂ **tsp. Tabasco sauce**
1¹/₂ **cups white wine**
1 **tsp. pepper**

Combine all ingredients to form brine. Then, soak 3-inch salmon
chunks for 8-10 hours. Remove and drain salmon. Smoke 1-2
panfuls of cherry, alder or apple wood and cook salmon in
smoker 8 or more hours, depending on thickness of chunks.
Remove fish when oil is not present on the fish and fish is firm.

Richard Bartlett
Davison, Michigan

Sweet And Sour Salmon Fillets

Serves: 6
Prep Time: 30 minutes

2 lbs. salmon fillets, cut
   into 2-inch strips
¼ cup flour
1 tsp. salt
   cooking oil
½ cup vinegar
¾ cup sugar
1 cup water

2 chicken bouillon cubes
1 large green pepper, cut
   into rings
1 cup pineapple chunks,
   drained
3 T. cornstarch
1½ tsp. soy sauce
1½ T. water

Roll salmon strips in seasoned flour. In frying pan, heat cooking oil and fry both sides of salmon strips. Drain strips on paper towel. In another deep frying pan, combine vinegar, water, bouillon cubes, green pepper and pineapple. Cook on low heat until sugar melts and green peppers are soft, about 10 minutes. In cup, combine cornstarch, soy sauce and water and mix with spoon. Add gradually to hot sauce. Stir until thick. Pour sweet and sour sauce over cooked fish. Serve with rice.

Gregory Rosson
Cleveland, Ohio

Salmon Steak On The Grill

Serves: 2
Prep Time: 45 minutes

2 salmon steaks, 1-inch
   thick
   butter
   garlic powder

   seasoned salt
2 small onions, sliced
   salt and pepper

Butter bottom of foil pan. Sprinkle both sides of steaks with seasonings to taste. Lay steaks in pan and top with onions and butter. Cover with foil and place on grill. Cook 20 minutes and turn over, removing onion and replacing with more butter. Cover and cook until fish flakes, about 20-25 more minutes.

Tom Polkey
Escanaba, Michigan

Snapper With Cheese

Serves: 6
Prep Time: 1 hour

2 lbs. snapper fillets	**1 tsp. mustard**
1 onion, chopped	**1 tsp. salt**
¹/₂ lb. of your favorite	**¹/₂ tsp. pepper**
cheese, grated	
1 T. butter	
1 cup milk	

Lightly grease fillets and place in bottom of baking pan. Sprinkle onion over fillets, then sprinkle cheese over onion. Mix rest of ingredients together in separate bowl and pour in pan. Place pan in preheated oven and bake at 350 degrees for 45 minutes.

Oswaldo Tapanes
Miami, Florida

Moore's Baked Red Snapper

Serves: 4
Prep Time: 15-20 minutes

1 large red snapper	**1 cup sharp cheddar**
2 T. butter or margarine	**cheese, shredded**
2 T. flour	**dash of cayenne pepper**
2 T. salt	
1 cup milk	

In deep, 1-qt. non-metallic casserole dish, lay fish fillet. Melt butter in medium saucepan. Add flour and salt, blending until smooth. Gradually stir in milk. Add ³/₄ cup cheese and dash of cayenne pepper, stirring constantly until cheese melts into creamy sauce. Pour this mixture over fish and add remaining shredded cheese on top of fish. Cook at 350 degrees for 25-30 minutes

Gary Moore
Eltopia, Washington

Baked Red Snapper

Serves: 8
Prep Time: 20 minutes

3 lbs. snapper fillets, cut
into 8 pieces
1 cup milk
1 tsp. oregano
1 medium onion, sliced
¼ cup olive oil
½ cup pitted ripe olives
¼ cup dry white wine
¼ cup lemon juice
2 T. capers
1 tsp. ground cumin
½ tsp. salt
¼ tsp. pepper
4 large tomatoes, chopped
2 garlic cloves, minced

Place fillets in shallow, glass dish. Mix milk and oregano and
pour over fish. Cover dish and refrigerate for 1 hour. In skillet,
cook and stir onion in oil until tender. Stir in remaining
ingredients except fish. Simmer (uncovered) until thickened,
about 15 minutes. Heat oven to 350 degrees. Drain fish and pat
dry. Place each fillet on individual sheet of aluminum foil. Spoon
some tomato mixture onto fish. Fold foil over fish and secure.
Place foil packets on baking sheet and cook at 350 degrees for
30 minutes or until fish flakes easily with fork. Serve with
cilantro and lemon wedges.

Mike Blackwell
Moorpark, California

Sole In Herb Butter

Serves: 2
Prep Time: 10 minutes

³/₄ lb. sole fillets
5 T. butter
¹/₈ tsp. salt
¹/₈ tsp. onion powder
¹/₄ tsp. fresh parsley, minced
¹/₄ tsp. dried thyme

1 T. mayonnaise
1 T. lemon juice

Preheat broiler. Butter baking dish and rinse fillets in cold water. Pat dry. Melt butter in saucepan. Add remaining ingredients to butter and stir. Place fish in baking dish and top with butter sauce. Broil 3-4 minutes, basting occasionally. Serve immediately.

Robert Rector
Arvada, Colorado

Microwaved Fillet Of Sole In Parsley Butter

Serves: 4
Prep Time: 5 minutes

1 lb. sole fillets
¹/₂ cup margarine or butter
2 T. flour
2 T. fresh lemon juice
1 T. snipped parsley

¹/₄ tsp. salt
¹/₈ tsp. celery seed

Place butter in 10-inch square casserole dish. Microwave on high power until melted. Blend in remaining ingredients except fish. Coat both sides of fillets with butter sauce. Arrange in baking dish and cover with waxed paper. Microwave on high power until fish flakes easily in center with fork.

Robert Rector
Arvada, Colorado

Striper Steaks

Serves: 6
Prep Time: 45 minutes

**6 striper steaks, 1-inch
    thick**
¹/₃ cup melted butter
¹/₂ tsp. salt
¹/₄ tsp. paprika
**1 tsp. Worcestershire
    sauce**
1 T. onion, grated

Place steaks in shallow, greased baking pan. Melt butter and add remaining ingredients except onion. Brush mixture over fish. Sprinkle with onion. Bake uncovered at 350 degrees for 25 minutes. Serve with tartar sauce.

Don Scott
Joplin, Missouri

Honey-Glazed Smoked Sturgeon

Serves: 6
Prep Time: 1 day

2 lbs. sturgeon fillets	⅓ of small bay leaf
½ tsp. salt	water
⅓ lb. dark brown sugar	pan-full of applewood
½ large onion, sliced	honey
1 T. soy sauce	
1 T. Worcestershire sauce	
½ tsp. black pepper	
½ tsp. red pepper	
1 tsp. dill seed	

Cut fillets into 1x6-inch pieces and put into large bowl. Add salt, sugar, onion, soy and Worcestershire sauces, black and red pepper, dill seed and bay leaf. Add just enough water to cover fish. Let stand for 12 hours in cool place. Place fish on cooking racks of smoker. Add wood to pan and smoke at 250 degrees for 5-6 hours. (Time may vary on smoker or types of fish.) After about 3 hours, brush honey over each fillet.

Mark Zawodny
Hood River, Oregon

Quick Cooked Sturgeon

Serves: 4
Prep Time: 20 minutes

1 lb. fresh sturgeon
rice flour
salt and pepper to taste
vegetable oil

Make slits in fillets crosswise, ¼ inch thick. Roll in flour and salt and pepper. Heat vegetable oil in large skillet. Fry sturgeon (no more than 3 minutes per side) until golden brown. Serve immediately.

Jay Christensen
Klamath Falls, Oregon

Sauteed Sturgeon

Serves: varies
Prep Time: 25 minutes

1 **sturgeon steak per**
person
olive oil
butter
¹/₄ **onion, chopped**
3 **garlic cloves, minced**
2 **eggs, beaten**

flour
bread or cracker crumbs
dash of nutmeg
dash of allspice

Heat oil and a bit of butter in skillet. Saute onions and garlic until garlic browns. Dip fish in beaten egg, then roll in flour and bread crumbs mixed with dashes of nutmeg and allspice. Saute steaks on medium heat for 3-4 minutes per side, turning once. Remove and serve when golden brown.

Bill Banducci
Concord, California

Favorite Sturgeon Meatballs

Serves: 4
Prep Time: 2 hours

2 **lbs. sturgeon, ground**
³/₄ **cup Italian bread**
crumbs
¹/₂ **onion, chopped**
1 **egg**
4 **T. olive oil**
red spaghetti sauce
(your favorite)

Mix sturgeon, egg and bread crumbs together thoroughly. Roll into meatball-size balls and brown in olive oil. Add meatballs to sauce and cook about 1 hour. Serve over pasta.

Gary Hamilton
Pittsburg, California

BBQ Swordfish Steaks

Serves: 6
Prep Time: 30 minutes

2 swordfish steaks
¼ cup onion, chopped
2 T. green pepper, chopped
1 garlic clove, minced
2 T. oil or bacon grease
8 oz. tomato sauce

4 T. lemon juice
2 tsp. Worcestershire sauce
2 tsp. sugar
1 tsp. salt
1 tsp. black pepper

Cook onion, green pepper and garlic in oil or grease until tender. Add remaining ingredients, except fish, and simmer for 5 minutes. Remove and allow to cool. Cut steaks into serving-size pieces and lay in single layer in shallow, baking dish. Pour sauce over fish and let stand at room temperature for 30 minutes. Remove fish, saving sauce for basting. Place fish on well-greased, heated grill. Cook 4 inches from medium coals for 8 minutes. Baste often and liberally with sauce. Turn and cook 7-10 minutes longer, or until fish flakes. Serve with sauce.

A. C. Donohue
Lexington, Kentucky

Grilled Swordfish

Serves: varies
Prep Time: 2 hours, 10 minutes

½ lb. swordfish per person
lemon juice
garlic powder

mayonnaise
oregano

Two hours before cooking, sprinkle lemon juice on each piece of fish and spread mayonnaise liberally. Season fish with garlic powder and oregano, cover and refrigerate before serving. Broil or grill 8-10 minutes per side, or until fish is cooked. Cooking time may depend on thickness of fish.

William Macera, Sr.
Worcester, Massachusetts

Stuffed Trout

Serves: 6
Prep Time: 10 minutes

6 trout
salt and pepper
2 cups dry bread crumbs
¹/₃ cup onion, finely
chopped
¹/₄ cup dill pickle, chopped
¹/₂ tsp. paprika
¹/₄ cup salad oil

Season fish with salt and pepper. Place fish in well-greased, shallow baking pan. Combine bread crumbs, onion, pickle and paprika and stuff into slits made in fish. Generously brush fish with salad oil and cover dish with foil. Bake at 350 degrees for 45-60 minutes.

Rob Richardson
Omaha, Nebraska

Grilled Stuffed Trout

Serves: 8-10
Prep Time: 45 minutes

1-5 lbs. fresh trout fillets
seasoning salt
¹/₄ lb. butter or margarine
2 lbs. stuffing (depends on
number of fillets)

Sprinkle seasoning salt on inside and outside of fish. Place 3-4 pats of butter inside fish; then do the same on outside. Stuff fish with prepared stuffing and wrap in aluminum foil. Place on hot grill. Cook 10 minutes per side, turning three times.

Clifford Ponchaud, Sr.
Shawano, Wisconsin

Seviche

Serves: several
Prep Time: 1 hour

2-3 **lbs. trout fillets**
2 **cups lime juice**
1 **green pepper, cubed**
1 **hot pepper, finely**
   chopped
1 **large onion, diced**
1 **garlic clove, minced**
1 **cup stuffed green olives,**
   finely chopped
2 **T. vinegar**
2 **T. lemon juice**
4 **T. olive oil**

$^1/_2$ **tsp. salt**
   pepper to taste
2 **large tomatoes, diced**
   just before serving

Flake fish and soak in lime juice for 24 hours. In separate bowl, mix all other ingredients except tomatoes, which are added just before serving. Keep both bowls in refrigerator. Drain fish and combine all ingredients together just before serving. Serve on your favorite crackers.

Ross Korpela
Carlton, Minnesota

Smoked Trout Cracker Spread

Serves: 8
Prep Time: 30 minutes

1$^1/_4$ **lbs. smoked trout**
3 **sticks butter**
1 **T. lemon juice**

$^1/_3$ **cup heavy cream**
$^1/_8$ **tsp. cayenne pepper**

Melt butter in saucepan. Blend all ingredients in food processor and place in large bowl. Cover bowl and refrigerate 8 hours. Serve with crackers.

W. M. Beck
Rockville, Maryland

Trout Baked In Cream

Serves: 4
Prep Time: 10 minutes

4 whole trout
2 T. fresh lemon juice
1 tsp. dill weed
1 tsp. salt
¹/₄ tsp. white pepper
1 pt. whipping cream
2 T. fine dry seasoned bread crumbs

To remove bone from baked trout, slip knife along entire length of backbone. Pick up backbone starting from tail-end of fish and lift up. Gently turn fish over and lift backbone off other side of fish. Wash and pat fish dry. Brush inside and outside of fish with lemon juice and sprinkle with dill weed, salt and pepper. Place in lightly buttered baking dish. Pour cream over fish. Sprinkle with bread crumbs. Bake at 400 degrees for 15 minutes or until fish flakes easily with fork.

Cecil Robinson, Jr.
Jacksboro, Texas

Brown Barbecue

Serves: 8
Prep Time: 30 minutes

4 lbs. brown trout
1 T. brown sugar
1 tsp. soy sauce
salt and pepper
1 stick butter, melted

Mix all ingredients (except fish) in melted butter. Pour into skillet. Add fish and brown on one side. Baste top of fish, then turn and finish cooking on slow, indirect heat for 20 minutes.

Michael Lesperance
Menominee, Michigan

French Baked Trout

Serves: 6
Prep Time: 1 hour, 30 minutes

6 trout fillets, halved	$^1/_2$ tsp. pepper
4 bacon slices	1 cup dry white wine
1 cup onion, chopped	3 T. butter
1 cup carrots, grated	
1 cup mushrooms, chopped	
2 T. parsley, minced	
$^1/_2$ cup ham, cooked and diced	
2 tsp. salt	
$^1/_2$ tsp. dried thyme	

Half-cook bacon and drain well. Cut into small pieces. Sprinkle bacon in bottom of shallow casserole dish. Mix vegetables together with ham and seasonings. Spread half the mix on bacon, add fish, and top with remaining vegetable mixture. Pour on wine and dot with butter. Bake at 375 degrees for approximately 50 minutes.

Joseph Burns, Jr.
Fort Lewis, Washington

Hickory Dickory Trout

Serves: 2
Prep Time: 30 minutes

$^1/_2$ lb. fresh trout fillets	2 tsp. hickory spices
3 T. butter	1 cheese slice

Melt 2 of the 3 T. butter over low to medium heat. Sprinkle hickory spice over butter. Lay trout fillets in pan. Cook 5-10 minutes, turning when one side is cooked. Lay strips of cheese on top of fish and melt. Remove and serve with wild rice.

Richard Beaupre
Westfield, Massachusetts

Trout Shore Lunch

Serves: 4
Prep Time: 15 minutes

6 fresh trout
salt and pepper
flour
cornmeal
peanut oil
6 potatoes, sliced
2 onions, chopped

Clean trout, leaving head on. Break backbone just behind head and pull toward tail to skin fish. With sharp knife, score meat on each side to backbone every 1-2 inches. Salt and pepper fish. Mix flour and cornmeal together (1 part cornmeal to 2 parts flour works well). Dip fish in flour and cornmeal mixture. Fry fish in peanut oil until golden brown. Meanwhile, in another skillet, fry potatoes and onions. Serve together.

Robert Dunn
Springdale, Arkansas

Chipped Trout

Serves: 6
Prep Time: 15 minutes

2 lbs. fresh trout
Italian salad dressing
1 cup crushed potato chips
$1/2$ cup cheddar cheese
$1/4$ cup melted butter

Dip fillets in salad dressing and place in single layer, skin-side down, in baking dish. Combine crushed potato chips and cheese. Sprinkle this mixture over fish, then drizzle with melted butter. Bake at 400 degrees for 10-15 minutes or until fish flakes easily with fork.

Lynn Gordon
Draper, Utah

Barbecued Trout In Fennel

Serves: 3-5
Prep Time: 20 minutes

6 pan-sized trout
2 leafy fennel bunches
1 oz. butter
$1/2$ tsp. herbs de Provence
$1/2$ tsp. ground black pepper
$1/2$ tsp. garlic salt
charcoal briquettes

Light coals and heat grill. Smear butter on large sheet of aluminum foil, making several small slits in foil. Place fish on foil and surround with fennel. Sprinkle with herbs, garlic salt and pepper. Wrap loosely around fish and place foil directly on coals. Cook for 12 minutes or until fish is done on one side. Turn and cook another 8 minutes or until fish is done. Serve with new potatoes and vegetables.

Steven Lowy
Beverly Hills, California

Oven Baked Trout

Serves: 4
Prep Time: 45 minutes

2 lbs. trout fillets
1 stick butter
1 T. lemon juice
salt and pepper

Place trout on aluminum foil. Spread butter on fillets, then drizzle with lemon juice. Season fish with salt and pepper. Fold foil around fish and bake at 350 degrees for 30 minutes. Serve immediately.

Steve Warner
Morrisville, New York

Bishop Baked Trout

Serves: 4-6
Prep Time: 20 minutes

6 trout fillets
juice of 1 lemon
1 tsp. salt
1 garlic clove, minced
1 cup dry white wine
2 T. parsley, chopped
2 T. green onion heads

2 T. seasoned bread
crumbs
4 T. melted butter

Wash trout and pat dry. Rub inside and outside of fish with lemon juice and salt. Place garlic in bottom of buttered, shallow baking dish, large enough to hold the trout in a single layer. Pour wine over fish. Sprinkle with parsley, green onion and bread crumbs. Spoon butter over fish and bake uncovered at 400 degrees for 20 minutes.

James Miller
Arcadia, California

Golden Fried Trout

Serves: 2
Prep Time: 15 minutes

8 small trout fillets
1 egg
1 T. water
1/2 tsp. salt
2 cups cornflake crumbs
1/4 tsp. pepper

enough oil to cover 1/2
inch in skillet

Beat egg with water, salt and pepper. Dip fillet in egg mixture, coating thoroughly, then dredge through cornflake crumbs. Fry in hot oil until golden brown. Drain on paper towel and enjoy.

Walter Phillips
Hemingford, Nebraska

Bob's Lake Trout

Serves: 4-6
Prep Time: 35 minutes

2-3 lbs. dressed trout
   salt and pepper
6 bacon slices
1 onion, thinly sliced
1 bay leaf, crumbled
3 T. butter
2 T. flour
¹/₂ cup fine cracker crumbs

Preheat oven to 375 degrees. Season trout with salt and pepper.
Lay bacon slices in bottom of shallow baking pan and layer
onion over bacon. Sprinkle with bay leaf and place trout on top.
Mix butter with flour and spread evenly over fish. Sprinkle
crumbs over fish. Bake uncovered 35-40 minutes or until fish is
golden brown and flakes easily with fork.

Bob Goudreau
Lynn, Massachusetts

Brook Trout Meuniere

Serves: 4
Prep Time: 20 minutes

4 brook trout   **parsley, chopped**
   seasoning flour   **lemon wedges**
3 T. butter
¹/₄ cup clarified butter

Dip fish in flour. Saute trout in 3 T. melted butter until firm and
nicely browned, then remove to hot platter. Add clarified butter
to the drippings in pan and let brown. Cover dish with chopped
parsley and pour the browned butter over fish. Garnish with
lemon wedges.

Victoria Starkey
Albany, Oregon

Bob's Baked Brookies

Serves: 4-6
Prep Time: 15 minutes

6-8 small brook trout
¹/₄ cup parsley
2 T. butter
2 T. flour
¹/₄ cup cheddar cheese,
grated
¹/₂ cup cracker crumbs

¹/₄ cup chives or green
onion, chopped

Preheat oven to 375 degrees. Grease shallow baking pan and lay parsley in bottom. Add fish. Mix butter and flour and spread on fish. Mix cheese, cracker crumbs and green onion and sprinkle evenly over fish. Bake 15-20 minutes or until fish is golden and flakes easily but is still moist.

Bob Goudreau
Lynn, Massachusetts

Steam Baked Trout

Serves: 6
Prep Time: 50 minutes

6 1-lb. trout
vegetable oil
salt, pepper and thyme
2 lemons, sliced
2 tomatoes, sliced
1 onion, sliced

Rub trout with oil. Sprinkle salt, pepper and thyme inside and out. Lay fish in oiled baking pan and cover with layer of sliced lemon, tomato and onion. Cover with foil and bake at 350 degrees for 30-40 minutes. Serve with lemon, tomato and onion as garnish.

Bill Segraves
San Diego, California

Baked Trout in Wine Sauce

Serves: 4
Prep Time: 25 minutes

4 lbs. trout fillets
1 cup dry white wine
juice of 1 lemon
¹/₄ tsp. paprika
1¹/₂ tsp. salt
2 tsp. parsley, finely
chopped
2 T. olive oil
3 T. melted butter

¹/₄ tsp. dried thyme
1 cup slivered almonds

Combine all ingredients, except trout and almonds. Arrange fillets in single layer in baking dish. Pour mixture over fish, and sprinkle almonds over fish. Bake in preheated oven at 350 degrees for 20-30 minutes.

Kurtis Feil
Lovelock, Nevada

Grilled Trout

Serves: 4
Prep Time: 15 minutes

2 lbs. trout fillets
1 stick butter
1 tsp. parsley
1 tsp. black pepper
1 tsp. salt
1 garlic clove, chopped

1 small onion, chopped
1 lemon

Melt butter and add parsley, pepper, salt, garlic and onion. Brush mixture over fillets. Wrap trout in aluminum foil and place on medium grill. Cook 10 minutes per side or until fish is white and flakes easily. Remove and sprinkle with lemon juice.

Jason Safcik
Peoria, Arizona

Barbecued Brook Trout

Serves: 4
Prep Time: 20 minutes

4 brook trout	**4-5 potatoes, diced and pan-**
1 onion, sliced	**fried separately**
lemon juice	
salt and pepper	
4 bacon strips	
parsley	
1 lb. fresh green beans	

Open each cleaned fish and place sliced onion and lemon juice inside. Salt and pepper inside and outside of fish lightly. Fasten bacon strip lengthwise onto fish. Grill on wire rack 10-15 minutes per side or until brown. Garnish with parsley and serve with green beans and potatoes.

Carlos Whitney
Greenville, New Hampshire

Fried Trout and Potatoes

Serves: 4
Prep Time: 30 minutes

4 trout, cleaned	**$^1/_2$ cup butter-flavored**
$^1/_2$ cup flour	**shortening**
$^1/_2$ tsp. each salt, pepper,	**4 small potatoes, thinly**
thyme, cajun spices,	**sliced**
cilantro and dill	

Mix flour and spices together. Dip trout in water, then roll in flour mixture until completely covered. Place shortening in skillet and add fish and potatoes. Cook on medium heat until fish is done. Place fish on platter in oven to keep warm. Fry potatoes until cooked. Place fish and potatoes in skillet. Cook another 2 minutes and serve.

Victoria Starkey
Albany, Oklahoma

Trout With Herb Stuffing

Serves: 2-3
Prep Time: 25 minutes

2-3 trout, pan-dressed	**¹/₃ cup green onions, sliced**
¹/₂ tsp. salt	**1 T. parsley, chopped**
2 cups herb stuffing	**1 T. pimiento, chopped**
¹/₃ cup melted butter	**2 tsp. lemon juice**
¹/₂ cup fresh mushrooms, sliced	**¹/₄ tsp. butter**

Wash trout and pat dry. In mixing bowl, combine remaining ingredients. Stuff mixture in long, lengthwise slit made in trout and place in steamer basket. Cover and steam until fish is completely cooked.

Robert Perry
Clifton, Colorado

Stuffed Trout

Serves: 2
Prep Time: 1 hour

1 3-4 lb. trout	**3 oz. mushrooms, chopped**
salt to taste	**¹/₄ cup butter**
1 T. lemon juice	**1 tsp. salt**
8 bread slices	**1 tsp. poultry seasoning**
1 medium onion, quartered	**¹/₈ tsp. white pepper**
2 cups celery, sliced	

Preheat oven to 425 degrees. Rub inside of trout with salt and sprinkle with lemon juice. Tear bread slices in blender until finely crumbed, and put in mixing bowl. Blend onion and celery until coarsely chopped. Add onion, celery, mushrooms, melted butter, salt, poultry seasoning and pepper to bread crumbs. Fill trout with stuffing and fasten with skewers and string. Wrap in foil and bake in shallow pan for 30 minutes. Open foil and bake 15 minutes longer. During last 15 minutes, baste with melted butter or margarine.

Gerald Jackson
Shoreview, Minnesota

Cheesy Trout Bake

Serves: 4
Prep Time: 45 minutes

1 lb. cooked trout, flaked or smoked	1 tsp. salt
2 T. butter	$1/8$ tsp. pepper
2 T. flour	
1 cup milk	
2 cups pasta, uncooked	
$1/2$ lb. cheddar cheese, grated	

Preheat oven to 375 degrees. Grease casserole dish. In saucepan, melt butter. Add flour and stir until smooth. Add milk, stirring continuously to avoid lumps. Heat until mixture thickens. Add trout, pasta, cheese, salt and pepper. Mix well. Bake 30 minutes.

Phillip Wright
Warren, Ohio

Sour Dill Mash

Serves: 2
Prep Time: 20 minutes

2 trout (without heads)	sliced cocktail onions, drained
olive oil	almond slivers
salt and pepper	
dill sprigs	
Jack Daniels Sour-Mash Whiskey	

In heated, oiled skillet, place trout. Season fish with salt and pepper to taste. Line fish cavity with dill sprigs and dribble with whiskey and sliced cocktail onions. Cover skillet and cook over low heat, 7 minutes per side. Garnish with slivered almonds.

Gary Mills
Winnemucca, Nevada

Mediterranean Trout

Serves: 4-6
Prep Time: 20 minutes

1 lb. trout fillets
rice
garlic powder
1½ sticks butter
small bottle capers
4 oz. sweet vermouth

salt, pepper and lemon
to taste

Cook rice and set aside, keeping warm. Place fish in broiler pan and sprinkle lightly with garlic powder. Coat fillets with butter, then place under broiler. When butter is melted, pour capers and vermouth over fillets. Baste fish frequently. Serve fish and sauce over rice. Salt, pepper and sprinkle with lemon juice to taste.

Jim Pickett
Tampa, Florida

Parmesan Trout

Serves: 4-6
Prep Time: 30 minutes

6 12-inch trout fillets
milk
salt
pepper
paprika
2 T. Parmesan cheese,
grated

1 cup cornflakes, finely
crushed
4 bacon slices
dry white wine

Dip fillets in milk mixed with salt, pepper and paprika. Add cheese to cornflakes, and dip trout in dry mixture. Lay bacon slices in bottom of greased baking dish. Lay fish on bacon. Sprinkle with salt and pepper and a dash of white wine. Bake at 350 degrees for 25-30 minutes.

Gerald Jackson
Shoreview, Minnesota

Trout and Herbs

Serves: 4
Prep Time: 30 minutes

4 trout
1/2 cup dry red wine
1/4 cup olive oil
1/4 cup water
1/2 cup onion, chopped
1/2 tsp. dried mint
1/2 tsp. dried rosemary

1/2 tsp. thyme leaves
1 bay leaf, crushed
1 tsp. salt
15 whole peppercorns
3 egg yolks, slightly
  beaten

Clean and dress fish. In baking dish, combine wine, oil, water, onion, mint and seasonings. Stir. Place trout in marinade, coating thoroughly. Let stand at room temperature for 30 minutes. Place fish in baking dish. Bring marinade to a simmer in saucepan and then pour over fish. Cover with waxed paper and bake at 350 degrees for 20 minutes. Whisk 1/4 cup liquid with egg yolks. Whisk egg mixture into boiling liquid. Heat mixture in saucepan until slightly thickened. Pour over fish and serve.

Roy McClellan
Church Hill, Tennessee

Trout Dieppe

Serves: 4-6
Prep Time: 10 minutes

1 1/2 lbs. trout
1/2 cup water
1/2 cup white wine
1 can cream of shrimp
  soup

lemon slice
parsley sprig
cheese, grated

Simmer (poach) fillets in seasoned wine and water mixture 4-5 minutes or until fish is white and flakes easily. Drain liquid and mix with soup. Heat this until soup is warm. Place fillets in shallow, baking dish. Cover with shrimp sauce. Sprinkle with grated cheese and broil lightly.

Harold Baker
Colorado Springs, Colorado

Fresh Grilled Tuna Salad

Serves: 4-6
Prep Time: 20 minutes

4 tuna steaks
¹/₂ bottle Italian salad dressing
¹/₂ bottle creamy Italian salad dressing
salt and pepper
1¹/₂ cups celery, finely chopped
1 egg, boiled and crumbled

¹/₂ onion, finely chopped
mayonnaise

Marinate steaks in salad dressings, (covered), for 1 hour. Remove steaks and cook on grill 6 minutes per side, basting frequently with salad dressings. After tuna has cooled, break into small pieces and place in large bowl. Add remaining ingredients, using enough mayonnaise for desired consistency. The flavor from the grill is dynamite.

Thomas Ruffin, III
Murrells Inlet, South Carolina

Tempting Tuna

Serves: 4-6
Prep Time: 15 minutes

4 large tuna steaks
¹/₂ bottle Italian salad dressing

¹/₂ bottle creamy Italian salad dressing
salt and pepper

Pour both salad dressings into large casserole dish. Place tuna in dish, cover and marinate for 1 hour. Salt and pepper fish. Place on grill and cook 6 minutes per side, basting frequently with dressing mixture. Be sure to cook on grill rack, not directly on hot coals.

Thomas Ruffin, III
Murrells Inlet, South Carolina

Tuna Seafood Salad

Serves: 4-6
Prep Time: 25 minutes

1 8-oz. tuna steak
6 oz. elbow macaroni
1 can lump crabmeat
$^1/_2$ can small shrimp
$^2/_3$ cup mayonnaise
$^1/_3$ cup onion, chopped
$^1/_3$ cup celery, chopped
1 T. lemon juice
   garlic salt to taste
   parsley to taste
   seafood seasoning to
   taste

Grill tuna steak 4 minutes per side, brushing with butter. Meanwhile, cook and drain macaroni. Place macaroni in large bowl and toss with crab, shrimp and cooked, flaked tuna. Add mayonnaise, onion, celery and lemon juice. Season with garlic salt, parsley and seafood seasoning. Mix well and serve.

Paul Oliver
Englishtown, New Jersey

Light Tuna Spread

Serves: 4
Prep Time: 15 minutes

6 oz. tuna
1 8-oz. pkg. light cream
   cheese
1 tsp. tomato paste

Drain tuna. Mix all ingredients thoroughly. This can be used as a sandwich spread.

Kevin Druzdzel
Moundsview, Minnesota

Favorite Walleye Fillets

Serves: 4
Prep Time: 30 minutes

16 **walleye fillets, cut into 4-inch pieces**
vegetable oil for frying
3 **cups flour**
1 **large onion, chopped**
garlic and onion salt
parsley flakes

1 **T. lemon juice**
2 **cans beer**
3 **handfuls cornflakes**

Heat 2 inches of oil to high heat in deep skillet or pan. Mix flour, onion, garlic and onion salts, parsley flakes and lemon juice into paste. Add 1 can of beer. Crush cornflakes and add to mixture. Stir with fork to consistency of light pancake batter, using as much of the second can of beer as necessary. If batter thickens while standing, add more beer. If batter gets too thin, add more cornflakes. Dip fillets in batter and gently place in oil. Turn over when golden brown.

Rodney Kemp
Rhinelander, Wisconsin

Garlic Butter Walleye

Serves: 4
Prep Time: 30 minutes

4 **walleye fillets**
1 **garlic clove, minced**
4 **T. butter or margarine**
parsley flakes

Place walleye fillets in baking dish. Melt butter in small frying pan and add garlic. Saute until tender. Pour over fillets and sprinkle with parsley flakes. Bake at 350 degrees for 15-20 minutes or until done.

Mark Roesler
Inver Grove Heights, Minnesota

Cheese-Covered Walleye

Serves: 4
Prep Time: 35 minutes

- **2 lbs. walleye fillets,
  skinned**
- **1 cup cheddar cheese,
  shredded**
- **¹/₂ cup milk**
- **2 T. butter**
- **1 T. flour**
- **¹/₄ tsp. nutmeg**

Place fillets in 9x12-inch baking dish and set aside. In saucepan on low heat, melt butter. Add flour, continuously stirring until thickened. Add milk and nutmeg and blend well. Stir until mixture thickens again. Add cheese, stirring until melted and pour over walleye fillets. Bake at 350 degrees for 20-30 minutes. Let cool for 3 minutes before serving.

Gregory Rosson
Cleveland, Ohio

Breakfast Walleye

Serves: 4
Prep Time: 10 minutes

- **2 lbs. walleye fillets**
- **2 T. bacon drippings**
- **2 T. lemon juice
  salt and pepper to taste**

Heat bacon drippings in frying pan on medium heat. Fry fillets for 10 minutes, turning once. Sprinkle with lemon juice when cooked. Serve with fried eggs, bacon strips and hot buttered toast.

Maitland Brempell
Iron River, Wisconsin

Southern Oriental-Spiced Walleye

Serves: 4
Prep Time: 30 minutes

1¹/₂ lbs. walleye fillets
¹/₄ cup soy sauce
2 T. sesame oil
1 garlic clove, minced
¹/₄ tsp. ground ginger
2 T. butter

Arrange fillets in single layer in shallow container. Mix soy sauce, oil, garlic and ginger and spoon over fish. Marinate for 15 minutes, turning once. Place fillets on buttered piece of aluminum foil on broiler pan. Place a pat of butter on each fillet. Place under preheated broiler about 4 inches from heat and cook for 3 minutes. Turn and cook for another 3 minutes or until fish is flaky.

Jules Boone
Christiansburg, Virginia

Basted Walleye Fillets

Serves: 4-6
Prep Time: 5 minutes

3-4 lbs. walleye fillets
2 T. margarine
1 tsp. seasoning salt

On large sheet of aluminum foil, brush half of melted margarine in center and sprinkle with half of seasoning salt. Place fillets on mixture and cover with remaining margarine and seasoning salt. Fold and seal ends, then wrap again with another piece of foil. Cook on hot grill about 10 minutes per side. Serve with your choice of potato and fresh salad.

Gary Miller
Pendleton, Oregon

Crunchy Fried Walleye

Serves: 4-6
Prep Time: 30 minutes

1½ **lbs. walleye**
1 **egg**
1 **cup evaporated milk**
2 **cups cracker crumbs**
⅛ **tsp. salt**
⅛ **tsp. pepper**
2-4 **T. vegetable oil**

In shallow plate or pie plate, blend eggs and milk, then combine cracker crumbs, salt and pepper. Cut fish into serving-size pieces. Dip fish in milk, then coat with cracker crumbs. In 9-inch skillet, heat oil. Fry a few pieces at a time, until golden brown, about 3 minutes. Turn. Keep cooked fillets warm in oven at 175 degrees until all are ready to serve.

Richard Paschke
Janesville, Wisconsin

Oregano Walleye

Serves: varies
Prep Time: 15 minutes

walleye fillets
butter or margarine
oregano
garlic powder
seasoned bread crumbs

Grease skillet with butter or margarine and heat at medium temperature. Sprinkle oregano and garlic powder in skillet to season butter. Saute fillets until flaky and turn once. Sprinkle bread crumbs liberally on fillets. Saute another minute.

Francis Stack
Lorain, Ohio

Pike Florentine

Serves: 4
Prep Time: 30 minutes

2 lbs. walleye fillets
2-3 T. melted butter
fresh ground pepper to
taste
8 oz. frozen spinach,
thawed and drained

¹/₂ cup Parmesan cheese
lemon wedges

Wash and arrange fillets on greased rack in roasting pan. Brush each fillet with melted butter and season with pepper. Arrange spinach over each fillet. Sprinkle with Parmesan cheese. Bake at 350 degrees for 20 minutes. During last 5 minutes of baking, turn on broiler until cheese browns. Serve immediately with lemon wedges squeezed over the top.

Charles Tanner
Aurora, Ohio

Walleye Soup

Serves: 5
Prep Time: 20 minutes

1¹/₂ lbs. walleye fillets
3 cups potatoes, diced
1 cup onion, chopped
1 cup celery, chopped
¹/₂ cup green pepper,
chopped
¹/₄ cup parsley, chopped

1 can evaporated milk
1 8-oz. pkg. cream cheese
salt and lemon pepper to
taste

Add first 6 ingredients to large kettle and add enough water so ingredients are covered. Boil until potatoes are tender, about 15 minutes. Lower heat. Add milk, cream cheese and salt and pepper. Do not boil. Heat and serve.

Lori Lynn Leathers
Isle, Minnesota

Rolled Walleye Fillets

Serves: 4
Prep Time: 30 minutes

4 walleye fillets
¹/₂ onion, chopped
Italian bread crumbs
1 pkg. cream cheese
1 large egg

Skin fillets. If too thick, cut again lengthwise. Mix onion, bread crumbs and cheese in bowl. Add enough bread crumbs until batter is thick and stiff. Lay a fillet flat and place a spoonful of batter on it. Roll it lengthwise. Dip rolled fillet in beaten egg and roll in bread crumbs. Repeat with other fillets. Fry in skillet on medium heat. Turn when brown. Serve.

Adelle Keech
Hale, Michigan

Walleye Royale

Serves: 2
Prep Time: 20 minutes

2 walleye fillets
lemon pepper seasoning
¹/₂ medium onion, diced
1 tomato, sliced
paprika
lemon slices

Place fillets on sheets of aluminum foil. Season with lemon pepper seasoning and cover with diced onion. Lay tomato slices on onion and cover fish and onion. Seal fish in foil. Place on hot grill or in oven and bake 15 minutes at 400 degrees. Open foil and sprinkle with paprika. Cook 5 more minutes (foil should be open in oven or closed on grill). Serve with lemon wedges.

Gerald Koth
Concord Township, Ohio

Scavenger's Walleye

Serves: 4
Prep Time: 30 minutes

4 **walleye fillets**
3 **T. lemon juice**
2 **cups red wine vinegar**
2 **T. olive oil**
3 **garlic cloves, minced**
4 **T. parsley, chopped**

$^{1}/_{2}$ **cup green onions, chopped**
2 **pinches of peanut butter**
1$^{1}/_{2}$ **cups tomato sauce**
salt and pepper to taste

Place fillets in shallow dish and marinate with lemon juice and red wine vinegar. Let stand 30 minutes in refrigerator. In large skillet, heat olive oil, garlic, parsley and green onion. Cook until tender. Remove from griddle and set aside. On griddle, place peanut butter and brown each fillet in it. Remove fillets and place in baking dish. Add tomato sauce, spices, lemon juice and cooked mixture from griddle. Bake at 350 degrees for 35 minutes. Cover with aluminum foil for 30 minutes and finish cooking if needed. Serve.

Charles Walouke
Mentor, Ohio

Herb Baked Walleye

Serves: 1-2
Prep Time: 20-25 minutes

1$^{1}/_{2}$ **lbs. walleye fillets**
1 **tsp. parsley**
1 **tsp. paprika**
$^{1}/_{2}$ **tsp. oregano**
$^{1}/_{2}$ **tsp. salt**

$^{1}/_{4}$ **tsp. pepper**
1 **T. melted butter**
lemon wedges

Place fish into greased, glass baking dish. Sprinkle seasonings on fish. Drizzle butter and squeeze lemon juice over fish. Bake at 400 degrees for about 20 minutes.

Ron Pasch
Freeport, Illinois

Yellowtail Veracruz

Serves: 6-8
Prep Time: 30 minutes

**3 lbs. yellowtail fillets
salt
2 T. lime juice
2 lbs. ripe tomatoes
$^1/_4$ cup olive oil
1 medium onion, peeled
  and sliced
2 garlic cloves, minced
1 large bay leaf
$^1/_4$ tsp. oregano
2 jalapenos, sliced
12 green olives, pitted and
  halved
2 T. large capers**

Rub fillets with salt and lime juice. Place in single layer in casserole dish. Set aside. Skin, seed and chop tomatoes and set aside. Heat oil and add onion and garlic. Cook in frying pan until soft. Add tomatoes and remaining ingredients (except fish) and cook 10 minutes. Pour sauce over fillets and bake at 450 degrees until done. Allow 10 minutes cooking time per inch of thickness, with 10 minutes being a minimum.

Coni Rohrer-Sansome
San Diego, California

Fish Cakes

Serves: 4-6
Prep Time: 30 minutes

24 herring
1 medium potato
1 medium onion
2 tsp. nutmeg
4 eggs
milk
salt and pepper

Grind fish, potato and onion together in food processor or in bowl with electric mixer. Add remaining ingredients. Slowly add salt and pepper to taste; the more salt added the thicker the mixture. When mixture is desired consistency, remove and shape into cakes. Fry in shortening. Batter may be kept 1-2 days in refrigerator, and fish cakes may be frozen after frying.

Arthur Runston
Sauk Rapids, Minnesota

Creamy Fish Bake

Serves: 4
Prep Time: 30 minutes

1 lb. fish fillets
1 can cream of shrimp
  soup
¹/₂ cup sour cream
1 T. onion, chopped
1 T. horseradish
¹/₄ tsp. paprika

Combine all ingredients except fish. Lay fish in bottom of baking pan and pour mixture over fish. Bake in preheated oven at 325 degrees for 30 minutes.

William Smith
Burlington, Wisconsin

Hungarian Baked Fish

Serves: 6
Prep Time: 1 hour

3 lbs. rockfish, backbone removed
4 bacon slices, diced
1 medium potato, peeled and cooked
3 large green peppers, sliced and boiled
salt and pepper to taste

4 tomatoes, cut into ¼-inch slices
1 tsp. flour
1 tsp. paprika
1 cup sour cream

Make crosswise incisions in fish 2 inches apart. Fill cuts with bacon pieces. Grease baking dish. Cut potatoes into ½-inch slices and lay slices in dish. Cover with pepper slices and season with salt and pepper. Top with tomato slices and season lightly. Put fish on top, flesh up, and sprinkle with combined flour and paprika. Bake in preheated oven at 400 degrees for 15 minutes. Spread sour cream over fish and bake another 5 minutes, or until done.

Joseph Burns, Jr.
Fort Lewis, Washington

Gordon's Fish Loaf

Serves: 8
Prep Time: 10 minutes

2 cups fish
2 eggs
1 cup soft bread crumbs
¾ cup milk
1 T. lemon juice

1 small onion, chopped
1 tsp. parsley
1 tsp. salt
½ tsp. pepper

Beat eggs lightly. Combine remaining ingredients and mix well. Bake in greased loaf pan at 350 degrees for 1 hour.

Lynn Gordon
Drader, Utah

Treacher's Style Fish & Chips

Serves: 6-8
Prep Time: 45 minutes

3 **lbs. fresh fish fillets** **enough buttermilk to** **cover fillets**	2 **cups pancake mix or** **self-rising flour**
1 **lemon, sliced**	2½ **cups club soda**
8 **oz. oil**	1 **cup flour**

Soak fillets in buttermilk. Refrigerate in covered container for 2 hours with lemon slices placed over fish. Heat oil in heavy 2½-qt. saucepan. Drain buttermilk from fillets. In another bowl, combine pancake mix and club soda to give batter the consistency of buttermilk. Dip floured fillets into batter, letting excess drip off into batter bowl. Deep-fry for 4 minutes on each side and keep warm in 250-degree oven until all fillets are fried. Chips can be made by cutting crinkle-cut frozen cottage-style potatoes in half and frying as you would French fries.

George Lain, Sr.
Elk Grove, Illinois

Broiled Fish A L'Orange

Serves: 4
Prep Time: 30 minutes

2 **lbs. fish steaks**	1 **tsp. salt**
2 **T. orange juice**	2 **T. butter**
1 **T. orange peel, grated**	
4 **tsp. Worcestershire** **sauce**	

Arrange fish on rack in broiler pan. Combine remaining ingredients and brush lightly over fish. Place under hot broiler for 10 minutes (depending on thickness of steaks), basting with remaining sauce.

Daniel Silvestro
New York, New York

Beer Batter (Fish & Seafood)

Serves: makes enough for 2 lbs. of fish
Prep Time: 40 minutes

1 cup flour	1 egg
¹/₂ tsp. baking powder	1 cup beer
1 tsp. lemon peel (dried)	1 tsp. vegetable oil
1 tsp. onion powder	
¹/₂ tsp. tarragon leaves, crushed (dried)	
salt and white pepper to taste	

Put flour in mixing bowl. Add baking powder, lemon peel, onion powder, tarragon and salt and pepper. Beat egg into flour mixture using whisk. Slowly add beer and whip until batter is smooth. Brush top with vegetable oil, then cover mixture with plastic wrap and allow to sit in warm place for 30 minutes. Heat oil in deep-fryer to 350 degrees. Dip fish or seafood pieces in batter allowing excess to drip back into batter. Deep-fry until golden brown. Serve with lemon wedges.

Earl Ball
Phoenix, Arizona

Kwik Fish Oriental

Serves: 4
Prep Time: 20 minutes

1 lb. fresh fish fillets	¹/₂ medium onion, chopped
¹/₂ cup teriyaki marinade	¹/₄ cup peanut oil
¹/₂ tsp. pepper	
1 T. garlic salt	

Marinate fish in marinade for 1 hour. Season fish with pepper and garlic salt. Saute onion in peanut oil, adding margarine if necessary. Add fish and cook thoroughly, about 5 minutes. Turn once during cooking.

Richard Graham
McCordsville, Indiana

Swiss Fish Quiche

Serves: 6
Prep Time: 60 minutes

2 **cups cooked fish**	3 **eggs, beaten**
1 **9-inch pastry shell**	$^1/_4$ **cup onion, chopped**
1 **cup Swiss cheese,**	2 **T. green pepper**
shredded	2 **T. pimiento**
2 **T. flour**	$^1/_2$ **cup cheddar cheese,**
1 **T. instant chicken**	**grated**
bouillon	
1 **cup milk**	

Bake pastry shell 8 minutes, then remove and cool. Reduce oven to 350 degrees. In bowl, toss Swiss cheese, flour, bouillon and milk. Beat eggs and add to milk mixture. Place fish, onions, green pepper and pimiento in cooked pastry shell. Pour milk mixture over fish in pastry shell. Cook for 40 minutes. Top with cheddar cheese. Place in oven 5 minutes. Let stand 10 minutes before serving. Serve hot.

Mrs. D. Sailer
Mauston, Wisconsin

Fillets In Coral Sauce

Serves: 4-6
Prep Time: 20 minutes

2 **lbs. fish fillets**	2 **T. lemon juice**
1 **tsp. salt**	1 **tsp. onion, grated**
dash of pepper	$^1/_4$ **cup butter**
1 **tsp. paprika**	

Cut fillets into serving-size pieces. Place fish in single layer in well-greased baking pan, skin-side down. Combine remaining ingredients and pour over fish. Bake at 350 degrees until white and flaky, about 10 minutes.

Marge Fong
Chatfield, Minnesota

Maine-ly Fish Chowder

Serves: 6
Prep Time: 1 hour

leftover fish (any kind)	**3 cups milk**
¹/₄ lb. salt pork	**1 can evaporated milk**
2 medium onions, chopped	
5 cups potatoes, diced	
1-1¹/₂ cups water	
¹/₂ tsp. salt	
¹/₄ tsp. pepper	
¹/₄ tsp. Accent seasoning	

Fry salt pork in pan until fat melts and turns golden. Do not burn. Remove pork. Add onions to fat and fry until golden. Add potatoes and water, then add enough fish to fit pot. Add seasonings, but do not stir. Bring to a boil, then cook at low heat until potatoes are done and fish flakes. Be careful not to break fish. Add milk and evaporated milk. Heat well, but do not boil. Sprinkle salt pork on chowder when served.

Vito Ancona
Lisbon Falls, Maine

Fish Steamed In Tomato Sauce

Serves: 4
Prep Time: 7 minutes

3 lbs. fish fillets	**2 T. onion, minced**
3 cups tomatoes	**³/₄ tsp. peppercorns**
³/₄ tsp. salt	**2 T. butter**
2 bay leaves	

Place tomatoes, salt, bay leaves onion and peppercorns in deep pot. Wrap fish in cheese cloth and place on rack in pot. Cover and steam for 9 minutes. Remove fish and strain sauce, adding butter. Pour over fish and serve.

Robert Schmitt
Ellenton, Florida

Fish Stew/Chowder

Serves: 6
Prep Time: 30 minutes

½ **cup any kind of flaky leftover fish butter**
1 **bunch green onions, chopped**
1 **garlic clove, chopped**
1 **cup white wine**
12-15 **oysters (optional)**
½ **cup small (or cubed) scallops**

½ **cup shrimp**
½ **cup crab flakes, cooked**
½ **cup canned clams**
1 **can potato soup**
1 **tsp. garlic salt with parsley**
2 **tsp. black pepper**
2 **qts. milk (half & half is richer)**

Melt butter in skillet. Saute onions and garlic until soft, then transfer to soup pot. Add wine to skillet. Saute oysters (about 3 minutes each side), then transfer to soup pot. Saute scallops about 2 minutes; add to pot. Saute shrimp about 2 minutes and add to pot. Add rest of ingredients and stir well. Heat and serve with sour dough bread or crispy oyster crackers.

Bruce Morse
Santa Cruz, California

Linguini And Fish

Serves: 4
Prep Time: 20 minutes

1 **lb. fish fillets**
2 **garlic cloves**
6-8 **T. olive oil**
1 **medium tomato, chopped**

½ **medium green pepper, chopped**
1 **lb. No. 8 linguini**
Romano cheese, grated

Finely chop garlic and saute in olive oil. Chop fish into ¼-inch pieces. Add fish to garlic in olive oil. Cook fish 2-3 minutes—do not overcook. Add green pepper and cook 1 minute. Add tomato. When tomato is heated thoroughly, serve over bed of linguini cooked al dente. Cover with grated cheese to taste.

William Trout
Des Moines, Iowa

Fisherman's Soup

Serves: 6-8
Prep Time: 30 minutes

1 lb. fish fillets, boneless
8 cups chicken broth
1 T. cornstarch, dissolved
in ¼ cup water
¼ lb. scallops, poached
3 cups white rice, cooked
salt and pepper to taste

¼ cup red pepper, diced
¼ cup green pepper, diced

In stock pot, heat chicken broth to boiling. Add fish fillets and cook 2 minutes. Gradually stir in cornstarch and water mixture, stirring constantly until slight thickening occurs. Add poached scallops and rice. Heat thoroughly. Season with salt and pepper and ladle into bowls. Top with red and green peppers. (To poach scallops: Place scallops and 3 T. lemon juice in non-stick skillet. Cover and cook 4-6 minutes or until just tender.)

Jerry Adams
Duluth, Georgia

Lemon-Fried Fish Sandwiches

Serves: 4
Prep Time: 1 hour, 30 minutes

8 fish fillets
lemon juice
2 T. garlic salt
2 cups flour
4 hoagie rolls

Place fillets in glass bowl and cover with lemon juice. (Fresh-squeezed lemons are best.) Marinate for 1 hour. Mix garlic salt and flour in bowl. Dip fillets in dry mixture and fry in hot oil. Make sandwiches on hoagie rolls with lots of mayonnaise, lettuce and tomato.

Mrs. Jeffrey Lapp
Wasilla, Arkansas

Avocado Stuffed With Seafood

Serves: 6
Prep Time: 30 minutes

¹/₂ **lb. leftover cooked fish, boned and mashed**	¹/₄ **cup chili sauce**
3 **avocados**	**few drops of Worcestershire sauce**
juice of 1 lemon	**few drops of Tabasco sauce**
¹/₂ **lb. mixture of any or all: shrimp, tuna, clams and crab, all mashed**	1 **onion, finely minced**
	parsley, chopped
¹/₂ **cup mayonnaise**	**salt and pepper to taste**

Split each avocado in two and take out nut. Sprinkle lemon or lime juice on each half so it will not discolor. Mix all fish together and set aside. Mix remaining ingredients and add to fish mixture. Fill each avocado half with this mixture. Serve on a few leaves of lettuce. Garnish with radish rosette or parsley leaves.

Vince Pugliese
Pittsburgh, Pennsylvania

Fish Casserole

Serves: 3 cups
Prep Time: 30 minutes

2 **cups fish fillets, parboiled and cut up**	**milk**
1 **cup cheddar cheese soup, condensed**	1 **T. parsley, chopped**
	¹/₄ **cup buttered bread crumbs**

Stir soup in 1-qt. casserole dish. Gradually add milk. Stir in fish and parsley. Bake at 350 degrees for 25 minutes. Top with bread crumbs. Bake 5 minutes more or until lightly browned.

Kevin Vergon
South Whitley, Indiana

Lemon-Stuffed Fish

Serves: 4
Prep Time: 30 minutes

4 fish fillets	1 tsp. salt
¹/₂ cup celery, chopped	pepper to taste
¹/₄ cup onion, chopped	1 T. melted butter
3 T. butter	paprika
4 cups croutons	
¹/₂ tsp. lemon peel, grated	
4 tsp. lemon juice	
1 T. fresh parsley	

Place fillets in greased baking pan. Cook celery and onions in 3 T. butter until semi-tender. Pour over croutons. Add lemon peel and juice, parsley, salt and pepper. Toss together. Spoon half the stuffing mixture on each fillet in pan. Top with remaining two pieces of fish, brush with melted butter. Sprinkle with salt and paprika and bake covered at 350 degrees for 25 minutes.

Brian Brower
Brainerd, Minnesota

Fish-Stuffed Peppers

Serves: 2
Prep Time: 1 hour

1 cup fish, ground	¹/₄ tsp. pepper
1 T. rice, uncooked	4 medium bell peppers
4 T. onion, chopped	1 large can tomato juice
1 T. celery, chopped	
¹/₂ tsp. salt	

Mix fish, rice, onions, celery, salt and pepper together. Pack mixture into cored peppers. Place peppers in deep pan and cover with tomato juice. Simmer over low heat for 1 hour.

William Thennes
Bark River, Michigan

Potato Fish Casserole

Serves: 4
Prep Time: 20 minutes

1 **lb. fish**	1 **small dried hot pepper,**
1 **medium onion, thinly**	**minced**
sliced	3 **T. olive oil**
2 **large baking potatoes,**	
thinly sliced	
salt and pepper to taste	
¹/₄ **cup parsley, minced**	
1 **garlic clove, minced**	

Layer half the onion and potato slices in oiled casserole dish. Season with salt and pepper. Cut fish into four serving-size pieces. Arrange over vegetables. Sprinkle generously with parsley, then sprinkle with garlic and hot pepper. Drizzle with oil. Layer remaining onions and potatoes over fish. Season with salt and pepper, then drizzle with remaining oil. Cover and bake at 375 degrees for 1 hour.

Roy McClellan
Church Hill, Tennessee

Super Fish Puffs

Serves: 3-4
Prep Time: 30 minutes

1 **lb. fish fillets**	**few drops of onion juice**
salt and pepper	¹/₂ **T. Worcestershire sauce**
1 **egg white**	
¹/₄ **cup Miracle Whip**	

Arrange fillets in greased 8-inch baking dish. Season with salt and pepper. Beat egg white until stiff; fold in Miracle Whip, onion juice and Worcestershire sauce. Spread over fish fillets. Bake at 450 degrees for 20 minutes or until fish flakes easily.

Roy Van Zant
Mulvane, Kansas

Poached Fish

Serves: 2
Prep Time: 90 minutes

1 **lb. fish**	¹/₄ **tsp. thyme**
¹/₃ **cup lime juice**	¹/₂ **tsp. allspice**
¹/₂ **tsp. cayenne pepper**	**bay leaf**
2 **garlic cloves, minced**	
1 **T. salt**	
2 **cups water**	
2 **cups dry white wine**	
1 **onion, chopped**	

Combine lime juice, cayenne pepper, garlic and salt and use as marinade for fish. Soak 30 minutes. Discard and remove fish. In skillet, combine remaining ingredients and bring to a boil. Simmer 5 minutes. Add fish. Simmer uncovered for 10 minutes or until fish flakes easily. Remove fish and cover with small amount of cooking liquid. Serve with steamed rice.

Dennis Ray Schneider
Round Rock, Texas

Grilled Bacon 'Rapped Fish

Serves: 4-6
Prep Time: 30 minutes

2 **lbs. fresh fish fillets**	2 **lemons, thinly sliced**
butter	¹/₂ **lb. bacon**
2 **tsp. paprika**	

Wash fillets and pat dry. Brush with melted butter and sprinkle both sides with paprika. Squeeze juice from 1 lemon over fish. Lay lemon slices over fillets and wrap in place with bacon slices, securing with toothpicks. Place on grill about 4 inches from coals. Turn fish once, removing when bacon crisps.

Phil Deardorff
Lawrenceburg, Indiana

New Hampshire-Style Fish Stock

Serves: makes 3 qts. stock
Prep Time: 15-20 minutes

3 lbs. fish, including heads, tails and bones	**3 garlic cloves, crushed**
2 T. fresh lemon juice	**8 peppercorns**
4 celery stalks, chopped	**1 bay leaf**
2 yellow onions, chopped	**1 tsp. dried thyme**
1 carrot, thinly sliced	**¹/₄ cup fresh parsley, roughly chopped**
2 cups dry white wine	

Place fish, lemon juice, celery, onion, carrot, wine and garlic in ceramic or glass pot with 3 qts. water. Bring to a boil and then reduce to a steady simmer, removing any scum that may rise to surface. After 10 minutes, add remaining ingredients and simmer for an additional 10 minutes over medium heat. When finished, strain through cheese cloth. Allow stock to cool before refrigerating or freezing. For an extra bite, add 2 T. Worcestershire sauce while sauce is cooling.

Steven Bennett
Meredith, New Hampshire

Smoked Fish Ball

Serves: several
Prep Time: 15 minutes

16 oz. fish, baked
8 oz. cream cheese
1¹/₂ tsp. liquid smoke
salt to taste
nuts or parsley

Bone and crumble fish. Mix with cream cheese. Add liquid smoke and salt. Mix all ingredients thoroughly. Roll ball in nuts or parsley and chill. Serve with crackers.

David Mathweg
Roseburg, Oregon

Fish Chips

Serves: 4
Prep Time: 30 minutes

> **4 white fish fillets**
> **2 eggs**
> **lemon juice**
> **3 oz. cornflake crumbs**
> **2 oz. flour**
> **³/₄ T. garlic salt**

Cut fish into 2x3-inch pieces, ¹/₂ inch thick. Mix eggs and lemon juice together in bowl. Mix cornflakes, flour and garlic salt in separate bowl. Dip fish in egg batter, then into dry mixture. Place breaded fish onto wax paper until all are breaded. Heat oil about ¹/₂ inch deep in frying pan. Test oil heat by dropping in small piece of fish, it should be golden brown in less than a minute. When oil is hot, cook fish until both sides are golden brown. Serve.

Larry Jenen
Oak Forest, Illinois

Garfish Balls

Serves: 4-6
Prep Time: 45 minutes

> **2 lbs. garfish meat, flaked**
> **¹/₂ cup yellow mustard**
> **¹/₂ cup vinegar**
> **1 lb. mashed potatoes**
> **2 large onions, finely chopped**
>
> **1 cup mixture of parsley, green onions and celery leaves, all chopped**
> **flour**
> **cooking oil**

Make sauce by mixing mustard and vinegar together. In separate bowl, mix fish, potatoes, onions and vegetables together and shape into 1¹/₂-inch balls. Roll in mustard sauce, then roll in flour and deep-fry.

N. C. Hanks
Crowley, Louisiana

Smokey Barbecue Fillets

Serves: 8
Prep Time: 45 minutes

- **4 lbs. fish fillets**
- **2 tsp. liquid smoke**
- **1 tsp. Tabasco sauce**
- **1 tsp. Worcestershire sauce**
- **enough water to cover fillets**
- **¹/₂ cup flour**

Cut fillets into 6-inch sections and place in shallow pan. Mix liquid smoke, Tabasco sauce, Worcestershire sauce and water, then pour over fillets and let soak in refrigerator for 4-6 hours. Heat gas grill to medium, or raise charcoal grill high enough for fish to cook slowly. Cover grill with tinfoil. Put fillets on grill, then add flour to pan. Cook slowly, turning often and basting with sauce. Cook until fillets brown and become flaky.

Tom Snyder
Concordia, Kansas

Cajun Fish

Serves: 4
Prep Time: 6 minutes

- **2 lbs. fish**
- **cajun-style seafood seasoning**
- **2 T. butter**
- **aluminum foil**

Place foil strip on outdoor grill. Tuck in edges so foil is secured. Poke small holes in foil, about 2 inches apart. Melt butter. Turn grill on high. Put fish on grill and spread butter over both sides of fish. Then, sprinkle cajun seasoning over fish. Cook 1 minute per side, covered with grill lid.

Gim McClarren
Lubbock, Texas

Oven Fried Fish (Heart Healthy)

Serves: 4-6
Prep Time: 15 minutes

1¹/₂ **lbs. fish fillets, cut into**
pieces
2 **egg whites**
2 **T. water**
³/₄ **cup cornflakes**
³/₄ **cup instant potatoes**
¹/₂ **tsp. onion powder**
¹/₂ **tsp. garlic powder**
¹/₄ **tsp. pepper**

dash of Mrs. Dash's
Spicy
canola or safflower oil

Beat 2 egg whites with water. In separate bowl, mix dry ingredients together and put in pie pan. Pour oil into another pie pan. Dip fish into oil, then into egg whites, then coat with dry mixture. Place on lightly oiled cookie sheet. Bake at 500 degrees for 10-12 minutes or until fish is flaky.

Grace E. Durling
Redlands, California

Heavenly Blues

Serves: 4
Prep Time: 20 minutes

2 **fillets of your favorite**
fish, thick
1 **medium onion, thinly**
sliced
lemon juice

soy sauce
salt and pepper
butter

Place fillets on aluminum foil. Place onion slices on fillets. Sprinkle liberally with lemon juice and a dash of soy sauce. Salt and pepper to taste. Add a few pats of butter to the top and seal foil. Bake at 350 degrees for 15-20 minutes.

John Cram
North Wildwood, New Jersey

Seafood Omelette

Serves: 1
Prep Time: 15 minutes

¹/₄ cup fish, cooked	**¹/₈ cup tomato, diced**
1 small green onion, chopped	**butter**
¹/₈ cup green pepper, chopped	**2 T. water**
	3 eggs

Saute onion, green pepper and tomato in butter. Drain off extra liquid and butter. Set aside. Beat water and eggs together and pour into hot frying pan until almost cooked. (Move cooked eggs inward, allowing uncooked egg to run to side of pan and cook.) Spread vegetables and crumbled fish on half of pan; flip other half over to cover. Brown lightly. Remove from pan and season. (Grated cheese can also be added with vegetables and fish.)

Jon Morris
Charlottesville, Virginia

Hot & Spicy Fillets

Serves: 6
Prep Time: 10 minutes

1 lb. of your favorite fish fillets	**¹/₂ T. vegetable oil**
³/₄ cup tomato, chopped	**¹/₄ cup lemon juice**
¹/₃ cup green pepper, chopped	**dash of Tabasco sauce**
¹/₈ cup onion, chopped	**³/₄ tsp. salt (optional)**
¹/₂ tsp. basil	
¹/₄ tsp. pepper	

Place fish in greased baking dish. Mix other ingredients together in bowl. Spoon mixture over fish. Cook (uncovered) for 10 minutes in preheated oven at 400 degrees.

John Mehok, Jr.
New Hope, Pennsylvania

Hot Fish & Pasta Salad

Serves: 4-6
Prep Time: 20 minutes

1 lb. fish fillets, cut into
strips
2 T. oil
¹/₂ cup broccoli
1 cup snap peas
¹/₄ cup red pepper, chopped
¹/₂ cup pearl onions
¹/₄ cup water chestnuts

¹/₄ cup bean sprouts
2 cups rotini pasta
2 T. soy sauce
1 T. Hoisin sauce

Heat oil and stir-fry vegetables. Meanwhile, boil pasta according to package directions. When vegetables are almost tender, add fish and stir-fry for a few minutes or until fish is white and flaky. Add remaining ingredients and serve with dollop of mayonnaise, if desired.

Thomas Stevens, Sr.
Independence, Oregon

Hawaiian Fish Kabobs

Serves: 4-6
Prep Time: 30 minutes

1 lb. fish fillets, cut into
1-inch chunks
1 1-lb. can pineapple
chunks
¹/₄ cup oil

1 envelope spaghetti sauce
mix
4-6 bacon slices

Drain syrup from pineapple, reserving ¹/₂ cup. Combine syrup with oil and spaghetti sauce mix. Alternate fish and pineapple chunks on 4-6 skewers, weaving bacon around them. Brush with seasoning mixture. Grill over hot coals about 10 minutes, until tender. Turn and brush with seasoning frequently.

Gerald Jackson
Shoreview, Minnesota

Oven Fish Chowder

Serves: 6
Prep Time: 2 hours

2 **lbs. whitefish**	3 **garlic cloves**
3 **medium potatoes, diced**	½ **cup white wine**
2 **medium onions, diced**	**water**
butter	1 **pt. half & half**
2 **bay leaves**	**flour**
salt and pepper to taste	

Place fillets in large, lightly-greased pan. Cover with potatoes, onions, butter, bay leaves, seasonings and cloves. Pour in wine and water. Place in oven and bake at 375 degrees for 1 hour, uncovered. Remove and cover with aluminum foil. Cook another hour at 350 degrees. Meanwhile, heat half & half in large pan to scalding. Remove and add enough flour to thicken, about 1 cup. Remove fish from oven and mix with sauce. Cook over low heat for 30 minutes, seasoning to taste. Serve in large bowls.

Art Verville
Farmingdale, Maine

Kevin's Fish Burgers

Serves: 4
Prep Time: 45 minutes

2 **lbs. fish fillets**	2 **cups plain bread crumbs**
1 **small onion**	**salt and pepper**
1 **egg**	1 **cup cooking oil**

Ground fish fillets. Chop onion in small pieces. Mix fish, onion, egg and 1 cup bread crumbs. Add salt and pepper to taste. Next, shape mixture into 6 patties and coat well with remaining bread crumbs. Heat oil in large skillet. Fry patties 2 minutes on each side or until done.

Kevin Druzdzel
Moundsview, Minnesota

Herb-Smoked Fish

Serves: 1 per fish fillet
Prep Time: 20 minutes

**enough fish fillets or
steaks as people
soy sauce
aluminum foil
bay leaves**

Place fish on pan or platter. Shake soy sauce liberally over fish. Form small, box-like pan with aluminum foil and add 6 bay leaves. Place fish and bay leaves on hot grill with lid closed. Grill 10-12 minutes or until fish is done, turning once after 5 minutes. (Bay leaves will smoke.) If bay leaves burn, add a few more when you turn the fish. Excellent with mahi-mahi, halibut, salmon or swordfish.

Gerald Koth
Concord Township, Ohio

Sesame Seed Fish

Serves: 4
Prep Time: 15 minutes

**2 lbs. of your favorite
fillets
salt and pepper to taste
vegetable oil
1 egg white
2 T. sesame seeds**

Preheat broiler. Salt and pepper fish. Broil on lightly-oiled cookie sheet for about 3 minutes. Turn fish over and continue to broil for 2 minutes. Remove fish from oven and dip fillets into lightly-beaten egg white, then roll in sesame seeds. Place under broiler again until seeds are golden.

Jack Hensley
Lincoln, Nebraska

Fish Orientale

Serves: 4
Prep Time: 20 minutes

3 lbs. fish	2 tsp. Tabasco sauce
1 tsp. salt	1 tsp. sugar
¼ cup oil	1 cup chicken broth, hot
2 tsp. ginger root, minced	
6 scallions, sliced	
1 garlic clove, minced	
2 T. oyster sauce	
2 T. soy sauce	

Cut fish into serving-size pieces. Rub in salt. Heat oil in wok; stir in ginger, scallions, garlic, oyster sauce, soy sauce, Tabasco sauce and sugar. Cook 1 minute. Add fish and brown on both sides. Add chicken broth. Cover and cook over low heat for 15 minutes or until fish is flaky.

Fred Kadow
Rensselaer, Indiana

Fish Parmesan

Serves: 4
Prep Time: 15 minutes

8 oz. fish fillets	2 tsp. fresh parsley
1 16-oz. jar Ragu spaghetti sauce	½ tsp. fresh marjoram
	½ tsp fresh thyme
2 T. Parmesan cheese	2 tsp. fresh basil
1-2 tsp. dried Italian herbs (or 1 tsp. oregano)	

Place fish fillets in baking dish. Smother in spaghetti sauce. Sprinkle with Parmesan cheese and herbs to taste. Bake 15 minutes at 350 degrees. Serve with noodles, French bread and garden salad.

Jan Rutledge
Killeen, Texas

Fish Fingers

Serves: 8
Prep Time: 30 minutes

3 lbs. any fillets
1 can beer
1 tsp. lemon juice
1 pkg. seasoned fish
coating
1 pkg. onion ring batter
mix
2 eggs
milk

Soak fillets in beer and lemon juice for 1 hour. Cut fillets into strips 1-inch wide. Heat deep-fat fryer to 400 degrees. Mix together fish coating and onion ring batter. Add 2 eggs and milk to desired consistency. Dip fish fingers in batter and deep-fry until golden brown. Great as a snack or entree.

Tom Snyder
Concordia, Kansas

Saucy Fish Fillets

Serves: 3
Prep Time: 30 minutes

1 lb. fish fillets
dash of pepper
1 10³/₄-oz. can cream of
celery soup

¹/₂ cup mild process cheese,
shredded
dash of paprika

Arrange fillets in single layer in shallow baking dish. Sprinkle with pepper. Bake at 350 degrees for 15 minutes. Cover with soup, sprinkle with cheese and paprika. Bake 15 minutes or more until done. Serve and garnish with parsley or lemon.

Kevin Vergon
South Whitley, Indiana

Fred's Fabulous Fish

Serves: 6-10
Prep Time: 20 minutes

2 **lbs. fish fillets**	1 **cup cream**
10 **oz. frozen broccoli**	1 **cup Swiss cheese,**
4 **T. butter**	**shredded**
1½ **cups chicken broth**	¼ **cup toasted sliced**
2 **T. flour**	**almonds**
salt and pepper to taste	

Cook broccoli according to package directions, then saute in 2 T. butter. Set aside. Cook fillets in 1 cup chicken broth until flaky. In 2-qt. rectangular pan, layer fish and broccoli. Melt remaining half of butter in saucepan and stir in flour and salt and pepper. Stir until smooth. Gradually add cream, remaining chicken broth and ¾ cup of cheese (after mixture has thickened). Pour sauce over fish and broccoli, then sprinkle remaining cheese and toasted almonds on top. Bake at 400 degrees for 10 minutes, or until cheese bubbles.

Fred Heckeroth
Alpine, California

Fast Fresh Fish

Serves: 1 per person
Prep Time: 20 minutes

1 **fish fillet**
dash of salt
dash of pepper
1 **T. butter or oleo**

Clean fish. Season fish with dash of salt and pepper. Put butter on top of fish. Place fish on plate, cover with napkin and microwave on high power for 3-4 minutes. Serve.

Al Brickner
Land O'Lake, Florida

Cooper's Fish Chowder

Serves: 6
Prep Time: 45 minutes

2 **fish fillets, chopped**	**salt and pepper to taste**
2 **onion slices, chopped**	2 **oz. sour cream**
3 **celery stalks, diced**	
1 **pkg. noodle soup**	
4 **medium potatoes, diced**	
1 **T. Old Bay seasoning**	
2 **T. vinegar**	

In deep pot, saute onions and celery. Add soup mix, 4 cups water and potatoes. Cook until tender. Meanwhile, boil 1 qt. water with Old Bay seasoning, vinegar and salt and pepper. Add fish and cook 10 minutes. Drain fish and add to soup. Add sour cream and cook an additional 10 minutes. Serve.

Mrs. William Sawyer
Athens, Pennsylvania

Fish Casserole

Serves: 4
Prep Time: 20 minutes

2 **cups fish chunks, cooked**	$^1/_2$ **cup melted butter**
1$^1/_2$ **cups crushed crackers**	2 **eggs, lightly beaten**
1 **cup celery, diced**	
2 **large onions, chopped**	
$^1/_2$ **cup parsley, chopped**	
1 **green pepper, chopped**	
salt and pepper to taste	

Combine fish, crumbs and vegetables. Add salt and pepper and mix with butter and eggs. Pour mixture into buttered casserole dish. Sprinkle with bits of butter and extra crumbs and bake for 30 minutes at 375 degrees.

Kurtis Feil
Lovelock, Nevada

Great Beer Batter

Serves: varies
Prep Time: 5 minutes

fish pieces
egg whites
bisquick
beer
¹/₄ tsp. cream of tartar

Separate eggs in bowl. In another bowl, combine bisquick and beer according to package directions, substituting beer for water. Mix batter with egg yolks. Beat egg whites until they form stiff peaks. Add cream of tartar and beat so peaks will hold. Gently fold egg whites into batter mix and dredge fish, vegetable pieces, etc. through batter, covering completely. Pan- or deep-fry immediately until golden brown.

Charles Tanner
Aurora, Ohio

Skewered Garlic & Fish Kabobs

Serves: 4
Prep Time: 15 minutes

1 lb. fresh fish fillets
1 lb. medium shrimp
1 stick butter
3 T. garlic powder
4 bamboo skewers
1 lemon, sliced

Clean and de-vein shrimp. Melt butter and garlic in pan. Wash fillets and cut into 2-inch squares. Align fish on skewers, alternating shrimp, fish and lemon slices. Cook on grill 20 minutes or until fish is done. Brush frequently with garlic butter, turning frequently. Squeeze lemon juice over kabobs then serve.

Ed Lindsey
Newbury Park, California

Fried Fish Balls

Serves: 4
Prep Time: 30 minutes

1 lb. fish fillets	½ tsp. salt
4 egg yolks	¼ tsp. pepper
4 egg whites	⅛ tsp. garlic
1 tsp. parsley	
1 T. flour	

Boil fish in water for about 5 minutes. Drain and mash fish with fork. Beat egg yolks until stiff. Beat egg whites until fluffy. In large bowl, mix together yolks, parsley, flour, salt, pepper and garlic. Add fish. Then, add egg whites. Make balls and place them in hot cooking oil until golden brown.

Gerald Jackson
Shoreview, Minnesota

Fish Ball Soup

Serves: 4
Prep Time: 30 minutes

2 lbs. fish
1 small onion
1 egg
1 cup bread crumbs
1 can chicken broth
1 celery stalk, chopped
4 carrots, sliced
4 large potatoes, chopped

In blender, chop fish and onion. Mix egg and bread crumbs together. Combine egg mixture with fish and onion to form walnut-size balls. Set aside. In pan, combine broth, celery, carrots and potatoes. Cook 15 minutes. Add fish balls and cook until vegetables are tender.

Edward Jaye
Garfield Heights, Ohio

Smoky Battered Fillets

Serves: 2-4
Prep Time: 30 minutes

2-4 fish fillets	**1 cup flour**
¼-½ cup milk	**salt and pepper**
2-4 T. liquid smoke	
1 egg	
cracker crumbs	

Soak fillets in brine in refrigerator for 2 hours. Mix milk, liquid smoke, egg and salt and pepper in bowl. Remove fillets and pat dry. Add flour and cracker crumbs to bowl of liquid smoke, with enough crumbs to thicken. Dip fish in batter and place in lightly-greased pan on medium heat for 5-8 minutes per side. Serve immediately.

Eric Weaver
Cheyenne, Wyoming

Leftover Fish Croquettes

Serves: 4
Prep Time: 30 minutes

3 cups leftover fish, flaked	**2 eggs, beaten**
salt and pepper to taste	**1 cup Italian bread**
dash of fresh paprika	**crumbs**
1 medium onion, minced	
dash of fresh parsley,	
chopped	
1 T. lemon rind	

Mix all ingredients in glass bowl until firm ball forms when compressed. Roll 2 T. of the ingredients into firm ball. Place balls in hot oil and cook until golden brown. Let cool for 1 minute, then sprinkle with salt and whatever other seasonings you desire. Serve.

Steven Bennett
Meredith, New Hampshire

Pickled Fish

Serves: 8
Prep Time: 1 hour

1 qt. fish
salt to taste
1 pt. white wine vinegar
2 cups sugar
$^1/_3$ box pickling spice
2 medium onions, sliced

Cut fish into bite-size pieces. Add salt (lots) to fish and cover with vinegar. Let stand 5 days, stirring each day. Wash with cold water and soak for 15-20 minutes. Warm mixture of sugar, pickling spice and vinegar to dissolve sugar. Cool mixture and add to fish and onions. Mix all together and put in jars with enough liquid to cover fish. Refrigerate for 2 weeks before eating. Keep refrigerated.

Rodney Strand
Leeds, North

Stir-Fried Fish Strips

Serves: 4
Prep Time: 30 minutes

$1^1/_2$ lbs. fillet strips
2 T. sesame oil
$^1/_2$ green pepper
$^1/_4$ red bell pepper
$^1/_2$ onion
4 mushrooms
your favorite spices to taste
$^1/_2$ oz. wine or sake

Place oil in large skillet or wok. When oil is hot, saute fillet strips until half-cooked. Put in vegetables (cut into thin strips or slices) and cook until vegetables are half-cooked. Spice to taste and pour in wine or sake. Cover and steam for 1 minute. Remove and serve with rice.

J. D. Gagliardo
Oxnard, California

San Diego Light Fish Bake

Serves: 4
Prep Time: 1 hour

4 **whitefish fillets, boneless**
vegetable oil
1 **large tomato, sliced**
1 **green pepper, sliced**
3-4 **green onions, sliced**
6-10 **fresh mushrooms, sliced**
2-3 **celery stalks, sliced**

$^1\!/_2$ **lemon, thinly sliced**
salt and pepper to taste
$^1\!/_2$ **cup white wine**
$^1\!/_2$ **cup Parmesan cheese,**
grated
$^1\!/_4$ **cup parsley**

Lightly oil 8x12-inch baking pan with vegetable oil. Make layer of mixed vegetable slices, and cover layer with fish fillets. Place a few thin slices of lemon over top, and make another layer with remaining sliced vegetables. Season lightly with salt and pepper. Pour wine over vegetables. Sprinkle with Parmesan cheese and parsley. Bake in preheated 350-degree oven for about 35 minutes.

Chuck Erkelens
Carlsbad, California

Rick's Barbecued Fillets

Serves: 2-4
Prep Time: 30 minutes

fish fillets
2-3 **eggs**
barbecue potato chips
1 **cup oil**
pepper

Beat eggs. Crush chips in bag. Heat frying pan with oil on medium heat. Dip fillets in eggs, then put in bag of chips. Shake well. Lay breaded fillets in hot oil and brown on both sides. Season with pepper.

Rich Rugroden
Waseca, Minnesota

Smoked Fish Omelette

Serves: 2
Prep Time: 15 minutes

½ cup smoked fish, flaked
3 eggs
2 T. milk
⅛ tsp. pepper
1 T. margarine or butter
¼ cup cheddar or Swiss
cheese, shredded

In small bowl, blend eggs, milk and pepper. In 10-inch skillet, melt butter over medium heat. Pour eggs into skillet. Cook until eggs are set, about 5 minutes. Sprinkle fish and cheese over half of omelette. With spatula, fold other half over filling. Cook until cheese melts; 1-2 minutes.

Peter Widrlechner
Mount Prospect, Illinois

Fish Patties

Serves: 4
Prep Time: 20 minutes

1 cup fish, cooked and   **2 T. flour**
flaked   **cooking oil**
1 egg, beaten
1 tsp. onion, minced
1 tsp. lemon juice
1 tsp. salt
pepper to taste
1 cup mashed potatoes,
cold

Beat egg and combine with fish, onion, lemon juice, seasonings and potatoes. Form into patties, coating with flour to shape. Fry in vegetable oil until golden brown and fully cooked.

Matthew Olexa
Bloomsburg, Pennsylvania

Smoked Fish Nuggets

Serves: 4
Prep Time: 1 hour

2 cups smoked fish, flaked	**1 T. butter**
1 T. celery, minced	**¹/₄ lb. (sharp) cheese, cubed**
1¹/₂ tsp. Worcestershire	**1 cup dry bread crumbs**
sauce	
1 egg, beaten	
¹/₂ cup mashed potatoes	
1 T. onion, grated	

Combine all ingredients except cheese and bread crumbs. Mix thoroughly. Form walnut-size balls and insert cube of cheese into each nugget. Roll in bread crumbs. Fry in deep oil at 375 degrees for about 4 minutes or until golden brown. Nuggets will keep in freezer for 3-4 weeks.

Julie Klawitter
Underwood, Minnesota

Leftover Fish Omelette

Serves: 2
Prep Time: 15 minutes

2 cups fish, cold and	**1 egg, beaten**
flaked	**4 T. cheddar cheese,**
2 cups potatoes, diced and	**grated**
cooked	
2 T. onion, minced	
pinch of tarragon	
dash of garlic powder	

Combine all ingredients (except cheese) in bowl. Pour into frying pan and cook until mixture becomes firm to the eye. When firm, sprinkle on cheese and fold omelette in half. Remove from heat and allow to set 2 minutes before serving. A few drops of lemon juice gives an extra zesty bite.

Steven Bennett
Meredith, New Hampshire

Fish Stew

Serves: 4-6
Prep Time: 15 minutes

2 cups fish, steamed or broiled	¹/₂ can whole potatoes, diced
1 pkg. egg noodles	1 tsp. garlic
1 can cream of mushroom soup	1 tsp. pepper
1 can cream of celery soup	¹/₂ tsp. salt
¹/₂ can carrots	
¹/₂ can green beans	
¹/₂ can peas	

Boil noodles as directed, then drain well. In same pot, add remaining ingredients. Warm on medium heat, stirring occasionally, and serve.

William Reddington
Wilmington, Illinois

Escabeche

Serves: 4-6 as entree, 10-12 as hors d'oeuvre
Prep Time: 24 hours

6-8 2-lb. fish fillets	1 T. orange peel
2 T. oil	¹/₂ T. cayenne pepper
²/₃ cup oil	¹/₂ cup onion, chopped
3 T. red wine vinegar	¹/₄ cup cilantro, chopped
1 T. lemon peel, grated	2 garlic cloves, chopped

Flour fillets and saute in 2 T. oil. Do not brown. In blender, mix remaining ingredients until smooth. Pour one-third of mixture into flat dish. Place fillets in single layer in dish and cover with marinade. Cover and refrigerate 24 hours. Serve cold with your favorite crackers.

Dennis Ray Schneider
Round Rock, Texas

Vegetable Baked Fish

Serves: 2
Prep Time: 30 minutes

1 **lb. fish fillet**	¹/₄ **cup water**
¹/₂ **cup zucchini, sliced**	1 **T. butter**
1 **green pepper, sliced**	¹/₈ **tsp. paprika**
1 **tomato, sliced**	
1 **onion, sliced**	
¹/₄ **tsp. salt**	
¹/₈ **tsp. pepper**	

Place half of vegetables in baking dish. Season fish with salt and pepper and place on top of vegetables. Cover with remaining vegetables. Add water, dot with butter and sprinkle with paprika. Bake at 350 degrees for 20-25 minutes.

Mike Devine
Loveland, Colorado

Italian Grilled Fish

Serves: 2
Prep Time: 25 minutes

2 **medium fish, dressed**
3 **oz. Italian dressing**
   rosemary
   thyme
   lemon pepper
   garlic powder
   onion powder

Place each fish on sheet of aluminum foil and coat with salad dressing. Sprinkle lightly with above seasonings. Wrap foil securely around fish and place on hot grill. Cook 5-15 minutes, depending on heat of grill. Fish should be completely white and flaky when removed. Serve with rice pilaf and vegetables.

Jon Morris
Charlottesville, Virginia

Fillets With Clams

Serves: 3
Prep Time: 30 minutes

2 lbs. fish fillets	**¹/₂ cup white wine**
flour	**3 T. tomato paste**
vegetable oil	**6-8 clams**
2 T. butter	
salt and pepper to taste	

Dredge fillets in flour, then brown in vegetable oil. Remove from pan and drain. Remove oil from pan. Add butter, oregano, salt and pepper, wine, tomato paste and clams. Cook on medium heat for 10 minutes or until clams open. Pour sauce over fillets and arrange clams on plate with fillets. Serve hot.

Rob & Larraine Barbarelli
Bronx, New York

Woodrow's Fish Stew

Serves: 2
Prep Time: 1 hour

2 lbs. fish fillets
4 bacon slices
2 large sweet potatoes
6 fresh tomatoes
4 bell peppers
4 medium onions
creole seasoning

Place bacon strips in Dutch oven. Slice vegetables and place in layers on bacon. Place fish on vegetables, seasoning with creole seasoning. Continue alternating layers until pot is full. Cover (don't add water) and heat on stove until bacon starts to fry. Turn burner down and simmer for 45 minutes or until vegetables are tender.

James Woodrow
Eutawville, South Carolina

Microwave Lemon Almond Fillets

Serves: 4
Prep Time: 10 minutes

1 lb. fish, skinned
¹/₂ cup dry bread crumbs
2 T. melted butter

1 tsp. lemon peel, finely grated
¹/₃ cup toasted sliced almonds

Place fillets in single layer in lightly greased, microwave-safe dish. In small mixing bowl, combine bread crumbs, butter and lemon peel. Mix well, then sprinkle on top of fish. Cover with almonds. Cover baking dish with plastic wrap, folding back one small corner to vent steam. Cook on high power for 3 minutes. Rotate a half turn and cook another 2 minutes or until fish is done.

Gabby Talkington
Richmond, California

Fish Loaf

Serves: 4
Prep Time: 45 minutes

1¹/₂ cups raw fish, boned and diced
1 tsp. dried onion
1 T. lemon juice
1 tsp. salt
¹/₂ tsp. pepper
1 can cream of mushroom soup
2 cups old bread (soak in water and squeeze)
1 can mushrooms

1 T. paprika
2 eggs, beaten
¹/₂ cup celery, diced

Mix all ingredients together and bake 45 minutes at 375 degrees.

Gerald Jackson
Shoreview, Minnesota

Microwaved Fish Fillets

Serves: 4-6
Prep Time: 20 minutes

2 lbs. fish fillets (any kind
of firm fish)
2 T. lemon juice
¹/₄ cup margarine (softened)
¹/₂ cup Parmesan cheese,
grated
3 T. low fat sour cream
3 T. onion, finely chopped
1 garlic clove, finely
chopped
4-5 drops of Tabasco sauce
¹/₂ cup Monterey Jack
cheese, grated
paprika
1 T. parsley, chopped

Skin fillets and cut into serving-size pieces. Place fish on microwave-safe dish and cover with plastic wrap. Drizzle with lemon juice. Microwave on high for 6 minutes. Vent plastic wrap to release steam. Carefully remove wrap. Mix margarine, Parmesan cheese, sour cream, onion, garlic and Tabasco sauce in 4-cup glass measuring cup. Cover cup with plastic wrap and microwave on high for 1 minute. Stir. Spread mixture on fish fillets. Cover fillets with plastic. Poke hole in plastic with knife blade. Microwave on high for 1 minute, 30 seconds. Remove plastic wrap. Sprinkle fillets with Monterey Jack cheese. Sprinkle on paprika and microwave on high for 30 seconds. Remove from microwave and sprinkle on parsley.

Grace Burling
Redlands, California

Index

sole in herb butter, 111
southern oriental-spiced
  walleye, 135

CAJUN
cajun catfish, 59
cajun fish, 155
cajun fried bass, 51
yellow perch jambalaya, 85

CARP
baked carp fillets, 58

CATFISH
blackened catfish, 65
broiled catfish, 59
cajun catfish, 59
catfish burgers, 61
catfish chowder, 63
catfish parmesan, 62
catfish stew, 63
chinese catfish, 60
fried catfish supreme, 64
pan-fried catfish, 65
pecan catfish, 60
salsa-baked catfish, 62
steamed catfish, 64
steamed spanish catfish, 61

CHOWDER
catfish chowder, 63
cooper's fish chowder, 164
fish stew/chowder, 147
fisherman's soup, 148
jackson's northern chowder,
  82
maine-ly fish chowder, 146
oven fish chowder, 159
pickled northern, 82

COD
cod melt, 66

cod potato loaf, 67
savory microwaved cod, 66
shrimp and fish casserole, 67

CRAPPIE
broiled crappie, 68
cornbread crappie, 69
crappie chips, 69
crappie tidbits, 68

FISH CAKES
bass cakes, 44
bluegill fish cakes, 57

FLOUNDER
fabulous cheese flounder, 72
fish packages, 72
flounder with cheese sauce,
  70
grilled flounder with crab, 70
sweet & sour flounder, 71
tarragon flounder, 71

FRIED FISH
bass fillets, 46
beer batter (fish & seafood),
  144
bluefish batter, 54
breaded italian bass, 50
cajun catfish, 59
cajun fried bass, 51
cornbread crappie, 69
crunchy fried walleye, 136
escabeche, 172
favorite walleye fillets, 133
fillets with clams, 174
fish cakes, 141
fish chips, 154
fish fingers, 162
fish patties, 170
fried bluefish, 56
fried catfish supreme, 64

SEND US YOUR FISH RECIPE

Title: _____

Serves: _____

Prep Time: _____

Ingredients:

_____
_____
_____
_____
_____
_____
_____
_____

Directions:

_____ fold here
_____
_____
_____
_____
_____
_____
_____
_____
_____
_____
_____
_____
_____
_____
_____
_____

Your NAFC Member# _____

Your Name _____

Address _____

City/State/Zip _____

North American Fishing Club
12301 Whitewater Drive
P.O. Box 3403
Minnetonka, MN 55343

(tape or staple here)

A Great Gift Idea...

The NAFC Members' Cookbook!

Order extra copies of the 1992 NAFC Members' Cookbook
for your friends and family. They make great gifts
—fun to read and practical as well!

You'll also like to have a second copy to keep
at the cabin or in with your camping gear.

Send your order in now and get yours at the
special Member's price of only $9.95 each.
(Non-members pay $14.95)

Send me _____ copies of the 1992 NAFC Members' Cookbook.
I'm enclosing $9.95 each (non-members pay $14.95).
Include $1.50 per order for Postage and Handling.

If paying by Check or Money Order, send this form in
an envelope with your payment to: NAFC Members' Cookbook,
P.O. Box 3408, Minnetonka, MN 55343.
Charge customers may cut out this page, fold and mail.
(Don't forget to put on a stamp)

Payment Method:
__ Check or M.O.
__ MasterCard
__ Visa
__ Discover Card

Card # _____

Exp. Date _____

Signature _____

Name _____ Member # _____

Address _____

City/State/Zip _____

CB92

North American Fishing Club
12301 Whitewater Drive
P.O. Box 3403
Minnetonka, MN 55343

(tape or staple here)